tinker, tailor, soldier, sailor...

the life of Colin Kerby OAM

'Tinker, tailor, soldier, sailor,
rich man, poor man, beggar man, thief.'
Old English children's rhyme.

First published in 2011.
Revised edition, 2012 The Lakehouse Publications,
10 Rosemary Row, Rathmines, NSW 2283 Australia

ISBN – 13: 978-146-3717216

Font: Calibri 10. Printed on demand in USA by Create Space,
a subsidiary of Amazon Books.
Cover design by Helen Marshall

All profits from the sale of this book will be donated to the
Hamlin Fistula Relief & Aid Fund (www.hamlinfistula.org.au)
PO Box 965
Wahroonga, NSW 2076,
Australia.

Price: AUD$20.00
Books may be purchased from Jan Mitchell
Email: jb.mitchell46@gmail.com
Website: www.writingsfromjanmitchell.com
Also from createspace.com and amazon.com

Tinker, Tailor, Soldier, Sailor....

The Life of Colin Kerby, OAM

By

Jan Mitchell

THE LAKEHOUSE PUBLICATIONS, AUSTRALIA

Dedication

To THE KELSON FAMILY:
Paul, Helen, Jacob and Amelia,
with love from Col and Judy Kerby.

Acknowledgements

I wish to express my gratitude to Colin Kerby for his willingness to tell his stories for publication and also to his wife, Judy Kerby for helping to keep Col on track with his memories. Judy has also performed a major role in checking and helping edit the manuscript. Her sharpness of mind and knowledge of English grammar and vocabulary has been invaluable.

I wish to thank the Lake Macquarie branch of the Australian Fellowship of Writers for their encouragement and assistance with critique and editing. Particular members of the group have given superb assistance: Helen Marshall for the cover design and for scanning photographs into the text; Linda Visman, Tina and Wes Batey, Linda Brooks and Sophie Bush for their critique; Roz Buckingham for sharing information from her father's diary about the 1937 volcanic eruption in Rabaul; Linda Brooks and Sophie Bush for technical information about internet publishing. Thanks also to Tina Batey for assistance with negotiating the publishing template.

My husband, Ian Mitchell, has provided loving support throughout the project. His technical expertise has helped me understand details of Col's diving and engineering achievements and assisted with making my descriptions comprehensible to non-engineers.

For proof reading, my heartfelt thanks go to Lisa Herring, with further assistance from Jamie Mitchell, Alan Herring and Dirk Visman.

Contents

Acknowledgements   iv
Contents page   v
List of Illustrations   vi
Introduction   vii
Preface   x

Part One: Early Years   1
1   Beginnings   2
2   Papua New Guinea   23
3   Budding Surgeon   43
Part Two: The War Years   65
4   Back to Melbourne   66
5   Kerby's Exclusive Confectionary   83
Part Three: Post War Melbourne   97
6   Man About Town   98
7   Showman   114
Part Four: The Nineteen Fifties   133
8   Beer, Sea Lions and Laundry   134
9   Romance   157
10 Bee Aircraft   171
Part Five: Medical Research   183
11 Cancer Research   184
12 Kidney and Liver Transplants   200
Part Six: Industrial Engineering   212
13 Boat Building and Engineering   213
14 Life Saving, Rescue and Salvage   236
Part Seven: Travelling   249
15 Sailing Away   250
16 Travels at Home and Abroad   265

Epilogue   284
Glossary   285
Author's Profile   289

List of Illustrations

1. Colin at nine with his bicycle, after riding from   11
    Melbourne to Ballarat.
2. Fourteen year old Colin with his homemade   15
    speedboat and outboard motor.
3. Colin and friend with homemade diving helmet.   21
4. Map of Blanche Bay, New Britain, showing   23
    Rabaul, Kokopo and volcanoes.
5. Volcanic eruption in Rabaul, 1937.   25
6   Col's three "boys'.   39
7. Col examining pathology slides at Rapindik   46
    Laboratory.
8. Col and his mates in uniform for New Guinea   53
    Volunteer Rifles.
9. Col's Scott Squirrel motor-cycle.   54
10. Slim and Col in their diving suits.   81
11. Kerby's Glucose Butterscotch package.   91
12. Boiler Certificate, 1956 and Steam Engine   108
    Driver's Certificate, 1970.
13. Candidate for Melbourne City Council.   108
14. Col cruising about town in his sports car, a   109
    1930 Austin 7 Meteor.
15. Col's mother, Ivy, beside the diving tank.   120
16. Slim and New Guinean assistants on dredge,   122
17. L to R: Slim, Col and two other divers,1950.   124
18. Col and his mother, Ivy Kerby.   135
19. Noble serving beer on Sunday, St Kilda Kiosk.   136
20. Noble Kerby with two of his sea lions.   149
21. Joan Roberts and Judy Lingard in Perth.   158
22. Alf Lazer and Col.   159
23. Col and Judy on their wedding day,   165
    27th June, 1959.
24 Col when he took over the Kiosk lease.   168
25. Early gyrocopter.   171

26.	Col in flight in their first Gyrocopter.	172
27.	Alan ready to fly the Bee Aircraft.	175
28	Judy with her show dog	179
29.	Armand Hammer, Sam Rose and Col Kerby.	189
30.	Jonas Salk: Photo he gave to Col.	195
31.	Col's miniaturised Kidney Preserving Machine capable of fitting into an aircraft seat.	208
32.	Professor Avni Sali.	215
33.	*Ooroo*, St Kilda Pier soon after launching, 1972.	216
34	Col and Judy on the Pier on their 25th wedding Anniversary, 1984. The St Kilda Marina is in the background.	225
35.	Judy with some of the Tivoli Girls at a reunion in the Kiosk.	227
36.	*Ooroo* moored beside the back of the St Kilda Kiosk, 1980's.	228
37.	Col inserting a lead ingot into the yacht keel.	229
38.	Plaque commemorating the Kerby Family's association with the St Kilda Pier and Kiosk.	234
39.	Col and Judy with the Tattersall's Award for Enterprise and Achievement.	239
40.	Judy Congratulates Col on the receipt of his Order of Australia Medal.	240
41.	The Order of Australia Medal.	241
42.	*Ooroo* anchored at Refuge Cove, Wilson's Promontory, 1991.	252
43	Col and mate working on bearing	256
44.	Col when he worked for Skilled Engineering.	257
45.	Col and Judy in 2010.	282
46.	Author photo	289

Introduction

I first met Colin Kerby in June 2001. On the marina pier, I saw a sprightly older man, close to seventy, I thought. He was slim, dark haired and fit looking. Usually he was wearing overalls with a BHP insignia when I saw him. Although we hadn't met, he would greet me with a happy grin.

'You've met Col and Judy, haven't you?' an acquaintance asked me one day. 'They live on the motor yacht, *Ooroo*. You must meet them.'

A few days later, Helen invited us to dinner on her family's boat. Col and Judy were there too. All the guests were live-aboards at the marina.

My husband and I were both feeling down. Col and Judy took it upon themselves to cheer us up. On many afternoons, we met on their boat or ours for afternoon tea. We became intrigued as Col regaled us with tales about pre-war life in Rabaul, Papua New Guinea, being a commercial diver, about his confectionary factory in Melbourne, about a laundry business and a photography business and later living on St Kilda Pier in Melbourne. It became obvious that both he and his father had little time for petty authority.

Next, he started telling us about experimenting on sheep in his purpose built 'garage' on the Pier and later, being head-hunted to work for Jonas Salk at his medical research institute in America. Earlier, Salk had developed the vaccine for polio. Later, he went into cancer research.

Judy talked about her life as a professional dancer with a company in Melbourne that had toured to Brisbane, Sydney, Perth, Adelaide and New Zealand. Col mentioned that he had worked for the theatre company too and that was how he'd met Judy.

They told us how they'd designed and built *Ooroo* themselves while they were living at the Pier. Judy said she'd designed and built the interior fittings and Col had designed and built the structure of the boat.

To start with, we went away with thoughts that this couple was very entertaining, but we questioned if they were in some sort of fantasy land. After all, we learned, Col was close to eighty. He was still working occasionally. Was he some sort of fabulist story teller? Yet, Col seemed very sane and healthy. How could one man have had so many careers – enough for half a dozen busy men?

One day, Judy brought out her 'scrapbook' to show us a newspaper cutting. This scrapbook was a very large foolscap ring binder, packed full of memorabilia about their lives. There was a second one, just as big. The two folders contained material documenting everything they had told us and more. This was no fantasy. Everything was true, including the time when the Governor of Victoria presented Col with the medal for the Order of Australia for saving lives.

Long after we'd sold our boat and left the marina, I would think about Colin Kerby and his incredible life. I would think to myself, *Someone ought to write a biography of this extraordinary Australian who has so energetically filled his life to overflowing with initiative and achievement.* About eight years later, it occurred to me that I could be that person. Tentatively, I broached the subject to Col. To my delight, he was one hundred percent enthusiastic about the project, although humble that I thought his endeavours worth recording.

Not only is Col a wonderful raconteur, he also has a wickedly dry sense of humour. I hope you enjoy his stories as much as I have.

Jan Mitchell, 2011.

Preface

The Salk Institute
for
Biological Studies

December, 1970.

TO WHOM IT MAY CONCERN.

MR. COLIN KERBY was employed by this organization from March 1970, until December 1970, whilst he was on Leave from Monash University, Australia.

Mr. Kerby became known to us in the bio-medical engineering field when we installed two continuous flow centrifuges that had been invented by him.

We employed Mr. Kerby to design another centrifuge, of a different type. We estimated six months at least were necessary for the design of this unit, however, Mr. Kerby designed, built and successfully tested this unit in nine weeks.

We took advantage of his remaining term with us for him to design several items of laboratory and research equipment we had been interested in designing on and off for years.

I took keen interest in Mr. Kerby's work and can say he is, at least in the field we knew him, inventive in the extreme, [sic] he has an outstanding knowledge of tributary fields, electronics, electrics, engineering, optics, scientific photography and equipment, tissue cell culture, body fluids, body reaction to implanted materials, etc.

In the field of sterilization, I consider him an expert.

He is able to push staff without friction.

The staff liked working with him.

He was a marked asset to our program.

He has the ability to control several projects simultaneously.

Signed

JONAS SALK.

Part one: Early Years

1 Beginnings

I stopped crying long enough to swear.

'Bugger the red-back spider. What about my thumb?'

I stood beside my sister, holding out my thumb for Dad's inspection. It was throbbing, though the bleeding had ceased. He stopped trying to distract me with the spider and examined my thumb more closely. I had chopped the tip off it.

'How did you do that, Colin?' Dad asked me.

'Hilda and me were in the dinghy near the paddle steamer,' I said.

Dad turned to my thirteen year old half-sister.

'I thought you were looking after the little lad, Hilda. So, what happened to his thumb?' he asked.

'We were just rocking in the dinghy, Dad, and Colin had his hand over the side. I suppose we rocked too close to the *Marion*, and he hurt his thumb when we bumped into it.'

'Yeah Dad,' I piped up. 'Just like Hilda said, it was the paddle steamer's fault.'

Dad looked back at Hilda. 'He's only three. It's up to you to look out for him,' he stated. 'Now, off you go and take the boy home to your mother.'

At my father's command, Hilda picked me up again and set off homewards. Dad was fencing for his brother that day, helping out on Uncle Ed's sheep farm at Foster, near the banks of the Murray River in Victoria.

My father and his brothers had all fought in the First World War, each receiving a soldier settlement block of land when they returned home, but Uncle Ed was more interested in politics than farming. Dad didn't know much about farming either, so he sold his block and moved over to help his brother.

Dad was born in 1899. When he left school at sixteen, he worked as a clerk for a company that handled bankrupts. He also had to go around and check on the liquidators and see how much money they took over the week. That job needed plenty of self-confidence. He was a beardless youth of sixteen or seventeen at the time. He told me about a visit he made to one business.

'Mister, you've been tickling the tills. There should be more money in the tills.'

'I'm not going to have a kid your age tell me how much I can take out of *my* till.'

'It's nothing to do with my age. I'm an official of the court here. You have to put that money back.'

Dad worked for just a couple of years after he finished school. The war had started already and he joined up with the army in 1917, as soon as he was eighteen.

Before the war, my father had taught Sunday school in the Methodist Church, but after the war, he became an atheist.

Dad was in the trenches in France by the time he was nineteen. Wounded in the shoulder during a bayonet fight, he was sent to hospital. While there, his superiors found out that he spoke school boy French, so they transferred him from active service to headquarters as a translator. He said he was happy about that, not because of dodging the bullets, but because he was away from the lice, mud, wet feet and cold. He learned colloquial French, he told me, so he could speak to the girls in France. I think he was being a bit romantic. He was fairly shy with the girls in his late teens.

All my father's brothers went to the war. Mack was a gold miner, so the army made him a tunneller in France. His army record said he repaired pipes in no man's land. The pipes were 'Bangalore torpedoes,' which held explosives. Mack received the Distinguished Conduct Medal [DCM] for this work, but he was killed shortly after, in an explosion at 'Hill 60' near Ypres.

His younger brother, Norman, was nineteen when he died at Anzac Cove in April 1915. He's listed on the Lone Pine Memorial. As well as Dad, two of his brothers, Roy and Ed, came back from the war. We didn't have a lot to do with Roy, who married his brother Mack's widow and together they raised Mack's son and their own child.

It was Ed who had the farm at Foster. He had served at Gallipoli, where he was blinded in one eye. They sent him to hospital in England, where doctors stitched his eye up. Then he went to the trenches in France as a major, received a bullet in the lung and went to hospital in England again. When he returned to the trenches, he was shot again in the same lung.

When I was a young teenager, I asked him, 'Did the second bullet hit the first bullet?'

'Oh God no, if it had done that, I wouldn't be here now,' he said.

When he was young, Ed was keen on rowing. While he was convalescing from his lung injury, he rowed for the military team against the Cambridge University team, winning the race. He was embarrassed by one of his loud comrades.

'There goes Kerby: One eye, one lung, one arsehole and he beats the lot of you.'

In 1919, Ed was elected into Federal parliament. He won by one vote against a man named Charles McGrath from Ballarat. McGrath challenged the result and a bye-election was held in 1920, which was won by McGrath It was while Uncle Ed was in parliament that Dad looked after his farm.

Ed still had a bullet in his lung in 1928, when it became toxic and he started to die. In those days, they weren't keen on doing lung operations, but because he was near death, they operated and removed the bullet. He survived the operation and lived until 1970. Instead of lead around the bullet, it had copper and nickel. A bone deposit had grown over it. His wife had it made into a brooch and my father told me it looked like a pearl.

Ed was a good fighter. Years later, he came down to our place at the St Kilda Kiosk with a black eye. Even the white of it was black. Somebody had been trying to gouge out his one eye.

'Who were you having a go at, Ed? Have you been arguing politically?' my father asked.

'Something like that, Noble.'

'How's the other fellow?' Dad asked.

'He'll have difficulty walking for a long time with those testicles.'

~

Dad was twenty-one when he married my mother, Ivy, in September 1920. She was twenty-nine and already had an eight year old daughter from a previous marriage in England.

When she was first married, my mother lived in Lancashire, but her husband drank and then beat her. She decided not to put up with that, so she sold all the furniture, took half of the money and bought herself and her young daughter passage to Australia, disembarking in Melbourne. When I became an adult, she asked me if I thought that she had done the right thing.

'Yes,' I told her. I didn't like it when women were beaten.

I was born on Armistice Day, 11/11/1921. Some people call it Remembrance Day At that time, we lived in Linton, near Mount Butte in the Ballarat area. When my mother told my grandmother that she and my father intended naming me 'Colin', my grandmother was horrified. A man called Colin Ross had murdered a girl in East Melbourne the previous year.

'Fancy calling my grandson after a murderer! Why not call him Adam? That's a much nicer name.'

Maybe she regretted having allowed my Grandfather to name my father Noble and one of his brothers Royal.

~

Mount Butte was where my father had his soldier settlement – twelve hundred acres with sheep. Neither Dad nor his brothers had any experience of farming. Dad sold out when Ed went into parliament. When he went over to South Australia to work Uncle Ed's sheep farm at Foster, we rented a house nearby at Mannum. Uncle Ed returned after his term in parliament. I was almost five years old when my father left, bringing the family down to Melbourne.

We returned for a visit to Foster one time. My uncle kept about forty ferrets in a cage. They were used for chasing rabbits. I went around the pen, pulled the latch up and opened the door. A wave of ferrets came out of the cage. I ran inside.

'The ferrets escaped,' I announced, pointing back to where they were appearing around the corner of the shed, walking in unison in their undulating way.

My sister picked up a wooden clothesline prop, using it to herd the ferrets back into their pen. Eventually, we locked them all back in.

~

In Melbourne, my parents sent me to a Methodist Church kindergarten in Fitzroy Street, St Kilda. About half way through the morning, the teacher said something to one of the older girls, who went out the back to a side room. I followed and watched as she plugged in something. It made hot water. *What a wonderful device that is,* I thought. *It cooks the tea.* At home, we were lucky if we had wood for a fire. I had come from the bush, where there was no such thing as an electric kettle.

At the kindergarten, there was a selfish bugger of a child who monopolised the rocking horse. He wouldn't let anyone else have a turn, so I hauled him off and hooked him. Because of this, my parents were asked to come to the school and take me away. I was violent, they said.

~

Dad found work on the railway. Because he'd had a fairly good education, the union made him a delegate, but he threw his weight about and the Transport Board sacked him after only a year. That doesn't happen these days with a union delegate. With my father out of work, my parents had to find a cheaper place to live. We returned to Ballarat for a short time.

Dad ran the mechanical workshop at the garage in Sturt Street. He was a fitter and turner, mechanic and engineer. Most people didn't have paper qualifications in those days. My old man had grown up learning these skills from his father and grandfather, who were mining engineers. Likewise, as I was growing up, he taught me. Later in my life, as I became very skilled, I taught him many things.

~

In 1926, when I was five, I started at Warrenheip Primary School and we rented a house on an orchard called Apple Farm. Later, we lived in Pleasant Street in Ballarat. There, Cassie C... teamed up with me. Cassie was two years older than me. She taught me quite a lot.

'I was sexually molested when I was five years old,' I tell people. They think a paedophile abused me. 'By the seven year old girl next door,' I add.

One weekend, Cassie and I went to a house that was being built in the next block. Cassie went inside. She came out with a packet of matches. Several trees, ready to be planted, were lying on the ground close to the house. I tried to blame Cassie afterwards, but she admitted only to striking the match.

'You held the branch down to it,' she said.

Bugger it. How unfaithful she is, I thought.

The leaves burned first. The tree caught alight. Then the house caught fire and to our horror, that burned too. We ran home to my place.

'Mum, Mum, we just burned a house down.'

'Oh, go inside and stop talking nonsense.'

Just then, the fire engine went past and she realized then that we weren't telling lies. She went to see Cassie's father.

'They set fire to a house over in the next street,' she told him.

'Leave it to me, Mrs. Kerby. I'll handle them.'

But Cassie's dad didn't come. No one came. We were never punished.

School Years

I attended a total of twenty-two schools as I was growing up. We would run short of money for the rent and have to leave our house and move on. The main districts we came back to were Ballarat, Northcote and St Kilda. The longest I attended any one school was about three years at Middle Park Central. I was there from when I was nine until I was twelve.

Back in Melbourne, we moved to Cramer Street in Preston and Dad worked in Brunswick for Drury's travel business. They had open air buses called "charabancs".

Soon after my father started work there, I decided to walk to Brunswick. It was a very long way for a six year old, but I wanted to see the place where he was working. On the way, I came to Pentridge Gaol. There was a man, a guard, walking along the wall. I was petrified. I stopped on the road and wouldn't go past Pentridge. A woman with a pram came along.

'What's the matter?' she said.

'I'm worried about that man.'

'If you haven't done anything wrong, he can't do anything to you.'

That didn't pacify me at all, because I felt guilty about the mischief Cassie and I had been involved in. Eventually, I raised some courage and walked all the way to the charabanc company. It was about three miles. My father was surprised to see me and let me explore one of the buses. He even let me sit up in the driver's seat.

Each bus had about twenty-five wooden seats and opposite each row of seats, was a little door. They had canvas sides and top.

Preston was the second state school I attended. There was a fire alarm on a power pole. I would break the glass and press the button, then wait for the fire brigade to come. After I'd done this twice, the firemen told me not to do it again. I can't remember what they threatened me with, but I stopped after that.

My third state school was Northcote. There, I 'palled-up' with a girl, the second of many females in my life, other than my mother and sister. After my exploits with Cassie, my mother was a little concerned about my association with girls.[1]

My mother was a weaver. While we lived in Northcote, she took a job in a woollen mill. I don't think my mother ever went out to work after that, except many years later at the St Kilda Pier Kiosk.

My mother had a miscarriage and went into hospital. Apart from a curette, she had four other operations on the same day, one of which was the removal of her appendix. While she was in hospital and then convalescing, my sister looked after me. Hilda was fourteen and attended St Kilda High School. She took me to school with her and I sat beside her in class.

~

[1] *When Col makes any mention of the women in his life, he remains deadpan, while Judy rolls her eyes, puts her hands over her ears and says 'I'm leaving, I'm leaving.'*

Dad Starts His Own Business

Dad formed his own company in 1928, taking passengers from Melbourne to Naracoorte, across the border in South Australia. He called the company Kerby's Passenger Service, bought three Austin 12's and hired two other drivers.

One day, while Dad was driving through Gordon, a country area near Ballarat, he knocked a man off his bicycle, breaking his leg. Dad needed a stretcher for the injured man. There was a shed nearby. He ran to the shed and ripped the door off its hinges. To Dad's great surprise, behind the door was a man defecating into a bucket.

One accident was bad enough. Because my father couldn't afford to pay extra for commercial insurance and the carriage of passengers, his policy covered only private, non-commercial usage of the vehicles. However, one of the other drivers also had an accident. The driver left the car at a garage for an insurance assessment. My father had warned his drivers to remove the company business card from inside the vehicle. The driver forgot and the insurance assessor found the card. The insurance company refused any payout. Now there were two cars out of action and my father had no money to pay for their repairs. He had to sell the business and look for other work.

Dad's next job was driving buses, but he was always keen to start his own business again. He knew a man called Rupert Mullane, who suggested they go into business together taking passengers. This time, they wanted to transport people by bus up Sydney Road in Melbourne.

A friend, Hampton, told my father that there was a loophole in the *Hackney Carriage Act* that allowed it. You could do it legally if you went about it the right way. He said The law said that you couldn't go into competition with the railways by carrying passengers, but there was another section, section 93, in the constitution that there mustn't be restrictions between businesses. My father had used this loophole for his business transporting passengers to Narracoorte. In that case, he was exempt from the law that one was forbidden to compete with public transport within Victoria, because Narracoorte was in South Australia.

In Hampton's opinion, they could exploit this again by running a bus along Sydney Road to the tram depot in Coburg, in competition with the tram. Together with Rupert Mullane, they consulted a solicitor called Autry.

'Yes, you can do it,' Autry told them.

Mullane was a colourful man with a politically litigious family background. Hampton and my father were carried away by his passionate enthusiasm. Together, the three of them bought a bus and began transporting people, charging two pence per section. However, this business didn't last long. Mullane, the originator of the idea and the solicitor were wrong. All three partners were prosecuted and charged with breaking the law. Fines were imposed, but because they couldn't pay, they became fugitives.

9

My Father Arrested

At that time, my father was standing for Melbourne Ports in the Federal Parliament. He was hoping to gain election to parliament, so that he would be immune from imprisonment. The police were looking for him to arrest him. As he was walking on the street one day, a policeman came by on a bicycle. He thought he recognized my father.

'Noble!' he called out.

Upon hearing his name, Dad turned around, giving himself away. The policeman arrested him at gunpoint. The old man thought the copper might accidentally fire the gun.

'For Christ's sake put that thing away,' he told the cop. 'It might go off.'

My father was sentenced to six years in gaol and his partners were sentenced to eight years. In the end, Hampton served fourteen months, Mullane served eight months and my father did six months in Pentridge. I remember visiting him there only once with my mother and sister when I was nine. My mother didn't take us with her again.

The Truth newspaper, took up my father's case. They ran a collection and raised enough money to pay the company's fines, which amounted to about eight hundred pounds. In the paper, they wrote about how Noble was a returned soldier and had been in the trenches. He told me before he died that those fines were quite extensive, but the donations covered all the money and court costs. Once the money was paid, he and his partners were released from gaol.

Mammoth Bicycle Ride

During May 1930, while my father was incarcerated, I rode my bicycle to Ballarat, seventy-two miles away, to see my Grandmother. I took nearly ten hours to ride there, but came home again in eight and a half hours, because it was downhill. That was published in the newspaper with a photograph of me. Apparently that ride from Melbourne to Ballarat was a record distance for a nine year old to cycle – a record that has never been beaten.

*Col at nine after riding his bike
from Melbourne to Ballarat.*

We moved to Albert Park in 1930 and I sold Heralds that year. The paper shop is still there in Albert Park. It has a sloping sill at the bottom of the window, where I would sit in the early sunlight. One morning, the whole thing shook, knocking me right off. I went home and told my mother.

'There's been an earthquake in New Zealand,' she told me.

I definitely felt it there in Melbourne. Later, when we lived in Rabaul, cups on hooks would jump when we had an earthquake.

~

When my father came out of gaol, he sold his transport business and we went to Ballarat again, to live with his family for a while. Once again, Dad worked at the garage in Sturt Street, but there wasn't much call for his services during the Great Depression. Mainly, we lived on Dad's meagre war pension, which at least bought us food.

During this period, my father used his spare time to design and build a special shock absorber for cars, which he patented in Australia and a couple of other countries, including France.

Grandparents

Dad and his brothers had grown up in Ballarat. His forebears had moved there from at Port Donald in South Australia, where my great grandparents were married. My great grandfather Kerby was born in Hamilton in Canada, where he had trained as a mining engineer and my great grandmother came from Ireland to South Australia as a free settler. My grandfather, James Macklan Kerby, was born on 18/8/1861. His birth certificate was signed by his mother with a cross, because she was illiterate.

At Port Donald, Great Grandfather worked for the Canadian gold mining company, Pierce and Co. where he eventually became Underground Mine Manager. Later, he moved with his family to Ballarat, where he undertook a similar position with another mining company, The North Woah Hawp Canton [or Co.]. He filled the top position there for a number of years.

Grandpa started in another gold mine at Ballarat in 1872, when he was only eleven years old. He was a pushy young man, who moved up through all levels of underground management becoming, like his father, Underground Mine Manager. The last mine operating in Ballarat was called The Last Chance. It had closed by 1925.

My grandfather was short and stout and I found him rather intimidating. He was fairly affluent by the 1920's and owned a large house. I've been to Ballarat many times over the past twenty years. Several of my family, including my great grandmother, are buried in the Ballarat cemetery.

We have a magnificent silver cup, which my grandfather won when he was captain of the tug of war team for the goldfield in 1899. My father was born the same day. To my father's absolute horror, his parents named him Noble Victorious Champion Kerby. He detested the name throughout his life.

Grandpa separated from my grandmother about the mid nineteen twenties. Claiming that he was chasing a string of women, she moved out. The gold was mined out by then, so Grandpa sold the big house, bought a fruit shop in the main street of Prahran, a suburb of Melbourne, and lived in the flat above the shop. Grandmother remained living in a smaller house in Ballarat.

Back to Melbourne

After the depression, we came back to Melbourne and my father started in a good position working as an engineer for Alstergren's timber company in Melbourne. His job was to service the 'Gerlinger' timber straddlers, which were used to move piles of logs.

At first, we lived at Middle Park, where. There was a section of Middle Park Central State School which was also a high school. I was twelve and started high school there. I didn't have any choice regarding subjects. The teachers just put me into the academic course. I was learning French and Latin. We did science too – physics and chemistry, but there was no biology. I liked science, especially physics.

There's a big market in South Melbourne near the Middle Park School. One day after school, I was near the market with a big bundle of plasticine in my hand. I was nonchalantly rolling up tiny balls of it, about as big as a pea, and throwing them into the air. I threw one wildly towards the market stalls. A Chinaman, who was serving in his stall, dropped everything and started feeling his lip. I realised I had hit him on the lip.

I felt guilty and when he looked at me, I ran. He ran after me. What saved me was the heavy, leather bag around his waist with his money in it. I ran across the schoolyard nearby, with him following.

'Me catch you, me kill you,' he called out after me.

I saw a teacher coming out of the school building and I ran towards him for protection. When he saw the Chinaman chasing me, the teacher ducked inside without me. I wasn't trying to hit the Chinaman; it was an accident. In Ballarat, there were a lot of Chinese from the gold mining days; my father had several Chinese friends. The Chinaman gave up and went back to his stall and I didn't go near him for a long time.

St Kilda

We liked living at St Kilda and moved back there before I turned thirteen. I often swam in the ocean pool. The pool had two landings, one near the beach and another on the seaward side of the pool. One day, a group of kids were diving from the landing at the shallow end, where the water was about three feet deep. After each dive, they returned to the landing to dive again. Later, I noticed the group had returned with another boy. He ran to the deeper landing and dived off. A small group of us watched with amusement as he floundered in the water, but soon it became obvious that he couldn't swim. I had been taught life-saving at school, so I swam over and pulled him out.

Because I had saved his life, I received a letter of commendation from the Victorian Department of Education. Later, I received a medallion for swimming six hundred yards fully clothed. That was only the first of many life savings I performed at St Kilda.

There was a Catholic High School in St Kilda and I continued my schooling there. I did well in chemistry, being presented with an award for that subject, by the Catholic Archbishop, for topping all Catholic schools in Victoria. He didn't know I was an atheist. I'm sure he thought I was a Protestant. Perhaps I wouldn't have received that award had he known.

I built a small speed boat and my father gave me an outboard motor for it that he bought from Alstergren's. I loved messing about St Kilda Bay in my boat. The last time I saw Cassie, I was fourteen. It was during the Easter holidays. I was playing about in St Kilda Bay with a little speed boat I'd built. It was only seven by three feet and had an outboard motor. I was doing close to seventeen knots, which was as fast as it would go - not bad for a motorboat in 1935. A ten centimetres high wave lopped against the side of the boat and we rolled over. In the water, everything looked green, then I came up again. I had to be rescued. A reporter on the beach saw me. When he photographed me, I said what everybody else says when they have an unstable vessel.

'I hit a submerged object, I told the reporter.'

There was a short article in the Sunday paper about the incident and a photograph of me, with my name and address.

14

*Fourteen year old Colin with homemade speedboat
and Ace outboard motor.*

On Monday, a knock came at the door. When I opened it, there stood a woman wearing a big hat. To me, she looked about twenty-eight.

Beside her was a skinny girl, who knew St Kilda and had come along to point out where we lived. They worked together.

'Do you remember me?'

'No, I don't.'

'Don't you remember Cassie C...?'

I turned around and ran down the hall, yelling out 'Mummm.'

That was the last I saw of her.

~

A school mate called Bobby Ward, also fourteen years old, and I started a business giving speed boat rides. We even had our own business card printed. We called ourselves 'Speed Boat Specialists.' We charged people one shilling and sixpence [about eighteen cents] for a ten minute ride in St Kilda Bay.

Bobby Ward enlisted for World War II and was sent to Malaya. He was killed the day the Japanese invaded the peninsula.

My mother went for a trip to England in 1935. My father said if ever he saved enough money, she could have a trip home to Lancashire. I don't know how he saved enough money to send her.

While she was away, the house was mostly empty; my sister was already married and I was boarding out. Only my father lived there.

Chemistry

At school, I had a mate called Weary. Weary's proper name was Graydon. That name didn't suit him because he looked tired all the time. Someone called him Weary Willy, and so that's what we called him. His mother objected to the name. When I went to his house, I'd start to call him 'Weary' and I'd have to stop myself. Instead I had to train myself to say, "Graydon."

Weary and I made a laboratory in my bedroom at the house. We concentrated on explosives. One of our explosives put Weary into hospital one day. We made a small cannon by taking a piece of galvanised water pipe, putting it in the vice and squeezing up one end. We drilled a little, weeny hole, 1/16 of an inch for a touch hole. We inserted two teaspoons of our saltpetre mixture down the pipe. Next, we put a small bolt inside for a projectile. We took it into the yard to light it. I was holding the match, ready to strike it.

'Will I light this, Weary?'

'No, you've lit all the others. I'll do it,' he said.

'All right, but don't stand behind it.'

Ignoring my advice, Weary stood behind the "cannon" and lit it. It went off all right! It blew back and a piece of pipe hit him on the eyebrow, giving him a decent sort of a cut. The bolt just fell onto the ground. I was knocked stupid by the concussion from the blast. He started to scream.

'Do something, you fool! Do something!' Then he started running around the yard.

'Murder, plain murder,' cried the neighbour, sticking his head over the fence. The concussion had killed the old man's canary.

My father emerged from the house. Weary had blood all over his head. I thought Dad was going to go crook over this. Instead he dealt with my friend's injuries and drove him to hospital. Weary had so many cuts on his head that the doctors clipped the skin together rather than using sutures.

I kept that pipe for years. I showed it to an acquaintance and this dolt broke off all the shredded pieces of pipe.

'It was a bloody good article,' I protested.

'I didn't know you wanted to keep it.'

'Well, I've kept it for years. And you go and smash it up.' I could have choked him.

~

Attending our school was a fellow named Duckworth, who travelled from twelve miles away across Melbourne. He went home and told his cousin what Weary and I had done. Duckworth and his cousin used to get a nut and screw a bolt into the end of it. Then they put about a teaspoon of gunpowder into the nut and hit it with a hammer to make a bang. His cousin was screwing one up one day when it went off and blew part of his thumb away.

Somebody living near us put explosives on a tram track and damaged a tram. It wasn't me, but it was interesting how the authorities came to ask me about it.

The police interviewed a teenager from Duckworth's suburb..

'Who taught you how to make gunpowder?'

'Duckworth.'

They went to Duckworth and asked him the same question.

'Colin Kerby in St Kilda.'

So they thought they were on to something, but about a fortnight before, The Age newspaper had published in a Do it Yourself section, how to make crackers with about a teaspoon of gunpowder. We were making it in Barnes' honey jars, heaps of it.

The Inspector for Explosives, a man named Todner, came down to our school and brought a copper with him. Weary was at school with these clips all over his head. They called him out of class.

'Who do you make explosives with?'

'Colin, over there.'

So they called me out too. They accused us of the tram track explosion.

'No, no, we don't do that kind of thing,' we protested.

'Where do you make this gunpowder?'

'In my bedroom.'

They came to the house and went into my bedroom. They saw jars of gunpowder all lined up along the shelf, about ten kilos of it. Todner was flabbergasted.

'Christ almighty!'

17

He took all the jars outside and poured the powder down the gully trap.

We were bloody annoyed, because we'd spent our pennies on the ingredients. It was useless once it was wet. The detective spoke to my father and admonished him for allowing me to make gunpowder. My father disliked petty authority.

'I'm not going to stop him. The Age published how to do it a fortnight ago.'

The recipe in The Age wasn't very effective really. Ours was much more powerful. We used potash instead of saltpetre. If you use potassium chlorite, it's even more powerful, more sensitive and dangerous, but potassium chlorite nearly killed me later and it stopped me going into the army during World War II.

We never found out who had put explosive on the tram track.

Puberty

By the time my mother went to England, I had reached puberty. By then, I had developed many interests which influenced my adult life. Chemistry and photography were hobbies. I loved building things, so I built my own cameras, including a small movie camera. I've already mentioned my speed boat, a small business, swimming and life-saving.

I also became very interested in girls. A family with three girls, Lois, Marj and Betty, lived across the road from us in St Kilda. Lois and I were both fourteen when we met and she became a lifelong friend. We are still friends today. Her mother insisted on calling her Loyss. It was only later I found out the name was usually pronounced Lo-is.

Their father was an impressive man. He had been blind since birth, being born with no eyes. He earned his living playing the piano in a local bar. To get to work, he would walk straight down the centre of the footpath, no cane, hands in his pockets. Often, I would watch him and he never deviated. He'd come to the corner, and turn – amazing!

Like all boys that age, I thought about sex frequently. I fantasised about Lois and when she and I were both fifteen, there was one night when, if I'd been a little bit more game, neither of us would have been virgins again. I just didn't have the courage. I couldn't reach the light switch and I wasn't confident enough with the light on.

In early 1937, soon after I reached fifteen, Alstergren's timber firm in Melbourne sent my father up to Rabaul in New Britain (part of Papua New Guinea). The company was interested in extracting timber from forests near there and Dad went as their Site Engineer. Mum and I stayed on in St Kilda, because I was still at school. While Dad was away, I still spent a lot of time at St Kilda Bay.

Later, Lois went nursing and I went to New Guinea. When I came back to Melbourne, I took her out again. She was living in a Nurses' Home then. One night, I was hiking her over the fence when the matron came out. This matron tapped me on the back while I had my hands on Lois's bum. I didn't know whether to let go or not. After all, matrons are pretty fierce people. I hoisted Lois over the top, then I wouldn't tell the matron the name of the girl. I said Mary somebody, like in New Guinea. Up there, the women were all called 'Mary'.

Lois became a matron. Married women were not permitted to work in public service occupations, like nursing or teaching but, after Lois married, she bought her own private hospital.

~

Diving Helmets
Deep sea diving fascinated me. I tried making a diving helmet from a ten-gallon rectangular kerosene tin. I cut a piece out of one side and screwed some celluloid (not perspex in those days) on the front. We glued it all around with Tarzan's Grip. I didn't have the money to buy the glue I needed. My friend, Bobby Bruin, went off somewhere and came back with the glue.

'Where did you get that?'

'I went down to the hardware shop.'

I put the glue around the helmet.

Under the St Kilda Pier, there was some lead-covered cable that I thought was defunct. I rowed under the pier in my little speedboat and, with some scissors and pliers, I chopped off about a yard of cable each time I went under. I finished up with a pile of it.

We had a wood stove in our house, but Lois's family used gas for cooking. We put the lengths of cable into a big pot on the gas burner. My idea was to melt the lead for diving weights. There was rubber under the lead and that caught fire. It created stalactites of rubber soot all around the whole house. We just about wrecked the house. I don't know why their mother was so kind to me. She didn't say anything much about it or forbid me from visiting them.

We made our lead weights. I fixed leather to the base of my homemade helmet and bent nails for hooks through the leather. I attached the weights to the hooks, to hold the helmet down below my shoulders. The air inside kept the water from getting in. With weights on our helmet, Bobby and I dived off St Kilda Pier, using a car tyre pump for our air supply.

I continued experimenting with diving outfits, changing from using the kerosene tin helmet to an ice cream can. The can was about twelve inches in diameter. The problem was it wasn't quite wide enough for my long nose. The can was round. I used a chisel to cut out a hole and glued celluloid over it for a visor. There was a trick to getting the helmet on or off. You couldn't put it on with your head straight. You had to lower your chin, or your nose wouldn't clear the jagged edge inside.

Col and friend with homemade diving helmet.

Lois was concerned I'd drown myself in this suit. Frequently, she would accompany me. Her chief concern was that the nails for my lead would become caught on some obstacle under the water and I would be unable to extricate myself.

One day, I was down on St Kilda Pier with Lois. A strapping young lad of about eighteen came along and, without speaking to me, picked up my helmet off the pier. He put it on and was walking about saying, 'I'm Ned Kelly.'

He didn't know the technique for getting the helmet off. While he was trying to get it off with his chin up, he cut his nose on the sharp edge. I decided I'd let the bugger suffer for a while for having taken it without asking. He thought he was calaboosed there forever, like the man in the iron mask. After he'd damaged his nose enough, he was out of control. I had to pacify him. I thought he might cut his nose right off. Eventually, he did as I told him; he lowered his chin and he took it off his head.

That's how I learned about diving and soon after that, my mother and I went off to visit Dad in New Guinea. We were supposed to return to Melbourne for me to continue my education, but that's not how it turned out and my interest in diving also had unexpected repercussions.

2 Papua New Guinea

*Map of Blanche Bay, New Britain, showing Rabaul, Kokopo
and island volcanoes: Matupi and Vulcan.
Scale: 1 inch to 5 miles.*

Alstergren's timber company sent a crew, including my father, to the island of New Britain in 1937, to commence timber felling operations at Put Put. When I had Easter school holidays coming up, my mother and I went on the P&O boat, *Neptune,* up to New Britain to visit Dad. We disembarked at Rabaul, the only port on the island.

At first, my mother and I lived about twenty-five miles from Rabaul, at the village of Kokopo, where accommodation was easier to obtain. Dad was living in the timber camp at Put Put, eighty miles away. He came to Kokopo on weekends whenever he could get a lift. I amused myself by learning Pidgin, so I could speak with the locals.

Eruption

Just over a month after we arrived in New Britain, there were two huge volcanic eruptions in Rabaul. We had gone into the town that day. About six or eight miles away, Matupi Island was spewing out ash. A fellow I'd met wanted to tow out his utility; it was stuck in the mud and ash a couple of miles out of town. I went with him in his truck for the ride. We tied a rope onto the ute to tow it out.

Just then, a volcano started coming up out of Simpson Harbour. We saw a local priest out in the bay in a sixteen foot dinghy with an inboard motor. The reef rose about four feet out of the water, taking him with it, boat and all. He stepped out of the boat and ran ashore on the new coral reef.

A mountain rose a thousand feet[2] as we watched, formed a crater and that started to erupt too. I photographed the eruptions with a little movie camera I had brought with me from Melbourne. We thought we should get out of there, so without untying the ute, we jumped into the truck and charged off. We nearly went through the windscreen. After disconnecting the rope, we drove back to town. By then, Matupi had started erupting large amounts of pumice. It was all very exciting. I don't think I realised the danger at first.

---

[2] The Golden Bear, *was in the harbour at the time. Her captain measured the height of Vulcan with his sextant. The new volcano was 670 feet above sea level. Source: John 'Jack' Faulkner's Diary.*

Volcanic eruption , Rabaul, 1937.

Mt. Namanula and the hospital for Europeans lie just inland from Rabaul. To escape from the eruption, everyone was running up that way ahead of me.

By this time I had learned a little bit of Pidgin. A native was running up towards the mountain, but then he turned onto a track heading down again.

'Where are you going?' I asked.

'I'm going to the church to pray,' he said.

'Never mind that. Run,' I replied in Pidgin.

Ash and pumice covered the church. In all, about five to eight hundred people were killed during the eruption. There was another big eruption in 1994. That time the wind was blowing the ash towards the town and buried Rabaul, but in 1937, the wind was blowing most of the ash away and the town survived, even though it was very thickly covered in pumice and dust, sufficient to damage many roofs. Until the eruption ceased, the white residents of the area, numbering about eight hundred, set up a tent community on the north coast. When everything settled down, they all returned to clean up the town. The new island mountain in the bay became known as Vulcan.

In New Guinea, most people used primus stoves for cooking. One day, I was given a faulty primus to fix. To test the stove, I pressurised the tank, primed the burner with methylated spirit and lit the pre-heated kerosene. The day was hot and I was dressed only in my bathing trunks. I lay on the ground, keenly watching the stove. I was unaware that pressurised kerosene was squirting out of a pinhole in the tube between the tank and the burner. The kerosene ignited and the flame was directed towards the fuel tank. While the fuel tank heated up, I was busy admiring the quality of the flame on the burner. The tank exploded. My face and chest were drenched in hot kerosene. Fortunately for me, I was not seriously burned. The air pressure from the explosion extinguished the flame. This was only the first of several times I came close to death.

The *Tilbura*

While Dad was working at Put Put, the Government called for tenders on the *Tilbura*, a forty foot Government launch without a motor. My father put a tender in for it and then went back to Put Put. After a couple of weeks, we received word to say our offer had been accepted. The boat we'd bought was tied up to the Government wharf at Rabaul and the government officials required us to take it away as soon as possible. At the wharf, they came down to show me which launch it was. They gave me the papers and, with a boat I'd hired, I towed the *Tilbura* back to Kokopo, where I anchored it.

Dad was fed up with staying in the huts with the other workers, because they boozed too much. He wanted me to bring the *Tilbura* to Put Put, so he could live on board.

I had become 'pally' with an older New Guinean, Bennie, who had a large native boat. It was about twenty-five feet long, a narrow, open boat with a mast and sail. I had an outboard motor that I put on his boat and we would play around with it. Bennie and I set off. We towed the *Tilbura* down to the beautiful little harbour at Put Put, then we sailed back to Kokopo in Bennie's boat.

~

A ropey named Bolsche was causing my father trouble at work. A ropey was the man in charge of all the wires on the site. He handled the wire and rigged it to go around the log. In those days, after they cut the timber down, they had to winch it out of the bush. There was a wire rope to a winch on a big tree a couple of miles away. On trees in between, the wire rope ran through blocks [pulleys] and a man ran with the log, as it was being winched. There was also a signal wire, which ran all the way to the winch site and worked a whistle. When the tree arrived at a block, the runner pulled the cord to the whistle and the winch-man stopped the winch. The runner unhooked the rope hauling the log, took it from one side of the block to the other and refastened it. At his signal, the winch-man restarted dragging the log. The repositioning of the wire ropes had to be done several times on a two mile drag. The modern way is to use a tractor to drag the log all the way.

The company was using native labour to clear the bush. If you belted a native, the rule was you must not hit him in the spleen area, because all the natives had malaria and if you hit them in the spleen area, they haemorrhaged and died. This injunction was not always followed and Bolsche bashed two natives, hitting them in the spleen area. Both natives died.

When Bolsche was charged and protested his innocence, my father wouldn't back him up. Dad complained that Bolsche was brutal to the natives. Instead of sacking Bolsche, Alstergren's sacked my father, who then had to leave the timber camp.

I arranged with Bennie for us to return to Put Put, pick up the launch and my father, then tow the *Tilbura* back to Kokopo. Later, Dad sued Alstergren's for wrongful dismissal and won the case. In the meantime, we were stuck in New Guinea with no income.

~

I was supposed to return to school in Melbourne, but I stayed on while my father searched for another job. We didn't have enough money to send me and my mother home. I was not upset about this. Life in New Guinea was providing many exciting experiences for me.

For six weeks after my father was sacked, our only income was his meagre war veteran's pension. My father didn't want me to work for the timber company, but just in case we stayed and I applied for a job there, I needed a first aid certificate. To work native labour in groups of more than ten and up to a hundred and fifty, you had to be qualified in first aid and Pidgin. Dad arranged for me to study first aid at the hospital for native patients at Bitalova, twelve miles from Kokopo.

First Aid

The man in charge of the hospital was called Mr Parry. He wasn't a trained doctor; he was a senior medical assistant. He had been medical assistant in charge of the Bitalova hospital since the Germans left after World War I. Mr Parry also taught the First Aid course.

First Aid was a complex course that took a minimum of six months to complete. During that course, I saw my first dead person and I watched my first post mortem. Seeing a dead person cut open fascinated me. The course involved much, much more than it does for First Aid in Australia. We were taugh you're taught to use a scalpel on relatively minor problems like abscesses and tropical ulcers.

'You'd better learn something,' Mr Parry told me and handed me a scalpel.

I took amputated a toe the second or third day I was there. Of course, Mr Parry was guiding my hand, telling me where to cut. The idea of being a surgeon intrigued me. Because of Mr Parry's efficient instruction, the operation on the Native's toe was successful. I passed my First Aid certificate by the time I turned sixteen in November.

Tropical ulcers were ghastly things, nearly always below the knee. On occasions, they became huge, covering the whole of the lower leg and the foot, infecting the bone. If not treated, these ulcers could kill the patient. That was before we had antibiotics.

Mr Parry had arrived in New Guinea in the early 1920's. He was an excellent surgeon. I've seen operations he did on feet that you wouldn't believe would ever walk again. Mr Parry would almost take the sole of the foot off, scrub up the flesh, then put the sole back on. It was incredible how fast and rough he was, yet his operations were successful. Most native surgery was performed by medical assistants because in New Britain, there weren't enough qualified doctors – only ten altogether for four and a half million natives – but there were over forty medical assistants. Later, I trained as a medical assistant at Rapindik, the very large native hospital near Rabaul.

While Mr Parry was at the hospital, the Australian Health Department sent out a doctor, a fair dinkum doctor. This doctor would give an anaesthetic, but that was all he ever did.

'Do you want me to do this?' Mr Parry would ask.

'You know more about it than I do, Mr Parry. You do whatever you need to.'

A few years later, I met Mr Parry at a New Year's Eve party. He'd changed so much, I didn't recognize him at first. It was only when he started asking how my mother was, that I took another look and recognized him. He had been a hefty man and he'd lost a lot of weight.

Pidgin

I had started learning Pidgin as soon as I arrived in New Guinea and eventually became very fluent. Despite my father's ability to speak French, he didn't speak Pidgin very fluently, although he wasn't too bad. Because he was cross eyed, the natives often thought he was speaking to someone behind them. My mother spoke Pidgin too. She would speak Pidgin to me and English to the Natives. It drove me mad. There was a three months gaol term if you taught the natives English. You weren't allowed to let them learn, because if they were serving you at table, you didn't want them listening to your conversation.

All government officials had to be fluent in Pidgin and when I became a government employee, I was an official. If you weren't fluent enough, twelve percent of your pay was held back until such time that you were fluent. I went to lessons during work time for a little while. When I passed, I received my twelve percent back-pay.

Pidgin is not as simple as many people think. It is quite an evolved language. For example, they have lots of words for mosquito. Many people who go to New Guinea think they're speaking Pidgin. If they're living in a town or city, the natives glean a bit of English. You get newcomers who are up there for three or four months and reckon they can speak Pidgin; they're not speaking Pidgin at all. They use a few words in Pidgin and the natives get the gist of what they mean. To get to learn Pidgin, you need to go to a courthouse and listen to a magistrate speaking, or better still, in Rabaul at that time, the Clerk of the Court. He'd been there since

World War I, and he spoke beautiful Pidgin. It just flowed. I went often to listen to him.

I had no trouble getting the natives to work for me, because I was quite fluent in the language, young, and the natives liked the idea of working for a young white man. Several of my friends there were natives.

To make just a little money, we towed the *Tilbura* from Kokopo into Rabaul and put a Dodge car motor in it. Dad and I lived on board at Rabaul. We ran a ferry service for natives, charging them a shilling to go from Karavia Bay to the market and a stick of tobacco, worth three pence, to go home again. Dad and I made a few shillings this way. It wasn't much money, but I found it fun.

Diver Kerby

A Japanese salvage firm came to Rabaul to raise an eighty foot schooner; it was actually a ketch. In New Guinea, all the boats were ketches (the aft mast is a little shorter), but schooner is the Pidgin word for it. The firm was called Nano Buki Kysho and they used fair dinkum salvage divers' suits, copper helmets and all. We had binoculars on board. Using these, I zealously watched those guys get dressed and then dive. If you haven't watched them go through the procedure, you couldn't do it. I watched them for about a fortnight. I saw exactly what they did. I thought I could do that too, so I went over to them. After my experience in St Kilda Bay, I was full of youthful confidence.

'I'm Diver Kerby from Moresby. Have you any work for me?'

I had just turned sixteen that month, but I knew they couldn't contact Moresby. It was four hundred miles away. Today, you could just ring up, fax or email and ask "Is this bloke dinkum?" But they couldn't do that then.

'Yes, we have one man going on leave. It would be good to have a replacement diver.'

I was so excited, I nearly fell over. There were two other divers. I watched them ever so carefully.

To put on the diving suit, you pulled the rubber suit or dress up to your chest. There was a false collar or bib that fitted inside, which stopped water entering your suit. You folded that collar over and then your attendant put the copper corselet on you and put the bolts through the holes. Next, the brasses went on over your shoulders. Then the weights were attached to your shoulders and to a belt around your waist. These weighed forty pounds each. The helmet went on last, 'clunk', and finally, the attendant attached the helmet to the corselet, securing the bolts with wing nuts.

We were putting camels [air tanks] onto the hull to float it up to the surface. The first task I had was to go down with an air hose, which I'd poke into the hole to fill the camel, then keep out of the way when it floated up. When it started to float, we added the rest of the air. Eventually, the camel would rise to the top. Where you don't have much tidal rise and fall, as in Rabaul Harbour, with only about forty inches [one metre] of tide, filling the camels with air was difficult. We had very little space underneath the camels for the hoses.

Whenever the visor in my helmet fogged up, I would wipe it clear with the end of my long nose. Over the six weeks, I developed a callous on the end of my nose, which remained there for a couple of years. Towards the end of my six weeks with the diving team, one of the other divers was clearing his visor in quite a different way. I was puzzled.

'Why are you doing that?'

'I'm clearing my visor.' He paused. 'How long have you been diving, Kerby?'

'Ah...ah...not long.'

'This is the spit cock.' He showed me a small tube on the side of the helmet. 'It works like this. You suck in a little water, put your face down to allow the water to clear away the fogging, then you blow the water out again.'

'Well, isn't that clever,' I said.

The team lifted the schooner up, pumped her out so she was floating, then they went home to Japan with all the information about Rabaul harbour, which they used to their advantage a couple of years later.

I earned twenty nine pounds [about $60] the first week of diving. I was elated. That was bloody good pay for a lad in those times. I loved the diving and I worked for the salvage team for a bit over six weeks. I dived in New Guinea again in 1950. By then, I had experience with salvage work in Australia.

Various Jobs

After being unemployed for about six weeks, my father found a job in Rabaul, repairing cars, doing valve grinds and other mechanical work. My father was making about twelve pounds a week as a mechanic. With both Dad and me earning, we were able to clear our debts. By Christmas, we were able to pay our servants and rent a house in Rabaul for the three of us.

After the Japanese left, I joined Dad working the copra ships. The overseas ships came into Rabaul to pick up the copra and usually there were about one hundred and fifty natives loading it. One of the casual jobs available was supervising the natives loading the copra, which was packed in one hundred and sixty pound bags. The sacks went into slings for the crane to swing up on deck. The other job was tally clerk. We worked alternatively at this. Having my first aid certificate qualified me for these jobs.

Ten or twelve of us in Rabaul worked on the ships. When we heard the rattle of an anchor chain going overboard, we'd race down to the depot to get our jobs. There was work for only eight of us, so unless we ran down there in a hurry, we missed out on the job.

~

My mechanical apprenticeship with my father started when I was ten and went on for many years. Back then, I was allowed to 'help' when he was running the mechanical workshop in Ballarat. There was an Italian workshop in Rabaul. In my spare time, I worked in their engineering workshop. Later, I worked in the Department of Public Works workshop. I'd go down there and tinker about. The mechanics taught me to grind crankshafts for them in my free time and I did shifts after my day's work. They eventually acknowledged all that experience and called it an apprenticeship. They sent me the certificate when I was back in Melbourne. For most of that work, I didn't get paid. It was all fun to me.

Sinking the *Tilbura*

The shipwright in Rabaul was called Izumi. He was Japanese and, as with the salvage team, was probably a spy. Izumi had several boats on his slipway. One of them was ready to go back into the water. He had been re-caulking the one behind it. It was nearly finished, so he ran them both off and put a native on board overnight to keep watch on the unfinished boat and to pump it out if it leaked. Izumi was going to put it back on the slipway again with the tide the next morning. The boat sank overnight and next morning, Izumi found the watchman hanging on at the top of the mast and the boat was on the bottom of the bay

My father did a deal with Izumi. If we could get the boat up, as part of our payment for salvaging it, we were to have the diesel engine cheap. We did that, taking the drowned Fairbanks Morse diesel out of that boat and putting in into the *Tilbura*. On the North coast, there was a company that cut timber and made it into rafts for transportation. They paid to have the rafts towed south to Rabaul. We thought if we had a more powerful motor in the *Tilbura*, we could do this sort of work.

We removed the Dodge and installed the bigger diesel, but we also needed lathe work done on the gearbox and propeller. We did a deal with the Italian workshop: if they would finance us for this work, we'd pay them when we started taking rafts. That was agreed.

As well, we arranged with Izumi to replace our deck. It was double layered and when it leaked, we couldn't tell where the water was coming in. We wanted a single layer deck. We told Izumi about the deal we had with the Italians and he agreed to the same deal.

It took us six months to get our boat finished. We brought the first raft of timber in and we were paid seventy pounds for it. We paid a few pounds to the Italians and to Izumi and we paid our natives. We hadn't been paying them for a few months, so they were owed wages of about eight shillings a month - about ten pounds altogether. They continued to work for us and we were all able to eat decent food again.

To our dismay, there were no more rafts after that. We did only that one raft with the *Tilbura*, but we still owed the Italians and Izumi money for the fitting out of the boat. They thought they weren't going to get their money. Before either of us obtained our government jobs, the Italians sued us for the balance owing. When the Italians did that, Izumi, to protect his investment in the boat, sued us too. That was the only property we owned.

The Police in Rabaul were about to put a writ on the *Tilbura*. They knew the papers were coming, so in the afternoon, they seized the boat, taking it to the government wharf. My father had the job of fixing the Police Chief's car. He told Dad they'd produce the papers the next day.

'Dad, we haven't been presented with any papers. Officially, she's still ours. I reckon we ought to sink her, just to spite them.'

'How would you do that?'

Originally, there were drains from the cockpit, down under the floor. We had taken the drain pipes out to enable us to store our four diesel drums under there. Short pieces of pipe still protruded inside the hull; we had plugged these with wooden bungs.

'I'll cut about a foot off a broom handle and I'll swim over, poke the piece of broom handle up each pipe and knock the plug out.'

I wanted to sink the *Tilbura* because I felt resentful the workshops wouldn't wait till we had earned the money to pay our debts. They were going to put the boat up for auction and we had no money to try to get it back, so if we sank the bloody thing, they wouldn't get anything out of it anyway.

'How will you get down there?'

'I'll swim out.'

'I don't want you swimming out there.' My father was imagining crocodiles in the harbour.

'All right. I'll use my mate's canoe.'

Then my father started to get sick. He complained about some tomatoes he'd eaten; but it wasn't the tomatoes. It was nerves. I realised years later, he had been worried sick about everything, including me going on the harbour at night. I thought it was a great adventure.

I borrowed a six foot canoe from one of my Kanaka friends and paddled out into the harbour, taking with me a hammer and the piece of broomstick. It was a dead calm night, so I paddled very carefully. I could see the armed guard on the wharf, walking up and down with a rifle on his shoulder. About twenty boats, all government launches and schooners, were tied up fore and aft between the wharf and piles a hundred feet out. The night watchman was guarding the whole lot.

I paddled alongside the *Tilbura* and found the hole easily enough. I poked my stick up and hit it with the hammer. Booooommmm. *God, the guard will hear that!* I was terrified I'd be heard or seen, but the hull was built of timber and it didn't reverberate as much as steel would.

I knocked the plug out without difficulty, but the water didn't enter, because the pipe was just above water level on the inside. I wondered what else I could do. I couldn't turn a forty foot boat over by myself. I paddled back and went up to the house to tell my parents what had happened.

'I'll go back tomorrow night.'

'Do it tonight or not at all, Col. By tomorrow night, it will be too late to scuttle her.'

'Well, I'll go back and climb inside, undo the connection to the motor, flood it until the stern goes down far enough to take water in, then re-attach the connection. I want to make it a bit of a puzzle for them why the hell the thing went down.'

'That's a good idea. Just don't be seen.'

I went back and climbed on board, all eyes on the guard. The hatch squeaked loudly as I pushed it back. My heart was pounding as I climbed inside. Crouching down beside the engine, I undid the water intake. When the water was up to my chest, I reconnected the fitting, tightening it up with a wrench. Finally, I paddled back to shore and put everything away.

The *Tilbura* sank in water about forty feet deep and it was about ten days before anything was said. I believe the reason for that was that the guard worked from three o'clock until eleven and it was about eleven o'clock that the boat sank. When the relief guard came on, the *Tilbura* had already sunk, so he hadn't seen it. The boat had come onto the wharf only the previous afternoon. That's why nobody raised a hue and cry.

I couldn't stand the tension. I nearly rushed up and confessed. All three of us were a mass of nerves until someone realised the *Tilbura* was missing. At first they thought we'd taken and hidden her somewhere. They searched all around the harbour, but they couldn't find the boat.

Izumi was a diver as well as a shipwright. I saw Izumi and the Italians on some boats and Izumi was diving. They found the *Tilbura*.

I climbed into the little canoe and paddled over to watch. Izumi dived down the port side. He swam all along the port side before he came up.

'There's no hole,' he said.

Then he went down again and swam along the starboard side. When he came up again, he spoke in Pidgin, 'There's no hole.'

They lifted the boat above water with a crane and pumped it out till it floated, but they still didn't know how it had sunk.

A couple of months after I turned seventeen, I was given an old motor cycle, so I needed my driving licence.

I went to the police station and Ron Phelan, the Sergeant, said to me, 'Do you know the *Tilbura* was sunk?'

'Oh, yeah, I heard about that.'

'Do you know who sank it, Colin?'

'No, no I don't. I've no idea. Do you know?'

'Yes, we know.'

That was the end of the *Tilbura* for us. She went to auction and was sold.

Motorcycles

The motorcycle I had been given was an eleven year old AJS, built in 1928. Mostly I used it for transport to and from work. The parents of the fellow who gave me the bike owned a copra plantation about forty-five miles away from Rabaul at Put Put. I rode down there once, along a bush track. About ten miles before I reached their plantation, I came upon a big crocodile. It was running like a pacer, both legs moved on one side and then both on the other side. It had been sun baking on the path and the motorbike frightened it. I accelerated out of the way fast.

I spent a couple of nights with my friend. On my return trip, just exactly where I'd seen the crocodile, the con rod broke. It went click-click-click-click as the con rod flapped about. I lay the bike down on the track, left it there and I ran. About twenty miles down the track, I came to another station.

My mother didn't have the phone on and my father was away working at Kaviang in New Ireland, so I rang the switchboard girl, whom I knew. She was one of two German half-castes in Rabaul. Like most half castes, they were both very beautiful women.

'This is Colin Kerby, I said. 'I can't get back home tonight. Could you please get a message to my mother?'

'Yes, I can do that.'

I told the telephonist what had happened and she did get a message to Mum. I stayed at the plantation for the night and my hosts gave me a lift home in the morning. Because of that incident, I missed a day of work.

Someone picked up the motorbike and brought it back to Rabaul for me. I ordered a replacement con rod from Sydney and fixed the bike up, then I sold it to a young Malay, who had a crippled leg. I told the Italian engineers that I had sold my bike to the Krannie [Pidgin for a Malay].

'Does he want to break his other leg?' one of them asked.

I bought another motorbike with a side car for ten pounds. It had belonged to a fellow who served four years in the World War I. After the eruption, the whole town was covered in pumice, dust and ash and so was the bike. It had been sitting like that outside his wrecked house for about a year. I offered this man seven pounds and ten shillings.

'I don't have any more money,' I said.

'It's not very much, is it?'

He had to wait until payday so that I could pay him a few more quid.

The Scott Squirrel was an exotic motor cycle, with a water-cooled two-stroke engine. It was noisy and fast; I had some fun on that bike.

The *Endoona Star*

The *Endoona Star* was run by a fully-fledged Captain and another white officer with a Master's Certificate. I was out one day with Bennie in his twenty-five foot open boat, about half way between Rabaul and Kokopo, when the Endoona Star went across my bow, maybe fifty yards away. Our boat was sailing very slowly, because there wasn't much breeze.

The *Endoona Star* had a line out the back. I assumed the line held a trailing log [a small propeller, used to measure speed through the water]. It caught in the bobstay of my friend's boat. Thinking it was a spinner for a log, I went forward to free it. Several white men were on the back of the *Endoona Star,* shouting at me. I was watching where I could see the line. I thought if I kept watching there, I'd see the spinner come up. But it wasn't a log. It was a bloody big hook and I didn't see it. It was hanging down. At that moment, I stood up, because I was getting tired and right then, this great big hook came over the bobstay at the bow. In doing so, it flicked the line clear of where it was snagged. I couldn't believe how lucky I was to have stood up at the moment the hook came over our bow.

The skipper of the *Endoona Star* should have gone astern and stopped the boat when they saw me with the line in my hand. I could have been caught like a big fish and torn out of the boat. Because I was on a native boat and I have an olive skin, they probably thought I was a Malay...they really should have stopped that boat no matter who they thought I was.

Col's Three "Boys".

The Duk Duk

One day, I was walking between Rabaul and Kokopo with Toviat, one of my 'boys,' a thirty year old servant/employee. We came upon a very large native village. At the village, a Duk Duk was due to arrive. He's a man dressed up, a mysterious priest-like figure that women weren't allowed to see. One of the European administrations insisted that women couldn't be barred, and should be allowed to see the ceremony. Some of them went along, but frequently hid their eyes.

I was standing discretely behind a tree, a little away from the village centre. The Duk Duk was dressed up in a costume with his arms hidden underneath. The costume covered him to near the tops of his thighs. It looked like a lot of leaves stuck onto the covering, giving the impression it was a fibre-glass frame. That was impossible, but it was some sort of stiff framework constructed to make him look like a very large chicken. He was very athletic. I could see his legs. He raced out of the bush and he started a most impassioned speech. All the women were turning their faces away, covering their eyes and saying "Oooohhh". I was taking all this in. The speech lasted for about seven minutes, then he turned and dashed back off into the bush.

Toviat was a Toloy from the local tribe.

'What did he talk about?' I asked him.

'He spoke of one man who went somewhere and did something,' Toviat said in Pidgin.

How's that for evasion? His culture prevented him from telling me more.

Salvaging the Pinnace

There was a fairly large inter-island boat in the harbour one night. It was anchored out and they had two pinnaces, about eighteen feet long, going back and forth between the boat and the shore. It was a dead calm night. They were using native crew and they weren't showing lights. One boat was coming one way and the other was going the other way. They hit each other and one rolled over and sank.

My father and I found out that Weaver was the crewman of the one that didn't sink.

'If you can point out where the boat sank and if we can swim down and see it, we'll give you two pounds.'

Two pounds was a hell of a lot of money for a native at that time.

'All right,' said Weaver.

Where it sank was fifty-four feet deep. We took Weaver out by dinghy one night. It was a pitch-black night and it was a way off shore. He was looking this way and that and his eyes were flashing in the darkness.

'Here!' he shouted suddenly.

We dropped a buoy. Later, I swam down and there it was. Incredible!

The boat belonged to W.C. Carpenters, a large firm like Burns Philp, who were an opposition firm in the islands. My father went to Carpenters' office to see McLean, the shipping manager, to ask for salvage rights.

Karl Wunce, the local plumber, was there waiting to see McLean. Although we'd kept it quiet up till then that we knew where the boat was sunk, my father let on.

'What are you here for Kerby?' Wunce asked.

'You know that boat that was sunk in the bay; we've found it. We want to buy it.'

Wunce went in to do his business with McLean and McLean said to him,

'That's Kerby out there. What does he want?'

'He's found the boat, that pinnace of yours that sank.'

My father was going to offer McLean some nominal amount like twenty pounds for the pinnace, if we could we find it. When my father walked into the office, he made his offer.

'But you've already found it,' said McLean.

'No, no, we have to look for it.'

'Wunce told me you'd found it.'

Carpenters sold the vessel to us eventually for fifty pounds. In the meantime, we dropped a buoy about ten feet below the surface. We'd taken fairly rough sextant sights, but then the buoy sank and I had to dive to find the wreck again. I found the pinnace eventually.

A native and I raised the boat, bailed out the water and brought it in close to the shore. It had a single cylinder Bolinder diesel in it. My father must have taken that engine back to Melbourne with him, because he had it later at the Kiosk on St Kilda Pier. You had to heat the cylinders with a blowtorch to start it. We lifted the motor out of the hull and, dangling it from the bow of the tug, we ran in close to shore. There was a big coconut tree there. We put a line from the coconut tree, across the sand and down to the motor, then attached a chain block we'd borrowed. The sand knocked our hands about while we worked the chain block, but we pulled the diesel ashore. The native who was working with me became mildly upset.

'My hand has water inside!'

He had blisters. I caught on only after he showed me his hands.

Laboratory Technician

About this time, I was offered a job working as a junior technician in the native hospital pathology laboratory. This happened soon after my father found a job with the Engineering section of the Public Works Department. They needed to build landing strips for aircraft. Dad was employed as engineer to design the layout and build airstrips at Rabaul first and then at Kaviang on the island of New Ireland. At Kaviang, he had to supervise the construction of huts for accommodation before they could even start clearing the land. He drove the bulldozer to level the land for the airstrips.

Two weeks before the Kaviang airstrip was finished, Public Works sent out another fellow to take over as head of the project. He was a stolid man, who had been a government employee for years, so he had one level of seniority over my father. Dad sent a protest that being so close to completion, he should be able to finish the project. When the Department refused, Dad resigned. World War II had been declared and Dad decided to enlist.

3 Budding Surgeon

'What's Colin doing for work?'

'He's working native labour on the ships.'

My mother was talking to a local man. Later I found out he belonged to the Masonic Lodge.

'What would he like to do?'

'He'd like a job of any sort here.'

'Yes, but what would he *like* to do?'

'Well, he's good at chemistry.'

'I'll see what I can do.'

Soon after, I received a call to see Dr Backhouse at the Rapindik hospital laboratory in Rabaul. Dr Backhouse was the Pathologist in charge, with two technicians. He offered to take me on as his junior technician.

'You can take over the blood transfusions.'

I had turned sixteen in November and it was early in 1938 when I started working in the laboratory. Every morning, the ambulance picked me up and drove me the four miles [approximately nine kilometres] down to the hospital. Later, I rode my motorcycle to work.

In those days, there were only four blood groups known: A, AB, B and O. From A serum and B serum, you obtain just four possibilities. We have more now, because the RH [Rhesus] factor was discovered. To group blood, we placed a sample on a microscope slide. Dr Backhouse showed me how to do it. He had this watch maker's eye-piece in his hand.

'Come over here, Kerby.'

He had some blood on a microscope slide.

'There's one type of blood that coagulates and one that doesn't.'

I'd seen a picture somewhere of the watchmaker putting the eyepiece in his eye. *Bugger holding it in my hand,* I thought, *I'll do it the proper way.* I didn't have glasses in those days. When he gave me the eye-piece, I put it in my eye. I thought I looked very professional. Then the eyepiece popped out, hit the microscope slide and the blood sample splattered. You should have seen Dr

Backhouse. He went round the lab for about ten minutes, picking things up and banging them down, to express his rage.

'Well, of course, Kerby, if you're going to stay in this business, you can't be ham-fisted all the time. You need to have a little bit of finesse about these things.'

'Yes Doctor. I'm sorry Doctor.'

The next time he had something he wanted to show me, he called me over.

'Now hold it in your hand.'

~

Dr Backhouse was talking to me one day and he asked me how old I was.

'I'm seventeen.'

'Have you turned seventeen?'

'No, I'll be seventeen next month.'

I thought I might have received a better category of pay being a year older. It turned out there were only two pay rates: adult (over twenty one) and junior.

About thirty years later, when I was in Melbourne, I was looking up a Sydney telephone number under 'B'. Suddenly, I saw 'Backhouse'. It was 'T.C. Backhouse, Dr' I was working at Monash University then. I decided to ring him up. By that time, he was over eighty.

'It's Colin Kerby, Doctor.'

'Ahhh. Look, I'm losing my memory. Can you give me a bit of a reminder?'

'Well, from 1938 to 1940, I was your junior technician in the biochemistry laboratory at Rapindik.'

'Oh yes, Kerby. I have a very clear picture of you – as you were then, of course. What are you doing these days?'

'I'm working in cancer research at Monash University. I'm stationed at Prince Henry's Hospital.'

'Oh, do you know Dr X?' he asked.

'Yes, I know him.'

I wish I'd known that connection at the time I was applying for work at the university, I thought. Until then, I hadn't realised the implication of Masonic Lodge membership; that gentleman in Rabaul, who had spoken to my mother, and Dr Backhouse were

both Masons. Dr X at Melbourne University probably also belonged
to the Masons.

Albumin Urea

As well as doing blood transfusions and grouping blood, I had to
learn histology.

Soon after I started at the lab, I tested my own urine and found I
had albumin urea. I did this test on myself and I took the test tube in
to Sid and Tom, the other pathology technicians. In the hospital at
that time, we had a Chinaman, who was close to dying. I showed the
test to the other two in the lab.

Sid looked up and said, 'Oh, he's a goner. Who is it? The Cong?'
You called Chinese Congs in New Guinea.

'No, it's mine. It's me.'

'Shit, it's not is it?'

'Do you have albumin in your urine, Sid?'

'No. It's not normal. That's a pretty solid dose of it.'

'What's the score?'

'A shorter life.'

'Well, how short? With that clarity, how long do I have?'

'Probably till you're thirty.'

'Oh, that's all right. That's thirteen years away. That's a bloody
long way off and anything could happen.'

While I was working at the laboratory, an insurance salesman
came up from Melbourne. He did the rounds to sell life insurance.
He came in to me and started his spiel.

'I've albumin urea, heavy deposits.'

'Oooh, have you. Are you sure?'

'Yes.'

So he folded his books up and left. I went back into the lab and
told the others.

'I rid myself of that fellow quickly. I told him I had albumin urea.'

'That's a good idea to get rid of those blokes.'

~

Another part of my job at the pathology lab in Rapindik was to
pick up samples from the hospital. I'd been going into the hospital
for a few months when, one day, I saw a scalpel on the table. I
picked it up and waved it in the air.

Col examining pathology
slides at Rapindik Laboratory.

'How about teaching me a bit of surgery? I rather fancy myself as a surgeon.'

The chief medical assistant looked at me thoughtfully.

'Yes, we could do with you actually. We're a bit short handed, but first you'll have to ask Dr Backhouse.'

So I went and asked him.

'Yes Kerby, but you'll have to do your histology here and your blood grouping and blood transfusions in the lab as well.'

I agreed. I'd do my lab work promptly and, if there were no blood transfusions on, I'd go across to the hospital.

New Guinea, with a population of a few million natives, was a German territory until the First World War. After that, it was mandated to Australia. Australia couldn't afford trained doctors for all the natives. In the case of Rabaul, the Public Health Department had three doctors and well over a million natives in the area. The Health Department put advertisements in the newspapers to get men to go up there to train as medical assistants. Some of the surgeons had been there since the First World War. They were all unqualified. Someone would teach them surgery and hospital work and they'd become medical assistants. That was what I wanted to train as.

I went to the hospital as often as I could. The staff started to teach me a few things and one day, they told me that Ian Kerr, one of the medical assistants, was going home to Scotland, on leave for three months.

'What if you did his work while he's on leave and after a while, we'll take you into the theatre and teach you some surgery?'

That was what I wanted. Suddenly, I had an ambition to be a surgeon.

'I'd like that. What work does Ian Kerr do?'

'He does the VD clinic.'

'Yes, I'll give that a go.'

'Can you get over here at eight o'clock in the morning? He's examining the Maries.' [female natives.]

'I'll be there.'

I didn't tell my mother what I was doing, because she was petrified that I might become interested in the native girls.

~

The VD Clinic

I arrived at eight o'clock and Ian Kerr was ready to teach me how to take the VD clinic. He had about twenty women lined up upstairs. The upstairs of the hospital was for inspections and examinations.

'Come on, Mary.'

The first Mary jumped up on the table. She'd been there before and knew what to do. She put her legs up in the stirrups.

He showed me an instrument.

'You call this a "vaginal speculum".'

He inserted it, then showed me the little knob to hold the instrument open.

'If you look in, using the torch, you can see the uterus.'

'What's that, Ian?'

'It's usually called the womb.'

He said, 'You take two samples from each Mary. Take one sample from here and this next one from the clitoris.'

'What's that?'

'That's this little gimmick here.'

I inspected the clitoris and it was certainly a small gimmick.

He also had a spirit stove to sterilize the instruments. He heated up a wire with a loop on a glass rod. After it was sterilized, he waited for it to cool.

'You need to be gentle. It's a pretty tender spot.'

The next one, I had a go at. Even though we had Vaseline for lubricant, it was bloody hard to get the vaginal speculum in and she yelped a bit. Soon, I had the hang of it.

'In Australia, they ask the women if they want the speculum warmed, but it's not cold here, so we don't bother. We haven't time for that anyway.'

So I took samples from about ten women that morning. I dared not tell my mother I'd been looking at women's fannies. She'd have sent me back to Australia. She'd seen a girl kiss me when I was about ten and that incident distressed her for weeks.

~

The next morning, the 'boys' were waiting upstairs. Ian Kerr pulled a card out of a file index and called out a name. The native came forward, whipped off his lap lap and bent down. Ian put on a rubber glove, and put his finger in the Vaseline bottle.

'You massage the prostate Col, so if there's any puss in there, it comes out the end of the penis. These are the slides we send over to the lab for you to stain. Your pathologist checks if the treatment is working and sends that report back to us.'

He put his hand on the native's back and put his finger up his anus.

'You massage the prostate and down the seminal vesicles at the sides.'

Then he removed his finger.

'Stand up and turn round,' he said to the native. 'Pick up your penis.'

The fellow did as he was told. Ian took a smear off the end of the penis and put it on a slide.

'That's what you get at the lab. Now Col, are you right now for the rest of them?'

'Oh, yeah. No worries.'

I had great confidence. It looked fairly simple to me. I put on a glove and took the next card. It was Michael. I called Michael over. He came up and about another eighteen were lined up watching. Michael bent over. I couldn't find his anus. I was going all the way up and down his crevice, trying to find a soft spot. I couldn't find it. I was starting to sweat. All the boys were looking at me as the new master. I thought, *They'll be asking: what does he know?* After a while, I thought, *bugger it*. So I pulled his cheeks apart. *Oh, it's right down there.* I'd been looking far too high up. It was right down beneath his spinal column.

I didn't take my eye off it as I inserted my finger into his anus. *Gotcha! Now that I'm there, I'd better make a good job of this.* I massaged up and down his seminal vesicles and then did some more. I took my finger out, pulled off my glove and picked up the glass rod with the loop.

'Right oh, Michael.'

I was about to ask him to turn round and pick up his penis, but he had the most monstrous erection I've ever seen. I'd only seen my own erections before this. *Jeeze, that doesn't look right*. While I was thinking about this, I looked up at him and he was gazing at me intently. *He's fallen in love with me*. I was a bit dry around my mouth and backed up against the small table with my gear on it. He was standing there and I was in the corner. I was a bit hesitant to take a smear from an erect penis. I thought it wasn't quite the right thing. While I was procrastinating, he grabbed his penis and started masturbating in front of us all. He was looking at me all the time. I thought this was getting a bit deadly.

'Hey... Hey...Hey...'

He ejaculated a copious amount of semen all over the floor. *Well, it's no use me taking a smear now,* I thought. *It'll be all sperm.*

'Put your lap lap back on, Michael.'

I went down downstairs to see Ian Kerr.

'He just grabbed hold of his penis and masturbated in front of me.'

'Ooh God. That's most unethical.'

'Yeah, well I thought he was rather rude.'

'Not him, you.'

'Me? It's the first time I've had my finger up anybody's bum. How was I to know?'

'Well how will you go now?'

'All right. I'll know how far to go from now on.'

So from then on, I was very careful.

I went back upstairs.

'Next.'

The next native grinned.

'Do I have to fire up too? That's a hard act to follow,' he asked in Pidgin.

'No, you'll be all right.'

From then on, until I became accustomed to the procedure, I'd go poke, poke, then look at their penis to make sure it wasn't stirring. Then poke, poke, and I'd take another look.

Ian went on leave and I did the VD clinic for three months. I was still sixteen.

Surgery

After Ian came back, the chief medical assistant took me into the theatre, where he instructed me in amputations.

'Most of your theatre work will be amputation of legs, because these fellows get really bad tropical ulcers. They become toxic.'

'Yes, I saw a lot of ulcers like that when I was doing my first aid course at Bitalova.'

'The ulcers can eat right into the bone and the patients become very thin,' Dr Parry said.

The main cause of death in New Guinea was from these tropical ulcers in the feet and legs, and we'd see some shocking infections. We had to get the patient's permission to operate. To do that, we had to be graphic. We were instructed to say to them:

'Look, you're going to die. After you die, we'll take you over to the cemetery and bury you under the ground. But if you let us cut that leg off, you'll probably get better. We'll give you a peg leg and you can go back to your village, where your wife will look after you and you'll live to be an old man.'

Not one of them ever knocked me back, although Trevor, one of the other 'surgeons,' knew of one case where permission was refused by the patient.

After I'd been doing theatre work for about six months, I was performing up to six amputations every Tuesday. Right from the beginning, I never had any trouble. The only difference was that the other fellows sawed through the bones and stitched up straight afterwards. I thought that a smooth edge on the bone would cause less pain, so I would smooth the edges with a file. Strangely, I never asked the natives if there was any difference in pain levels. It took me about ten minutes longer, because I had to file both the tibia and the fibula. The others said I was putting chips into the wound, but I thought the chips could work their way out. I just didn't like straight sawn-off bones.

In those days, they would just tie the veins off and hold them down. Anastomosing wasn't invented them. That's when two blood vessels are joined up with little stitches all the way around. It was during the Second World War they discovered that procedure. You couldn't do a transplant now if you couldn't anastomose. Before the war, we had to rely on collateral circulation to take over.

An amputation was a very simple operation. I'd cut back the skin so that I had a flap to go around the bone. I'd sever the bone close up. I'd stitch the muscles and tendons, close off the blood vessels, then I'd fold the skin over and stitch that. We also put a drain in. Later in life, when I became involved in very decent surgery like liver transplants, there was a discussion in The Lancet about whether you should put drains in or not. We used drains and I can't remember an amputation ever going bad – not in our hospital. I did most of the amputations for a long time and let the other fellows off. Some of them were pretty neat surgeons. I never saw an abdominal operation, but I've seen fingers amputated. Removal of fingers – that's tricky.

~

Peg legs were supplied in dozens and they cost nine shillings each. The public works made them using native labour. They were all the same, made out of three or four pieces of timber. We adjusted the length for a short man by cutting some off the bottom.

I phoned the Public Works Office one day.

'That's a lot of money for those wooden legs.'

'Yes, but we have to knock off doing other work to make these.'

'What if I ordered a gross?'

'Yes, that would be cheaper.'

'Well they're nine shillings each now. What would they come down to if I ordered a gross?'

'Six shillings each.'

I sent them a requisition form for a gross. A truck full of peg legs arrived.

My boss was aghast.

'Jesus Christ, what have they done?'

'I ordered a gross.'

'Why did you order a gross?'

'Well, instead of nine shillings each, they're six shillings each.'

'That's all right, but where are we going to store them?'

'I thought your office looked pretty good.'

War

In September 1939, the Second World War began. When my father resigned from The Public Works Department, he decided to return to Melbourne to enlist. My parents left Rabaul in November, just after my eighteenth birthday. To start with, I remained living at our house, with my servants. Every night, I went to the Pacific Hotel to eat dinner. When the lease on the house ran out, I moved out and found board with the Andersons. Theirs was a luxurious house, probably the second best house in Rabaul after the Administrator's.

Dr Backhouse volunteered for war service too. My work continued at the laboratory and the hospital. Apart from me, there were the two senior technicians working at the lab: Sid Tee and Tom Evans.

While I was in Rabaul, I joined the Volunteers, along with several

Col and his mates in the New Guinea Volunteer Reserve.

mates, including the other technicians. I would ride my motorbike to the meetings. When I went over to Bulolo on the main island of New Guinea, I attended meetings with the army volunteer group there too.

Col's Scott Squirrel motor cycle.

Meeting the Administrator's Wife

We had a big fire with explosions one night in 1940. Perhaps it was a foretaste of the bombing to come. W.C. Carpenters' warehouse and offices burned up. Half of Rabaul came out to watch. I was standing next to a woman wearing a hat and what I thought was a rather inelegant dressing gown. It was three o'clock in the morning. I started chatting to the woman and found out my companion was Lady McNicol, the Administrator's wife. Later on, she invited me up to Government house for a meal. I had several meals up there. Somehow, she found out that I didn't drink alcohol. This impressed her. In New Guinea, white people drank a lot of whisky and other spirits.

'You mustn't drink. It's dangerous,' my mother had told me.

I've seen my father drink a beer, but only occasionally. Ironically, it was my mother who became an alcoholic later in her life.

I went to the pub frequently in Rabaul.

I would bang on the counter and say, 'A passion fruit soda please.'

A Malay worked behind the counter – a really nice fellow. He knew my order was always a passion fruit soda, or if I was buying a beer for someone, it would be a beer and a passion fruit.

~

The first time I went to dinner at the McNicol's, we had cherries and cream for dessert. There was only one dairy man in Rabaul and cream was very expensive. I'd been taught to spit out cherry pips into my spoon and put them aside. Lady McNicol started to eat her desert and she didn't put out any pips. Wondering if I'd been brought up wrongly, I ate my cherries pips and all. The phone rang and when the Administrator went out to answer it, Lady McNicol also left the room, so I was just sitting there. When the native who was serving at table came in, I asked what happened to the pips.

'Does the Missus eat the pips?'

'No. We removed her pips before her plate was brought to the table.'

Delivery

Although I was still eighteen, at times I was left in charge of the hospital at night. It was a two-hundred-bed hospital and they were pretty rough wards; just planks and a couple of blankets – no mattresses.

One evening, a woman came in escorted by her friend. Was she pregnant! I reckoned, with my experienced eye, she was about twelve months pregnant. We had four doctor boys [native medical assistants / nurses] on duty that night.

'What do you do with pregnant women when they come in?' I asked one of them.

'You should know, Master.'

'Well, I don't.'

'Put her up top.'

That meant upstairs.

The woman couldn't speak Pidgin, but she had a female friend with her who knew a few words.

I was writing a letter to my sister and I didn't want to be interrupted, so I went back to my letter. I checked on the patient occasionally. About two o'clock in the morning, she let out this yell which frightened the hell out of me. I raced up stairs. She was sitting on the floor playing with a bit of fabric.

'What's going on?'

'What's the panic?' her friend answered.

'She yelled.'

'What do you expect?'

I pulled the medical book off the shelf and looked up what to do with pregnant women. It said to heat up water, so I told the Kanaka to cook up some water on the big primus stove. He did that and then it went cold.

About six o'clock, the patient was yelling and yelling, so I went upstairs. She gave birth on the instant. Bang!

I did all the right things. The book said to get a couple of forceps, some artery scissors and some twine. It said how far from the umbilicus to cut the cord, so I did all that and tied it off.

I wasn't particularly distressed, but then she started to deliver the placenta. I didn't know what it was. I didn't know anything about a placenta. I'd heard my mother talk about afterbirth, but I thought it was a bit of blood. I thought, Christ, is that her liver? I didn't know whether to stuff it back or pull it out.

The woman with her was putting her hand on the patient's stomach, so I thought I'd do the same thing. Both of us had our hands on her stomach. As she bore down, she eventually delivered the placenta. To verify what it was, I thought I should wrap it up in newspaper to show somebody in the day shift.

The book said to wash the baby, cover it in olive oil and no matter how clean the mother is with regard to VD, put 'Argeroll' in its eyes. I found the big bottle of 'Argeroll', which is a tar-like disinfectant, and looked to see what the dosage was.

Imagine the scene. I've this kid washed, then I've put olive oil on its skin and I was chasing it up and down the table. He was bawling his head off and I held his head under my arm and poured 'Argeroll' into his eyes and just about drowned the poor little bugger, but the 'Argeroll' went into his eyes.

The day staff began to arrive at half past seven.

'How did you go last night?' the boss asked me.

'Oh, you know…. By the way, I had a confinement.'

'Shit. You haven't done one before, have you? How did it go?'

'It was all right. I have a sample here of what she produced. I want you to check it to see if it's all right.'

'Good idea.'

I knew I'd done the right thing there.

'Did you have any trouble?'

'No, no. It all went well.'

'What sex is the baby?'

'I'm buggered if I know.'

I never thought to look at its genitals. If I'd done so, I'd probably have grabbed them as it slid towards the end of the table.

That birth was the most memorable, because it was my first. After that night, I helped with many more deliveries.

~

Another night, at 2.00am when I was on duty, I decided to give the patients some entertainment. I was eighteen and the only white person on duty. I decided to ride my motor bike through the ward, thinking it would cheer up the patients. I started the bike and rode into the hospital. The ward was long, with a corridor down the

55

middle and beds lined up along each side. I rode the bike to the end of the ward, then turned around and revved out again. There was a lot of oily smoke left behind, because the bike was a two-stroke. I was shocked to find that the patients didn't appreciate what I'd done. They were coughing on the smoke.

Next morning, the medical assistant in charge was checking the patient charts. He wanted to know why, in one ward, everyone's blood pressure and respiration rates showed irregularities. I just hadn't realised until that night, how sick the patients in the hospital were.

'We had a bit of an earth tremor in the night, 'I told him. 'Didn't you feel it?'

Antibiotics

Bayer brought out the first antibiotics, Bayer M&B 693 and sulphonamide. They had done all their animal trials, but they hadn't tried these drugs on humans. They made an agreement with the Australian and Portuguese governments to use both the New Guinea natives and the Portuguese in West Africa for their human trials. We received M&B 693 and sulphonamides about the same time. Like antibiotics, sulphonamides are also used to treat infection

One day, when I was working at the lab, they sent for me to go to the hospital.

We've a new 'anti-bee-otic.'

'What's that?'

'It's a new drug called M&B 693. It's supposed to be very good. It hasn't been used in the southern hemisphere before. As the youngest in the unit, you can be the first to administer it.'

'Right oh. What do I do?'

'There's the victim.'

'What's wrong with him?'

'Gonorrhea.'

'What's the dosage?'

'Two tablets every four hours.'

So I gave the patient two tablets.

Once we started using the antibiotic, our death rate and consequently our post mortem rate fell dramatically. No one had ever used M&B 693 on humans, and we were doing the first human trial. We were just learning and some people died when they developed haematuria. [blood in the urine]. We kept a careful check on the patients and we found the method to stop the deaths. We passed this information on to Bayer. As soon as the patient started to pass blood in his urine, we'd take him off the antibiotic treatment and give him a rectal saline drip. We didn't know why a saline drip into the vein didn't work, but administered rectally, it saved the patient's life. They needed one or two litres over a couple of days. Perhaps that was too much saline solution to administer through a vein.

If the patient died, at the post mortem I could feel grit like sand through the kidney. We found that the antibiotic was forming crystals in the kidney. The dosage of M&B 693 was two tablets every four hours. We were also using sulphonamide, which was in tablets too, but we were fairly sure it was the M&B 693 causing the haematuria.

Sometimes, we saw massive tropical ulcers that extended from knee to ankle and all over the foot. Antibiotics were unsuitable for treating these. Instead we found a miraculous treatment for tropical ulcers. I don't know how the treatment originated. We would make a saturated solution of potassium permanganate and scrub the ulcerated area. In extreme cases, we had to anaesthetize the patient with chloroform. We called this treatment PPC or potassium permanganate cauterization.

Legalities

Our coroner, Mr Mantle, was also the magistrate. He was a glorious looking man, elderly, about six foot five, white headed and straight as a ramrod. He used a walking stick, which was the symbol of the white master.

If a native died in hospital, any of the staff who had been attending to him could sign the death certificate; but if he died a violent death outside the hospital, the coroner had to see the body.

I had an ambiguous case. I had been attending to a patient who had rheumatism. We would send him with a doctor boy [native assistant] to walk about a hundred and fifty yards down to the volcanic hot pools on the shore and leave him there for a while. The doctor boy would wait to help the patient back.

One day, I sent that patient down to the hot pool and a shark bit him, tearing out his femoral artery, along with the thigh muscle. The doctor boy tried carrying the man back to his ward, but the artery was spurting blood everywhere. He died on the track coming back. Because he was a hospital patient, I signed the death certificate.. About three days after they buried him, the Chief Medical Administrator asked if the Coroner had seen the body.

'No, he hasn't. He was a hospital patient.'

'But Colin, it was a violent death.'

'Well, that's border line, isn't it?'

'No. The coroner's put in a request; he wants to see the body.'

'Oh Jesus, he's been in the ground for three days and you know how hot that ground is.'

'It's your blunder. You go and dig him up. Get a couple of calaboose to help you.'

[Calaboose is a Pidgin word for prisoner. These were prisoners assigned to work at the hospital. They wore red and white striped lap laps.]

'Take a couple of calaboose to dig him up. Do you know where the body is?'

'Yes, I do. I told them where to bury him.'

We went to the cemetery. The calaboose dug down, revealing the body, which was wrapped up in a blanket. They put a rope round the arm of the corpse, which pulled off the trunk. We had a trolley with huge cart wheels on it to take the bodies down to the cemetery. Eventually, the calaboose loaded the body onto the cart.

I led the way up, the prisoners pulling the cart behind them. We took the body to the mortuary and then I rang Mr Mantle and said the body was there for inspection. He came up in his car

'Is he over in the mortuary, Kerby?'

'Yes Sir.'

'You'd better come over with me.'

I stood up on the concrete slab, just outside the door, where the body was lying. Mr Mantle asked me to open the door. He walked up backwards, until he was outside the door.

'Kerby, if I turn round now, will I see the body?'

'Yes. Mr Mantle.'

He swung around, then back again.

'Right, I've seen the body. You can bury him again.'

~

I became a government official when I worked at the laboratory. Government officials were required to watch floggings. Usually the offence was sexual stuff, including being lesbian. That was a carry-over from the German days.

One day, my friend Bennie was reminiscing to me about the Germans. Bennie had lived under their rule when he was a young man.

'Strong men, strong men.'

'Not like us?' I asked.

'No. They strong men. If you convicted, they ask: "What you want? A year in gaol or ten strokes of the kunda?" ' [A cane.]

'How long was the cane?'

'With his hands, Bennie indicated about a metre, by a centimetre and a half. The canes were left over from the German administrators, who used metric measurements.

A native could be flogged and released. The natives preferred to be flogged than to go to gaol. It was over then. Even during German rule, the floggings were undertaken by the native police boys. One police "boy" would have a short stick. He'd indicate where the native was to be hit and the other police boy would strike him with the cane twice in the one spot. The second stroke would break the skin. When my duties involved watching a flogging, we took the victim straight to hospital afterwards.

I carried a drug called "Coramine" with me to the floggings. If the prisoner collapsed, I had to inject him with this heart drug. After the punishment, we'd treat the wounds at the hospital. He went home when he was healed.

I also went to court to give evidence when I was working at the laboratory. Mainly I went to Court to give evidence about natives, usually house boys, who masturbated while looking at small white children. If the parents found out about it, they would tell the police, who sent the child's bedclothes down to the laboratory where I worked, to examine them for semen. The native would be charged with attempted paedophilia.

Mr Mantle, the coroner, thought he spoke good Pidgin, but he wasn't very good at all. I gave the pathology report to the court.

'The bed clothes were brought down for examination. I did a nitric acid ring test on the sample. It indicated semen. I did an ultra violet light test. It indicated semen.'

Mr Mantle would just sit there impassively. Then I'd finish off my report.

'The specimen smelt like semen.'

'It smelt like semen. Six months!'

Later on, when the Japanese came, Mr Mantle was captured. They let him make tea for the interned white men. He was such an imposing looking man; I heard later that the Japanese never disrespected him. He died on a Japanese ship, the *Monte Video Maru*, on the way to Japan. An American submarine torpedoed it and everyone on board died. They lost two thousand people, which was the biggest maritime catastrophe ever involving Australians. I've a book with all their names in it. I had blood grouped them all at the start of the war and I knew most of them. Tom Evans, the lab technician who worked with me, died on that ship too.

~

We did approximately two hundred post mortems in a year. I would go with Dr Backhouse to do the post mortems and take notes. When Backhouse knew he was going away to war, he taught me to do them. We had one of the fellows from the hospital take my notes. If I was stuck during a post mortem and couldn't find out what killed the patient, I could call one of the two private doctors, a man who had done some pathology, to come and help me out.

One day in 1940, I spoke to Dr Brennan, the Director of the hospital, about my pay. He didn't do any surgery; he was an administrator. I had been working at the hospital for over two years, doing a lot of the amputations and post mortems. At eighteen and a half, I was starting to develop something of a swelled head about my skills. My father had told me it was time I came back to Melbourne and joined up with the army, but I wanted to stay. I went to Dr Brennan.

'How about giving me a rise?' I said.

'No. NO!'

Several of the fellows were outside the office listening to my request.

'No, I'd have to pay you as an adult,' said Dr Brennan. 'That's what you're asking me to pay you. I can get an adult for what I'd be paying you.'

'Yes, but look at some of your adults. Look at X. He never does any surgery. He's drunk every night and apart from that, he has association with the Maries.'

I didn't get a rise. He stood up and walked away.

Some of the fellows had been listening and one of them told me his opinion.

'You're bloody well worth it. Tell him to go to buggery.'

I thought about it for a few days, then I went to the lab and asked Sid to type me out a resignation.

'All right. Are you sure you want it?'

'Yes Sid, write it for me please.'

He typed it out. I remember he wrote in the resignation: 'I wish my resignation to take effect at the end of my leave.' I wouldn't have thought of that. They were very silly to accept my departure, because they were short of staff. I left in spring 1940.

That evening, I went up to the pub and banged on the counter to obtain service.

'A whisky please – a double whisky.'

The Malay serving blanched. He thought I was going to drink it. He reached for the bottle.

'No, no. Give me a passion fruit, please.'

Bulolo

Soon after I'd resigned from the hospital, I met a man in the pub. He told me he was working on the gold dredge in Bulolo. I asked him how much he was earning and it was a bloody sight more than I had been. I travelled by ferry from Rabaul to Lae on the main island of New Guinea. From there, I flew on a Junkers transport plane to the Bulolo gold field. Also on the flight were a cow and a billiards table. I stayed with the fellow I'd met in Rabaul and asked for a job, but there was no position available.

A strange thing happened though. While I was there, a telephone mechanic died. He had climbed onto the roof to fix the phone for one of the offices. Another electrician had used telephone wire to run 240 volts. When the mechanic undid the telephone wire, it was live and he was electrocuted. Another electrician was working on one of the dredges. They took him off the dredge and put him into the electrical section and I replaced him on the stern of the dredge.

We worked an eight hour shift – three eight hour shifts a day, seven days a week, every week: eleven to seven; seven to three; and three to eleven. Christmas and Good Friday were the only days the dredges didn't work. I stayed there for four months.

Whenever I was on graveyard shift (eleven to seven), I'd be so tired when I came off, frequently, I'd just flop into the bed without undressing. Every day, the dredge master had to get up five minutes early to come down and wake me up, because I'd sleep through the alarm. I became deeply fatigued on that job. The work was hectic and noisy. There was a hooter system for communications. If the dredge master wanted something, he'd press the enormous hooter. That's probably where my industrial deafness came from.

Eventually, I couldn't take the dredge work any longer and it was time to go back to Melbourne. I left Bulolo with a pocket full of money. Even the normal week's pay was a lot more than I had earned at the hospital, and then there were penalty rates on top of that.

On the twenty first of February, 1941, I arrived back in Melbourne. I had left as a school boy; I returned as a young man intending to study Medicine, but after I'd enrolled, I found it didn't challenge me.

When I wrote to the Engineering section of the Public Works Department in Rabaul to ask for my certificate in Fitting and Turning, they kept their promise. The certificate arrived promptly.

World War II was still raging. The Japanese had bombed Pearl Harbour in Hawaii, and then they were threatening the Western Pacific too. Wondering if I should enlist, I went for a medical examination with the army.

Part Two: The War Years

4 Back to Melbourne

When I came down to Melbourne in February 1941, I didn't know whether to study medicine or join the army. While I was in Rabaul, I had joined an organisation called the New Guinea Volunteer Rifles. I went to those meetings a couple of times in Bulolo as well. The NGVR had groups all over New Guinea. Oddly enough, this classified me as a soldier.

My Dad was keen for me to join up. He'd joined the army as soon as he arrived back in Melbourne from New Guinea and was working in Records. The old man was rather good at clerical work. He'd been a clerk for a year or so when he first left school. In Records, a one-armed Colonel, who had been in the First World War, was in charge. The Colonel told me once that before my father worked there, if anyone wanted some information from the files, they had to write in; but after Dad worked there, people could ring up and ask for a soldier's record and he had the data at his fingertips.

I did a medical for the army and they asked me if I'd ever had malaria. I told them I had had it several times.

'I've had sub tertian, benign tertian and quartan.'

'What's that?' they asked.

'That's the three phases of malaria you can get.'

'What about dengue fever?'

'Yes, I've had dengue.'

They always told us in New Guinea that dengue doesn't kill you. It's known as "break bone fever."

They knew absolutely nothing about malaria. The army was worried about both the malaria and that I had albumin urea, so I was rejected.

~

My rejection didn't bother me a great deal. Instead, I enrolled at Melbourne University to study Medicine, but after my experiences in New Guinea, I found the introduction to the medical course so boring that I left after two months. Following that, I had to apply to Manpower for work. You couldn't just take a job during wartime.

You had to go to Manpower and they sent you to the job where you were needed. They looked over my qualifications.

'You've done Chemistry?'

'Yes. I received an award for Chemistry in High School. I also worked in a pathology laboratory in Rabaul for two years,' I said.

~

Manpower sent me to teach chemistry to leaving certificate level at a coaching college in the Rialto building, a very big building in the centre of Melbourne, just two blocks from the Town Hall. While I was at the college, I enrolled as a student too. I studied French, Latin and physics. I was quite good at Latin but I was never any good at French. I loved physics and chemistry. The college called physics 'natural philosophy'.

'What's this natural philosophy?'

'It's physics.'

'Well why do they call it natural philosophy?'

'Sorry, I don't know.'

If I'd had my time over as a schoolboy again, I'd have done natural philosophy and nothing else. If only you could have just done it as a single subject. I became pretty good at physics just studying it by myself.

~

April 24th 1941, is a date I'll never forget. It was the second time I nearly lost my life. I was teaching Chemistry to a class of about twenty students in a lab on the first floor. Down the back of the laboratory, there was a senior master taking some other sort of class. I was up the front of the big room, where the practical laboratory equipment was. At the back of the room, a double door led outside. One door was open. The other door was still bolted into the bricks.

The item in the curriculum required me to show the students how to make oxygen. The demonstration involved mixing into a test tube, equal parts of potassium chlorate and manganese dioxide. As I made the oxygen, it bubbled up into the cylinder. To show the students it contained oxygen, I dropped in an ember. Instead of just glowing, the bloody thing exploded. I felt a bang in my leg, looked down and saw that the flying glass had gouged my thigh and cut into my flesh. Blood was pumping out through my trousers. I realised that the glass had cut my femoral artery. I was wearing a shirt with a stiff collar and studs, a tie and a suit. *If that's in my groin, I'm dead,* I remember thinking, *because I can't hold that artery.*

The Master was a senior teacher, who owned the college. He came wobbling up.

'What happened, Kerby?' he asked.

'I'm afraid it hit me in the femoral artery, Sir.'

He looked down and I was bloody from head to foot. To demonstrate, I took my thumb off the artery and it went 'swish.'

'A doctor, an ambulance!' he shouted.

He spun around, then he ran out the door. All the students, both his class and mine, except for one girl, rushed out the door too and, in their rush, stripped the door off its hinges. One girl stayed behind. By this time, I'd fallen onto the floor.

'Are you all right, Sir?'

'You'd better go. I'm going to remove my trousers,' I told her heroically.

She left. I pulled my trousers down and another student, Don Rabinov, came back.

'Can I do anything for you?'

'Yes, undo my collar.'

I must have been getting rather weak. He squatted down next to me and asked again.

'What did you say?'

'Undo my collar.'

He undid the studs. (I learned later that he wanted to gain entry to medical school. Don eventually became a doctor and later a surgeon. He also became a lifelong friend. I went to his funeral in 2005.)

The next thing I knew, there were two dopey looking ambulance men standing there with a stretcher. They were just looking at me, not making a move.

'Do you have a tourniquet?' I asked.

'No.'

'For Christ's sake, go and get one.'

One of the ambos went away and came back with a tourniquet. He put it on my leg and I had a look down at the wound. It was about three inches down my thigh, so, to my great relief, the tourniquet worked okay.

We were on the first floor. They put me on the stretcher, which was seven feet long, but the lift was only six feet. The bloke in the front marched up to the lift. He walked inside, but the doors couldn't close. My head was still sticking out into the corridor. The automatic door was trying to close.

'Gadoink, gadoink, gadoink...'

'Ray, we'll have to go down the stairs,' said the fellow by my head.

They reversed out. Those fellows weren't very smart, but it was wartime. The Ambulance Service had to take whoever they could get. They took me down feet first. I reckon about half a litre of my blood gushed all over Ray's blue uniform coat. I don't know why I didn't pass out. I was extremely aware of everything that was happening. I found out later that anybody having a severe haemorrhage is excessively alert – until they pass out. They took me outside and put me in the ambulance. I went through the traffic lights to the hospital, the bell ringing. After I arrived at the emergency department, a girl fed me a cup of tea with a spoon.

While I was lying on the stretcher in emergency, some fellow came by and looked hard at me.

'Are you usually that colour?'

'Well I don't know what colour I am at the moment, but I've just come down from New Guinea and I have a suntan.'

The tourniquet was still on and my pants were off. The army Records Office where my father worked was also in the centre of the city. Someone rang him and he came to the hospital. They tried to get in touch with my mother, but the Kiosk had no phone. They sent a policeman to tell her I was injured and in hospital.

It was afternoon and the shift changed at three o'clock. Having just recently come down from New Guinea and also being in shock, I felt quite cold. I was wearing two pairs of long johns, which the staff took off, because they were saturated with blood. Someone wrapped them up in newspaper and gave my mother the parcel to take home with her. While she was travelling home in the tram, the blood dripped out of the newspaper, onto the floor.

~

67

When the shift changed, an arrogant young resident doctor came in. I was in the emergency ward, lying quite comfortably on a stretcher. He had a kidney dish with suture thread in it, a needle and forceps. I couldn't believe his intentions. I nearly died from this idiot's actions.

'You're not going to suture it,' I said.

'Yes, yes.'

'But it's a ruptured femoral artery!'

'Mmmm, yes.'

He took the tourniquet off and threw it in the corner of the room. I looked down and I could see the artery pumping again. Fortunately for me, he had enough bloody sense to call for help. A female doctor came through – a woman of about forty-five or fifty.

'Where's the tourniquet?' she asked.

'Over there,' said the resident.

She picked it up and put it back on.

'Look out for his hairs,' said the resident.' Keep his hairs out of the way.'

'Never mind my hairs, you numbskull, just put the tourniquet on,' I said.

There was an intercom in the room and a nursing sister spoke into it.

'Is the Lord Sumner Theatre ready? We are anticipating a fatality.'

I had enough energy left to be sarcastic. 'That's nice.'

They took me out on a trolley, but the lift had just started on its way up. It was one of those with a wire mesh around it. The dopey young doctor called out.

'Miss Higgins, we have an emergency here. Can you bring the lift down please?'

She brought it down again, emptied it and they put me in.

I was aware of being placed on the operating table. I remember regaining consciousness in the ward next day. I still have a large hollow in my thigh where muscle tissue had been blown away. The nurses told me I had been in theatre for three hours, patching that. They just tied my artery off. They didn't anastomose it, because they didn't yet know how to do so. That was to have serious implications for me many, many years later.

If I used the bedpan, a nursing sister had to stand beside me. It was a bit embarrassing for a young man, but she had to stay beside the bed with a tourniquet, in case I bled.

I received four blood transfusions altogether. I looked down at the transfusion equipment and saw that there was no bubble-trap. It was antiquated. We used better gear than that on the Kanakas in New Guinea. We kept the glass Glaxo bottles, which originally came with glucose or saline solution in them. When they were empty, we sterilised the bottles in the autoclave and we reused them for blood transfusions. In case we had a bubble of air in the transfusion line, we would take a length of glass tubing, heat it with a Bunsen burner, push it together, then we put a finger over one end and puffed down the tube. That way, we'd have a sphere in the glass in the middle of the tube. If an air bubble came through with the blood, it would go up into the bubble-trap and not into the patient.

I looked down and, because I didn't have a bubble-trap on the tube into my hand, I was agitated. The doctor arrived to do his afternoon rounds.

The Sister in Charge of the ward approached.

'This is the doctor who set up your blood transfusion.'

'Don't you chaps use a bubble-trap in your transfusion gear?' I asked.

'What, what…?' The doctor stood there, open mouthed. Here was a nineteen year old admonishing him for his transfusion equipment. He was a fairly old doctor of thirty six or so.

'No bloody bubble-trap. Christ! What if I get an air bubble in here?'

He took off and left me still protesting.

My mother was the same blood group as me, so she gave the blood for my transfusions. I copped malaria from that – the worst case of malaria I ever suffered.

'He knows how to treat it,' my father told them. 'He'll be all right.'

My father brought in my Atabrin, a fabulous anti-malarial drug.

When I went home to convalescence, the doctor spoke to Dad.

'He seems to know what he's doing with his pills.'

'Yes,' my father reassured him. 'He knows the dosages.'

I'd always looked after myself with Atabrin. The disadvantage is that it makes your skin go yellow. My mother wouldn't use it because of that.

I recovered fairly quickly from the blood loss after four transfusions, but my leg took months to heal. The explosion had blown a large piece of muscle out of my thigh and I was on a walking stick for a long time. I was still using the walking stick when I went for my second medical to join the Australian Infantry Force [AIF]. By then the military were trying to conscript more people.

'What's the walking stick for?' they asked, when I limped in.

I showed them my hospital medical report.

'Christ! We're not that desperate.'

My second rejection by the army didn't unduly upset me. With so many men away at the war, there were plenty of opportunities in Melbourne for an energetic and enterprising young man.

~

After my parents had come down from New Guinea in 1939 at the start of the war, they bought the lease for St Kilda Pier Kiosk. Their plan was that my Mother should run the Kiosk. I wrote to them that I didn't think buying the kiosk was a good idea, because Mum became seasick so quickly. I remembered that, when we went across St Georges Channel between New Britain and New Ireland on the *Tilbora*, my mother was very seasick. I thought when Mum looked out the window and saw the waves in St Kilda Bay, she was bound to be seasick, but she never was.

Before I came back to Melbourne, my father had written complaining how some dreadful bastard had cut all the telephone wires to the Kiosk from under the pier. Of course, when I did that, the wires were all hanging down, apparently broken in places. When I came back home, I told him how I had done it for the lead and cooked it up into diving weights at my girlfriend's place.

I didn't return to teaching the chemistry class. When my father knew that the army had rejected me and I could stay in Melbourne, he requested a transfer to New Guinea. While Dad was away, I lived at the Kiosk helping Mum. St Kilda Pier had been one of my favourite haunts during my early teens. Now it was my home.

My interest in physics continued and I went back to the coaching college to continue my study of physics. Don Rabinov, who had been one of my chemistry students, was in the same physics class. We became friends. I also became lifelong friends with another student in the class, Alf Lazer.

~

My dad transferred straight from the Records office to active service in the army. Because he'd worked in little boats in New Guinea, they put him into Water Transport. He travelled up to Clifton Gardens in Sydney, to the naval base there. After some training, they put him in charge of a boat, AS 28, and gave him a crew of eight to take it up to New Guinea. His rank was Warrant Officer First Class, top of the Non-Commissioned Officers. He sailed North to Milne Bay, near Lae, while the Japanese were invading New Guinea from the north. At Milne Bay, he transferred to Gunnery, where he trained briefly on Owen guns, then he took a small group of men, perhaps only two or three, inland close to the war zone. Their task was to report by radio whenever Japanese aircraft passed over, heading south. My old man did a pretty good job of that surveillance and his superior recommended him to be promoted to Lieutenant. There was opposition in Canberra about it, because he was cross-eyed.

'We've looked at WO1 Kerby's record, and he's cross-eyed. Because his appearance would be unbecoming to that of an officer, we are refusing his commission.'

The Commanding Officer wrote back:

'That might be so, but when he was two hundred miles ahead of our front line at Salamoa near Lae, sending us information about Japanese movements, he was extraordinarily helpful.'

A letter came back from Canberra, approving his promotion.

Dad was in New Guinea during the early part of the Pacific War, 1942 and 1943. By 1944, he was back in Melbourne with two pips on his shoulder, a Lieutenant. That year, he tried standing for parliament again as a candidate for the
Services' party. I never worked so hard in all my life as when I helped him with that campaign. Arthur Caldwell beat Dad by about 12,000 votes. Dad's was the lowest vote.

My father said he represented an exclusive part of the electorate. His slogan was 'Drop the deadheads and clear the numbskulls out of the Government Administration.' He never did have time for petty authority and regulations.

In 1944, my grandfather died. My mate, Alf Lazer, travelled up to Ballarat with me. I went to the funeral service and afterwards, met up with Alf in the public bar of the hotel where we were staying. When I walked into the bar, the barman commented to Alf, 'Here's Col now. You couldn't mistake him for anyone but Noble Kerby's son.'

Street Photographer

I was very keen on photography from way back. I took both my still camera and a movie camera with me to Rabaul and, while I was there, I modified another movie camera, a sixteen millimetre, to take 3D film.

As soon as my leg was sufficiently healed, I applied for a job with Leicagraph as a Street Photographer. It was a fairly high quality street photography business. When I worked for them, they insisted on calling me Tony.

'What's your name?' they asked when I applied for work.

'Colin.'

'Oh no, we have someone called Colin. We'll have to call you something else. You look like a Dago. Let's call you Tony.'

That's how I became Tony. Later, a fellow called Anthony came to work there. They went through the name routine with him as well.

'We can't call you Tony. We've already a Tony here.'

They called him Bill. We kept in contact with him. Those names remain to this day. Ion, a friend from that era, still calls me Tony. Bill died about eight years ago, so Ion's about the only one left now that calls me Tony.

~

As well as helping my mother with the Kiosk, I decided to buy my own photographic business – a street photography business – with the money I had made on the gold dredge in New Guinea. A couple of photography businesses I looked at were studios, but I wasn't skilled enough for that. I bought an existing street photography business to get the processing equipment.

72

If you start a business, you have to have somewhere to hammer in a nail and hang up your coat. If you buy an existing business, the coat hook is already in place. By buying that business, I obtained everything I needed: the dark room equipment, cameras and lots of other things that were almost impossible to get otherwise, because it was wartime. I employed photographers and I went out on the streets too, taking photographs and handing out cards. I finished up with seven cameras double-shifted, fourteen men in all. When the Americans came on R and R [rest and recreation] from the Coral Sea and took out local girls, they wanted photographs together. It was very lucrative.

At the time I started, we were allowed to take the photograph in the street, but we were not allowed to give out business cards. I was fined many times at ten pounds each time. My men were fined too, but they were getting a good income and could afford to pay the fines.

The taxation was on advertising our photography. The government fellow told me that showing the proofs was advertising and he wanted to charge me ten percent for that. I said I wasn't going to pay it. From the year dot, photographers have shown the proofs to the customer and not been taxed for it. There could be a situation where you don't sell one out of the thirty six on the sheet. But no, the sales tax department wouldn't have it. I had to go up and see them. Matthews, the honest inspector I was dealing with, was called in by his department head. The attempt to tax us might have been the Department Head's own idea. There were thirteen street photography businesses in Melbourne at the time. I had so many men working for me, mine was the principal one. There must have been a hundred photographers on the streets altogether in the 1940's.

I had an argument with the head of the sales tax department over the levying of this tax. The man had a bullet-shaped head. I leaned over his desk.

'No, I'm not going to pay it.'

'I'll take you to court. What the magistrate will decide is ...'

'Just a bloody minute, what the magistrate will decide is a matter for conjecture.'

Matthews was standing there. He agreed.

73

'That's quite so, Mr Kerby.'

Bullet Head was Matthews' boss. I continued to berate Bullet Head.

'When a customer makes an order, they get the proof as well as the enlargement. This tax is just fishing and parsimonious.'

'Will you leave us, Mr Matthews?'

When Matthews had gone, he continued to me. 'Listen, you're a bloody nuisance. If you keep your trap shut, I won't go after you, but don't tell any of the others.'

For the first time in my life, I kept my trap shut.

'Fair enough, it's a deal.'

They all paid extra tax and I didn't. How do you like that? He did an illegal deal.

Prior to that, I was sometimes taken to court. The district prosecutor in Melbourne at that time was named Bennett. One day, when I was in court, the magistrate asked a very impertinent question.

'Mr Bennett, is there anything we can charge this man with? I want to put him in gaol.'

'No, Your Honour.'

I would grin around the court and generally act cheekily. They could charge me no more than ten pounds.

I kept the photography business going for some years. I had three shops for it. I called the one in the Empire Arcade, Lavish. The photography almost ran itself. All I did was oversee it.

Night life at The Kiosk

When my father returned home from his army service in New Guinea, many American soldiers were in Melbourne for R & R leave. Dad installed a polished steel floor on the Kiosk verandah and held dancing there at night. Servicemen and locals enjoyed dancing all the current fashions to music from gramophone records. One young woman wore a full skirt and whirled so energetically as she danced, that her knickers were on view. She told me much later that she sewed buttons on her knickers, so they looked like eyes. I can remember seeing that when I was about twenty.

Salvage Diver

One day in 1943, I found out that the Government wanted the *Kakariki* salvaged. About six years earlier, in 1937, an island trader, which plied from Melbourne to Tasmania, ran into the *Kakariki,* sinking her in Port Phillip Bay. Back then, when I rode my pushbike around the foreshore, I could see the mast sticking up above the water. The *Kakariki* had been a small coastal trader. When she went down, she had a cargo of timber in the hold.

I applied for the diving job with the salvage firm, citing my experience in Rabaul. In 1944, a team of eight began cutting up the wreck. There were two divers, me and a chap called Slim. He and I became the best of mates.

I bought the latest available diving gear, though it wasn't as good as the Japanese had supplied. I found too, that I preferred the method the Japanese used to get a diver into the water. They picked you up from the platform with a crane and deposited you onto a ladder; you only walked down the ladder to the water's surface and dropped off. The method used in Australia was to seat the diver on the deck and dress him completely except for his face glass. Someone walked him across the deck to the ladder, where they screwed on the face glass. The diver walked down the ladder into the water. That method was more awkward, because the gear was as heavy as I was. Walking across the deck was very difficult.

Our job was to break up and remove the *Kakariki* from the bay. By then, the ship had been underwater for seven years, so her cargo of timber was waterlogged inside the hull. This made it very difficult to work. There were girders from the deck to the bilge and we had to get inside to cut them with oxy torches. It was extremely dark in the hold and we had to battle our way through the timber to get to those girders.

There was a degaussing unit about two miles away. Such a unit was a necessity in wartime. It was used to reduce the magnetic field of a steel ship, thereby lowering the risk of magnetic mines being triggered by the vessel. Our detonations upset their unit. They said we were allowed to use only two sticks of nitro-glycerine each time we had to blow. Instead, at times, we used much more. Every time we blew, which was whenever we couldn't cut with a torch, the degaussing blokes would come charging up in a launch and accuse us of using more 'gelly' than we were permitted.

'We're only using two sticks.'

We couldn't cut through the shaft. It was too big. We used a whole case of gelignite either side and fired them both together. We cut the superstructure off at the mud line, using oxy and explosives. The structure weighed about 300 tons. We had enough camels [buoyancy tanks] on it to lift 450 tons. Pell, the dive master, was puzzled.

'I don't know why the bloody thing won't come up.'

'I think when we are cutting, sometimes we might be cutting a bit fast and the slag runs around the back and re-welds.' I said. 'That might be the problem.'

We were using the oxy torch under mud, so it was impossible to see. You have to hold your finger around the torch and just feel whether it has gone through the steel. If it doesn't go through, the flame comes out and burns your finger, so you know you've missed. When it goes through, there's no flame, so you move along to the next bit. If you come to a mussel — bloody mussels, they're a problem — the oxy won't cut beyond that either, so you get a back blow there too.

'Mmm...How do you think we can fix that, Col?'

'I think we should take down a piece of wire and run it along the cut.'

Pell agreed we should try.

We had problems with the positioning of the *Helen Moore*, the salvage boat. The person in charge often let the boat drift over the wreck. I frequently complained about the boat drifting over our work area. Just prior to the final dive, I leaned over the side and looked straight down at the wreck. Yet again, the dive boat was drifting over the *Kakariki*. I asked the crew to move the boat back, which they did.

Slim and I went down once more. There was a big steam winch on the bow of the *Helen Moore*. The surface team lowered the camel with a small crane. I was crouching down on the deck of the *Kakariki* near her deck winch, with chains and big shackles ready to attach the twenty ton camel we hoped would lift the superstructure out of the water.

While I was attaching the camel, Slim went down about another twenty feet to the mud line. He slid the wire around the cut and found a piece of half inch plate about eighteen inches long that hadn't been cut at all. Without informing me that he was going to do so, Slim cut the last section away. I was standing on the deck, when suddenly the superstructure gave a wobble. I felt uneasy, so I went to the edge to look down at Slim. I was looking at his air bubbles when, suddenly, the whole four hundred tons of the superstructure started coming up through the water.

I shot upwards, but I couldn't see and I thought I had fallen off the deck into the interior of the *Kakariki*. Instead, I was jammed up against the hull of the *Helen Moore*. My air supply suddenly stopped. I was prepared to die. Next, I felt myself being dragged. Just at that moment, I broke surface. The change in air pressure caused my diving suit to expand, making movement difficult. My arms and legs were held out straight, like the 'Michelin Man'. That was my third brush with death. I rose so fast, it was fortunate that I wasn't crushed between the two boats. I could have been killed had the dive boat not been moved back just before we went down.

Then Slim shot up to the surface too. The topside of the dive boat was about five feet off the water and our boarding ladder had been wrenched off the *Helen Moore* when the top of the wreck crashed into it. Everyone on board was trying to get hold of Slim, to pull him onto the deck. He was a heavy, muscular man and in his dive gear, he weighed an extra one hundred and fifty pounds. The crew started hauling him on board. Slim was wearing a twenty-five pound lead boot on each foot and the youngest crew member, a well-muscled teenager, caught one boot, put it under his arm and marched across the deck. Slim's other leg was still hanging down the side of the boat. I was looking at his crutch. We had diver to diver and diver to surface communications. This teenager was pulling Slim's foot and I could hear Slim screaming as his legs were stretched further and further apart. Eventually, they pulled Slim on the deck and rolled him over like a barrel of beer. His arms were flopping about in all directions. After that, they pulled me up.

We cut up the rest of the hull. The whole boat was about nine hundred tons. There was a newspaper report and photo about the wreck and salvage of the *Kakariki*. It claimed that Diver Kerby came up and said, 'Everything's all right.'

What I actually said when I came up was, 'Everything's a bloody mess.'

We spent six months cutting up that ship and moving it out of the bay. We dumped the steel between Altona and Kroit Creek. The job was finally finished in early June, 1944, close to D Day, before the war's end in Europe.

Slim was surly and taciturn when I first met him. Not long before, his wife had died of tuberculosis and he was grieving and depressed. Slim had been a naval diver for some time. He was often very edgy until he remarried and had a family. He and I became firm friends and remained so for the rest of his life. He died of a stroke in Cairns, in 2002, aged 86. After diving on the *Kakariki*, he came and worked for me as a photographer.

Slim and Col in their diving suits.

A friend of mine had a very posh café in Collins Street. The whole basement was empty, so I rented the area to use as a dark room for my photographic business. During lunch hour one day, Slim was working in the dark room. He was wearing only sailor's bell-bottom trousers and his feet were bare. At six foot two [188 cm] and being very athletic, he was a fairly good looking bloke. He liked wandering about without a shirt, showing off his pectorals.

Slim spied a very large rat. He chased it with a broom around the basement. It ran up the stairs into the café, which was full of people eating lunch. Slim chased after it, running across the tables. He caught the rat and killed it in a corner.

The café owner was distressed about this and when I came in that afternoon, I had to pacify him as best I could.

As well as working in my photography lab, Slim helped out in the confectionary factory and also helped me obtain a salvage job in New Guinea in 1950.

5 Kerby's Exclusive Confectionary

While I was still working on the *Kakariki* in late 1943, I went down to discuss with the Department of Rehabilitation how they could assist me to set up as a confectioner. I used my experience as a member of the New Guinea Volunteer Rifle Brigade to help me. Many of the men from the brigade went on to perform active service with the AIF. I didn't tell them I hadn't done that and that I had already purchased a photography business. Nor did I tell them we needed sweets to sell at the Kiosk.

'I served in the army overseas. What about some help to re-establish myself as a confectioner?'

'That's fair enough. You'll have to go down to our expert on confectionaries.'

They told me where to find their man. I went to see this confectionaries expert, an old bloke, who had been making sweets all his working life. He was the specialist who knew what allowances one should get. Because it was wartime and there was rationing, they had to issue me with permits to buy my ingredients. I thought that the permits covered three months' supply. I was no confectioner. When I was a kid at school, I would cook up vinegar, sugar and water and make toffee, smash it up and eat it. I loved it. It doesn't work that way when you're doing it commercially, because it doesn't have a shelf life.

'How much sugar do you want?'

'Half a ton.'

'Oh, that won't go very far. We'll make it three tons.'

He was talking usage per month, and I was thinking, that's a ton a month for three months.

'That's all right. '

'How much glucose will you need?'

'I'm a bit out of touch,' I said. I was supposed to be a confectioner trying to re-establish myself and I had never heard of glucose.

'You'll need a barrel. That weighs 560 pounds, I think. Coconut, licorice... Can you come back next week to collect the permits?'

I told him I was working on a salvage job.

'I'm between the devil and the deep blue sea.' Then I realised what I'd said and apologised profusely.

I received my permits and quotas and I went out to CSR [Colonial Sugar Refinery] and gave them the permit for the sugar and glucose.

I rented a factory in the city, twelve hundred square feet upstairs on the first floor. It was one hundred and fifty yards from the Police Headquarters and opposite the museum. I had the factory for five years, starting in 1943 and selling out in 1948. I had to render all the bricks. The Department of Health wouldn't let you have un-rendered walls, so we had to chip all the bricks to make the render stick.

I had hemi-spherical, copper kettles made. Each of those pots held a seventy pound bag of sugar. They sat over big, black, cast iron gas rings. I ordered a table, fourteen feet long and four feet wide, supported on trestles. Galvanised iron was too difficult to obtain in wartime, so I found a sheet of zinc to cover the table top. I soldered it up and built one and a half inch steel fiddles around the edges of the table. A year or so later, I ordered a water cooled table. The water flowed in channels under the surface, cooling the toffee.

A Jewish refugee friend, Roy, was working for me. He was a really skinny fellow and weighed about what my weight is now – nine stone [fifty-six kilos]. The day the sugar was due to be delivered, I had to attend to some other business for a short while.

'I'm waiting for the sugar delivery. I have to go away for about an hour. You're in charge, Roy. If they come before I get back, tell them to put it over there.' "Over there" was up two flights of stairs to the first floor. There was no lift in the building.

The semi-trailer pulled up only ten minutes after I'd left. The driver knocked on the door and spoke to Roy.

'I've a load of sugar.'

'Very good, just put it over there.'

'Twelve feet from the truck, that's all mate. Union rules. That'll be about there.'

He pointed to the doorway. There was a vestibule there and he filled it up with bags of sugar. Roy agreed, because he knew I needed the sugar and he was afraid the driver would take it away again. There are 32 bags to the ton. I had received two tons straight off and now he was delivering another four tons. It's lucky he wasn't delivering three months' supply – nine tons. The other tenants could scarcely get in or out of the building. Roy wasn't strong enough to carry the bags up. They were too heavy for him. When I came back, I carried all the sugar upstairs – 128 bags of it. You should have seen the mess. I just dropped it inside the door.

The barrels of glucose came from CSR too. They came in the back way. We had a little hand truck and we brought them in on that. The biggest problem I had with the glucose was getting it out of the barrel. There was a big bung in the barrel, but I didn't know how to get the main lid off.

When we first started making sweets, I went down to Myers to buy a large can for cooking marshmallow snowballs. I didn't know what I was buying. My father saw me walking back the half kilometer from Myers to the factory, carrying this container on my shoulder. He pulled his car up beside me.

'Why are you walking along with a shit can on your back?

'I want a pot like this to cook snowballs in,' I said. It seemed I had bought an outdoor dunny can.

When we first made the snowballs, we had a broom stick with a whisk tied on the end with wire. We belted hell out of the boiled glucose with this whisk; that's how primitively I started out. Later, I had a water-cooled beater professionally made by a very nice firm that did fabrication. It was a beauty; the beater would handle about one hundred and fifty pounds of marshmallow in the pot.

I bought a confectionary cook book: Home recipes for confectionary. I thumbed through this book. What will I make? Licorice allsorts? I liked those, so I thought I'd try some. I bought sheets of licorice about two feet by one foot. They came in half-hundredweight bundles [just over fifty kilos].

The instructions were to lay out a sheet of licorice and paint it with gelatine and water. There was a big drought on in Queensland, and it was hard to get gelatine, which is made from boiled calves' hooves. Make your fondant. Put the fondant on top of the gelatine. Place another layer of licorice on top and leave overnight. Next day, cut it up with a knife. I looked up fondant: Sugar, glucose, water. Cook it at 308 degrees Fahrenheit. Pour it out onto a slab and use a paddle to work it until it goes creamy. I made an implement a bit like a six foot canoe paddle. You need a handle long enough to grip with both hands, because there's about one hundred and fifty pounds of the mixture on the table to be worked. I sharpened the end so it would slide underneath.

I cooked up the first batch. When it was cooked, I poured it out on the table and it surfed down to the end and started to go over the edge, so I rushed to that end of the table, picking it up. Then the mixture surfed back to the other end. It was pouring over both edges and out under the fiddles, where they weren't sufficiently close to the table and at the corners. I had stalagmites of glucose on the floor. I ran around for about four or five hours until it cooled enough. If I had made clamps on the fiddles, much less mixture would have poured underneath.

When the mixture had cooled sufficiently, I shoved my paddle into it and it stuck there. I did the best I could, but I couldn't get it right. I put my gloves on and put on some oil to knead the mix. Confectioners' gloves are leather, and like gauntlets, they come up to your elbows. It's a wonder I didn't get stuck in the fondant. It was no bloody good. I had put the sheet of licorice down and put the fondant on top and another sheet of licorice on top. The book said to leave it overnight. Come back next day to cut it up. When I came back next day, the two sheets of licorice had stuck together and the fondant had spread out all over the equipment.

After a long time, perhaps six weeks, I had wasted a huge amount of ingredients. You had to use things within the period of time of the permits. You couldn't bank them up. The book said if it fails, put it aside to reuse in the next batch, so I put it on a tarp on the floor in the corner. I finished up with about four tons of gluey material on the tarpaulin with newspaper over it. The health inspector came up and he took one look.

'What's that?'

'That's going to the tip. '

'I'll stop here until it goes.'

He doesn't know anything about confectionary manufacture, I thought. *That was going in the next batch.*

There was a high school just up the street, not far away from where I was. I went up there and spoke to the Domestic Science teacher. I took some licorice allsorts with me.

'How do I make this stuff?' I asked.

'It looks to me like a paste. '

'How do you make a paste?'

'You cook up sugar and water and glucose, then you put icing sugar in it and that thickens it up,' the teacher explained.

Once I put the icing sugar in, the fondant thickened and was okay. I was able to make my licorice allsorts. Eventually I was making twelve tons of confectionary a week and I had about twenty women working for me. They worked at one end of the factory and the machinery was at the other end.

I bought a machine to make icing sugar. It had a shaft which spun with little hammers attached to it. As you poured sugar down the funnel, the hammers crushed up the grains. If you put the sugar through once, it made caster sugar. The second time through, it became very fine icing sugar.

~

I found out that confectioners are very tight-mouthed. They don't give away their secrets. I found only one who was pretty liberal, but most weren't. From that confectioner, I bought a mangle that made boiled lollies. Half of the shape of a lolly was on the top roller and the other half on the bottom roller. We cooked the sugar and glucose and when it was cool enough, we dumped it in a lump on the water-cooled table. As it cooled more, we could pick it up and bend it over so that the softer material on top slid over the sides. At that point, we turned it over again. When we had kneaded it like this a few times, we caught the lump of mixture onto a big taffy hook hanging above the table. We pulled the taffy repeatedly, until we had formed a long fat python. You could even write words on the toffee at that stage and they would come out in the middle of the lolly.

When the taffy mixture was ready in a snake shape, we laid it lengthways on the table and fed it through the rollers which formed up the lollies. There was no drive chain, just the rollers and bearings, not even a handle. I had a spare five-horse power motor, so I thought I'd put that on the mangle. I rigged up the motor and some belts. The rollers were geared so they always came round in the right position. I started up the motor.

There was a bucket for the lollies to go into. I fed the python of taffy into the mangle and in about two seconds, it went boom. The whole bloody lot went through at once. It was like a Gatling gun shooting sweets the length of the factory, smashing the windows and peppering the women employees. One woman lost a tooth. This machine was doing 1,440 revolutions per minute. The noise it made was really deafening. You needed ear protection. The machine was designed to wind the taffy through by hand. It needed to be geared down when motorised, so I geared it down ten to one. That didn't make any difference. The lollies still went through at the same rate. The workroom was still like a war zone, so the women took their morning tea next door.

I ended up putting a gear box on that motor, which took it down by 150 times. That worked and it handled an enormous amount of taffy. With the electric motor on, we could probably have made a hundred tons a week. I sold the toffees in bulk to a fellow with a wrapping machine. Later, I bought my own wrapping machine.

My snowballs put me on the market. They were the roughest looking snowballs you ever saw – balls of marshmallow covered in chocolate and coconut. I would sell an order into a shop, say ten boxes and before I left the shop, three quarters of the stock would be sold already. When people saw me delivering and because confectionary was so scarce during the war, they would queue to be served. The marshmallows always sold out. I called my product Kerby's Exclusive Confectionary.

~

Half way through all this, I realised that I could make much more money if I sold the sweets in cartons. I went to a firm call Farrow, Falcon Press. Most paper and cardboards were rationed in wartime. They had a ration of white line slip. It is a very light cardboard, with white paper stuck on it and a waxy kind of finish. Even though they were a very big firm, their quotas were taken up and they didn't have enough to make my cartons. They made me up a few cartons and I was paid double the price for sweets packed that way. I never wanted to sell un-boxed sweets again. We needed to make our own cartons.

Making our own Cartons
Having decided to start a carton business, I rented a complete building in the next block, with a shop out the front. I bought a

printing press and a cutting platen. Dawson and Payne made these printing presses called Stick Over. You feed your cardboard in, it is picked up on the roller and taken across the printing inks, then it comes out the other side. The Stick Over moves the card out of the press onto the pile and takes the next sheet of cardboard. After the sheet of card is printed, it goes into the cutting platen.

I had Slim working for me at this time. Slim and I were trying to get the Dawson Payne Stick Over printing press to work. We were using maroon ink. A friend called Michael Betts was over too. He wasn't working for me; he was just visiting. Mike was asleep on the stretcher just out the back near the kitchen.

Slim and I were working away and we had ink all over ourselves. I went out to the kitchen to make a cup of tea. When I returned, Slim was giggling. All three of us had an eye for a gag; we were energetic young men in our early twenties.

'What's up?' I asked Slim.

'Have a look at this.'

He took me outside and down to the corner. We were one building away from Little Lonsdale Street. For a century, Little Lon had been the brothel area of Melbourne. Down near the lamp post, he'd rubbed his hands on the concrete and made it look like blood. He'd dipped a rag into the ink, and dripped it from the rag all the way to the building on the other side of us and had it running right into the doorway of the next building.

'Jeeze. That looks too good,' I said. We'll have the coppers down here. '

Slim looked at it again and realised how deadly it appeared.

'Do you think so?' he asked me.

'Bloody sure. We'll have the coppers down here in no time.'

We went inside and had a cup of tea, expecting the police to arrive very soon. I'd had stippling done on the window so no one could look in. I scratched a little hole so we could see out. There was a copper with his helmet on down under the light post, just standing there.

'Slim, there's a copper down there already.' This worried him.

'They'll have us under observation, I said.

We heard a bang out the back. Two coppers came over the fence. We looked out the window and there was a fellow there in a suit as well as a constable in uniform beside him. I opened the door.

'Come in.'

They both came in and looked at Slim.

'What's that on your hands?'

'It's blood. He just killed a man,' I said.

The copper took his helmet off. He looked through to the other room and there was the stretcher with a body lying on it, covered by a sheet. Michael had the sheet over his head.

Slim blustered.

'It's paint. No, it's not, it's ink. '

The detective took five steps through to the backroom and pulled the sheet down. Mike sat up. The young copper was right beside me. He obviously thought that if either of us made a move, he would stop us. We showed them the ink. I didn't say anything more. I left Slim to try to explain it all, but he wasn't very good at explaining. To start with, Slim had gone back and tried to wipe the ink off. That just made it all look worse. The copper had followed the ink up the street to the next building. He pulled something out of his pocket and dug a card into the red mess, putting it into a sample bag to examine for human cells.

~

Once we had the printer going, printing the cardboard wasn't so very difficult. Cutting out the boxes was a different story. Firstly, you draw up the shape of your carton and with a jigsaw cut out the pattern in three quarter inch plywood. Secondly, you put the ply into a frame with koins on the sides, which are like a double steel frame with a special screw between the frames that you tighten to jam the plywood inside. This frame sits inside the cutting platen, under a heavy, motorised press. There are long knives like razor blades for cutting out the cardboard and similar knives the same width, but blunt to make the creases for bending. These are set up in the plywood. When it is all correctly adjusted in the platen, you slip the cardboard over the plywood and bend it with little benders.

You pick up your printed cardboard and when the machine is opening up, you put the card into the machine. The motorised heavy press comes down automatically: "Clunk". It pushes the cardboard down onto the blades to cut it. So it doesn't stick on the knives, you put on little pieces of cork, which push the cardboard up again off the knives. When the lid comes down, it compresses the cork, but when it opens again, you have to remove the card and put in another piece. One person takes the card off the platen and the other person puts the next sheet in. The knack is to put that card in before the press comes down again, squashing your fingers.

The big day arrived when we were going to produce these cartons. The knives were sharp and the motor was on. The press was quite powerful and there was no safety guard on those platens. The press could crush your hand. We tossed a coin as to who was going to put the card in and who was going to take it out again. Slim lost, so he had to put the cardboard in and I was to take it out. We had our pile of printed card. Slim put one card in. I didn't have the courage to take it out, so that was no good. We changed places. I put it in, but Slim was frightened to put his hand in to take the card out again. So that was no bloody good either. We tried for all of one day. Finally, I had an idea.

'We'll disconnect the motor. I'll drill a hole in the flywheel and I'll wind it around very slowly until you get accustomed to it.'

The flywheel was really big, about two foot six inches across. I wound it and "clunk", the press came down. It was hard work. We did this all one afternoon. I decided we should try it with the motor on, but I'd flick the switch, to keep it going slowly. I flicked the switch. It was a little bit faster. Slim put a sheet in and I pulled it out. I flicked the switch again. We did this all the next morning. After lunch, we put the belt back on and started up the motor. About three o'clock, I looked across at Slim and the machine was going "clunk, clunk, clunk". Slim had a cigarette in his mouth; he was putting the sheet in; I was taking it out; he was putting another one in. All within two days, we'd trained ourselves.

Kerby's Glucose Butterscotch package.

I didn't have a machine to glue the edges of the carton, but a woman, who is very dexterous with her fingers, can fan the sheets out, about ten at a time, brush them, fold them up and stick them down. A good woman can do almost as many boxes as a machine. From then on, we had plenty of cartons and I never sold any more confectionary loose. I stopped making the boiled lollies, but continued with licorice allsorts and concentrated on marshmallows in cubes. I gave up the snowballs.

To cut the marshmallows, I had a long blunt stainless knife. The Masonite trays were two foot by four foot and had rails on the sides. The cutting blade was two feet long by four inches wide and one millimetre thick, with a piece of wood along the back for pressing down. The women would look at the tray then go bang, bang, bang. No measurement. They were that bloody accurate. They'd do half a tray this way, then tip the tray up and coat them in coconut. We did both pink and white.

I made a very dangerous looking blade for slicing the licorice allsorts. It was a long, very sharp knife, with wood along the top. We needed to wipe the blade occasionally with water. While wiping the blade, one woman cut herself very badly, right through the nail. These days, Work Safety wouldn't allow a knife like that.

Chocolates

I employed an excellent enrober (decorator of chocolates) for dipping chocolates. This woman was top notch at her job. The chocolate came in big slabs that melted at between 98 and 103 degrees Fahrenheit. We had a little timber tray with glazing paper on it. The fondant, shaped to the right size, was sent to the enrober. She dipped the chocolate and decorated the top. The woman was about fifty-five and she'd done this sort of work for about thirty years.

She'd pick up the fondant in her gloved hand, roll it in the chocolate and put it on the glazed paper. When she'd done about two dozen, she'd pick up the little fork and wind that about over the chocolate, making the design on the top. Some, she'd do the design just with her gloved finger. She didn't get her hands into the chocolate. The women all wore special gloves.

That one woman was so good with the chocolates, I would hire her out to the big shops. They'd put her in the window, or next to a special stand inside the shop, where people could watch her work. I profited both ways, because I also had a stand of chocolates for sale in the shop. Apart from the Kiosk, I sold my confectionary to theatres, department stores and the cinemas. Myers would send a good looking girl up to beg me to sell them more. I sold those chocolates for a long time, which gave me great satisfaction.

~

I had a firm make the boxes for the chocolates, because they required a different kind of box and it had to have cellophane on it.
I decided to call our chocolates *Blue Voodoo*. Slim was horrified when I told him.

'You just sued a bloke for copying your marshmallow box. Now you want to call your chocolates *Blue Voodoo*. How is *Black Magic* going to let you get away with that?'

Black Magic was a famous brand of chocolate being made at that time. Slim was referring to a company I had sued, because they imitated my confectionary boxes. This competitor went to Farrow, Falcon Press and ordered boxes very similar to mine. They called them *Marathon Exclusive Confectionary*, in the same colour and same script as mine. I went into a shop in Lonsdale Street, where I saw them up on the shelf. *I didn't know we sold here,* I said to myself. The next day, someone told me about Marathon, so I sued them. The judge said one man's article couldn't look like another man's article. They had even used the same shade of red as well as the same script.

'With my chocolates, the box is blue, not black,' I told Slim.

~

For a while, there was a gas strike on and you could use the gas only from eight o'clock until nine in the morning. I went to a scrap yard and bought an industrial vacuum cleaner metal barrel about a yard in diameter and one and a half yards high, with a flange around the top. I cleaned it all up. I could boil six hundred pounds of sugar for marshmallows in one go. I had big gas jets under the pot and I could do all the cooking in three quarters to one hour. It would keep hot all day, so I never stopped production.

When my old man came back from New Guinea in 1945, he came and helped out at the confectionary factory too. He was impressed with the success of my confectionary business. Later on, he bought a small factory of his own and started to make confectionary for the Kiosk.

~

A Burning Issue

In Melbourne one day, just after the war was over, Slim was driving one of the big confectionary vans through the city. Petrol was scarce and rationed. I had a twenty gallon petrol tank in the cabin and a spare can holding another two gallons. The truck ran out of petrol, but it was still in gear. I thought maybe we could open the cap and pour some petrol in. I looked at Slim and he wasn't smoking so, just as we came over the hump of the bridge over the Yarra, I started to pour petrol into the tank. As we were coming down towards the main intersection with Flinders Street, I spilt some. It ran down through the hole by the gear stick and fell onto the hot exhaust pipe.

The petrol ignited and the flame came up into the cabin. The two gallon can was on fire in my hands. Slim was still at the wheel. I looked around in panic at the windows, wanting to throw the petrol can out of the cabin before it exploded. Slim's window was open, but his head was in the way. I went wooosh, towards the window with the can, but I hit Slim's forehead with it and gashed him quite badly. The petrol was burning in his face and Slim was stamping his feet on the pedals.

The small amount of fuel I'd poured into the tank started the motor up again. It was in top gear, so the truck was leap-frogging down the street. It would stall and then start up again.

There was cop on point duty at the intersection. Slim couldn't stop. The cop had his hand up as the truck kept coming towards him. He kept retreating with his hand up. In the end, Slim took hold of the can and hurled it out of the window. We had about four or five boxes of marshmallows on the seat beside us and Slim hurled these out the window too, even though they weren't burning. I took off my leather jacket and put the flames out with it. The traffic cop came up as I opened the door.

'I was going to offer you two pounds for your truck while it was on fire,' he said.

There was traffic everywhere. That was a very busy intersection, right in the heart of down-town Melbourne. I took Slim up to the hospital to get his head stitched. Slim was lying on the trolley. A sister came by and spoke to me.

'What are you here for?

'I'm here with my mate, to give him moral support.'

'You can give him moral support out in the waiting room.'

From where I was standing in the waiting room, I could still see Slim's feet at the end of the trolley. I could tell how many stitches they were putting in by the dancing of his feet. He had four stitches, then they gave him a tetanus injection and he scratched for two days with the rash he developed. I don't know why they needed to give him a tetanus injection, because the wound had been burned clean.

~

Mussels

In summer, confectionary drops off, so to keep my employees together, in 1947, I looked for something else to keep them busy. I spent a lot of time on The Pier and I knew that many fellows came and gathered mussels there. They used a wire net basket with sharp teeth on it to dig the mussels off the piles under The Pier. I thought that with my diving gear, I could get mussels from all over the bay. There was a mussel-o who had a fatal accident when he was riding his motorbike. He had a factory, a full-fledged mussel outfit, so I went to his widow and arranged with her to rent the factory.

I decided to use my staff to bottle mussels for me. Other people would go to the bottle-o to get used pickle jars. They washed the jars and put vinegar in with the mussels, then a cork, which they waxed. I bought proper jars with square, tall sides and proper screw tops from Australian Glass. I ordered a nice label to be made and called the product Kerby's Ocean Rock Mussels.

I would collect the mussels off the women's baths at St Kilda, next door to the pier. The fellows on the Pier couldn't get out there. The first day, I had two or three men with me and we brought in about one and a half tons of mussels. I did the diving and they packed the mussels into hessian bags and stacked them onto the truck. I had a cement mixer on the pier to break apart the clumps of shells. We had mussels galore.

I had a big diver's knife and I thought, *if any bloody shark comes near me, I'll jab this knife at him.* I'd never seen any fish while I was diving, but I thought I'd heroically drag my knife out and attack a shark. One day, I turned around and there was a big white head next to me. Instead of dragging my knife out, I let out a scream and tried to get away. I've no idea what sort of fish it was.

We took the mussels to the factory and dumped them there. My staff was at the factory ready to bottle them. I went back just before knock off time and the women had packed only eleven bottles of mussels during the whole day. The widow of the mussel-o showed the women how to open the mussels, but they couldn't get the knack of doing it. They weren't dexterous enough to shuck the mussels out of their shells. I had four and a half tons of mussels that I took back and dumped into the sea. The operation wasn't profitable and I shut it down fairly quickly.

The newspaper had reported on it and announced that someone was going into the mussel business in a big way, but I lost so much money on it, it was pathetic.

The next year, I did another deal with the widow of the mussel-o. I dived for half an hour each morning, and supplied enough mussels for her to bottle. Those, I sold to Myers. We both made some money out of that deal. My women were keen, but they just couldn't manage the task. For ten years after I'd closed down the business, Myers would ring every summer to ask for mussels.

~

A representative for Red Tulip came to me.

'Would you be interested in a merger?'

I checked up on them and they weren't very big, not even as big as me.

'No, I'm not interested.'

I didn't know until quite recently, they joined forces with a friend of mine. Eventually, they bought him out. I really missed out there. Red Tulip became quite big and well known.

~

Eventually, the taxation bothered me enough that, in 1948, I decided to sell the confectionary business. Two Jewish men bought it. I stayed with them for a while, showing them how everything worked. One took over the factory and the other went out as salesman.

Slim and I were still in our mid-twenties and we wanted to have some fun. I had an idea that would give us some adventure.

Part Three: Post War Melbourne

6 Man About Town

My Friend the Thief

I had a friend called Bill Jones, who was a thief. I met him very early on in the forties. He was a boner at the abattoirs. Bill had a fabulous personality and I liked him, but he could be shifty. He stole from wherever he worked. Although he worked hard, he always seemed to want more money. I suppose he was a kleptomaniac.

While I was friendly with Bill, he started to go out with a very sincere young woman, whom he married eventually. She didn't know he stole. Val was a very devout Catholic. He was a Catholic too. I was best man at their wedding.

I knew several members of her family. I had five of them working for me for some years. I employed them in my businesses: photography, confectionary and later, dry cleaning.

Bill's wife had a terrible time during the birth of her first child. Bill was unhappy with the doctor. He went to a nurse for advice.

'Who's the best obstetrician in Melbourne?'

Bill went to that doctor's rooms and charged through the waiting room and into his surgery, where he was attending to a patient.

Bill took him by the arm.

'Forget all this. You're coming with me. My wife's in trouble. I need you to help her now or she'll die. You're coming with me.'

He dragged him out of the rooms. The surgeon had enough sense to know he was dealing with a dangerous man, so he went. He told all his patients to re-book and come back later.

Bill took the obstetrician to the hospital. In three quarters of an hour, he'd done a caesarean on Val, saving both mother and baby. Subsequently, he did five caesareans on her, delivering five more babies.

~

I gave Bill some advice one day.

'Listen, if you ever get caught with your thieving, don't you try to talk your way out of it. You're not too smart. If you were smarter, you wouldn't be a bloody thief. So if the coppers ever get hold of you, don't try to deny anything. You haven't enough brains to do that. Just say, "I admit nothing." And keep saying, "I admit nothing," until your barrister gets to you.' That was probably the best advice he ever received in his life.

My father gave him a job selling some confectionary he was making then. I gave him some of my confectionary to sell too. My father's sweets sold for two shillings a box. Bill travelled all over Victoria selling for us. Then I found out he was selling them for two and three pence. He was pocketing the extra three pence. I became suspicious and decided to check up on him.

'Give me your books.'

'No no, I haven't written them up yet.'

When you use cash receipts, you don't have to write your books up. You just write the receipt, so I realised he must be overselling. I did a tour around one of his runs and he was charging everyone two and three.

He didn't rob from me, but because he did rob my father, I gave up my friendship with him. I had great respect for his wife though and kept in touch with her for decades. I would ring her up every year on her birthday.

A couple of years went by and I received a phone call from Val one day. She was very distressed.

'The police came and arrested Bill.'

'Where is he? What Police Station?'

'Russell St.'

I went up to Russell St. It wasn't because of Bill. I knew he'd been up to something. I told Val it wasn't for him; it was for her, because I respected her. She had nobody else to go to.

I went up to the watch house.

'Do you have Bill Jones here? Can I see him?'

'He's been here for three hours, but he won't tell us anything.'

Aha, he's taken some notice of me, I thought.

'It's five o'clock. He's going to be re-questioned at eight o'clock, so if you come back at half past eight, you can bail him.'

I agreed. As an afterthought, they offered for me to talk to the detective in charge and told me his name. I went to the station across the road.

'You have Bill Jones here.'

'Yes. Are you a friend of his?'

'Yes.'

'We're going to talk to him again about eight o'clock. Will you go back to the watch house and see him and tell him to talk to us about what's going on.'

The detective rang the watch house and told them to let me see him. I thought they'd put us in a nice little room together to have a chat, but they didn't. They opened a door. There were bars with wire netting over them. Two or three feet away, there was another wire netting fence and I could see through into the yard, which was illuminated. I could see perhaps fifty men milling about. The policeman came and stood beside me. It was all I could do to pass good wishes through the fence. I'll never forget this copper. He was huge, with a great big gut and he stood there impassively, like a totem pole as though he couldn't hear what we were saying. Somebody inside called over the loud speaker: 'Bill Jones.'

Bill came over and he looked terrible. He needed a shave and he was white.

'Hello Bill. How are you going?'

'How am I going? I'm in bloody gaol.'

'They're going to talk to you and question you again this evening. I'll come back after that and bail you.'

'Good.'

So I went. The thing was, I'd seen him and he hadn't been beaten. They made a mistake in letting me see him. When I came back, I had to take a JP with me. They called Bill out of the yard, and when he came out, he looked awful. I was shocked. Even the whites of his eyes were black. I thought he was blind.

'Jesus Christ, what's happened?'

He was not saying anything, but he was a mess.

The JP was looking away.

'Look at him, look at him,' I insisted.

The JP wouldn't look at Bill. He had a Bible with him and he just kept looking at the Bible. I bailed Bill and took him outside.

'Go over to the station now and make a complaint.'

'No no, I want to get away.'

'If you don't go now, they'll say you had a fight after you left here and you won't have a leg to stand on.'

That was the usual technique and still is.

'No no, I want to get away. My chest's hurting badly.'

'Did you get belted in the chest?'

'Yeah.'

'You might have busted a rib.'

I took Bill up to the hospital and stayed in casualty with him until they took him in. I gave him some money for a cab home and I left.

Then it came to the court case. I had been to see his barrister. Bill was charged with receiving stolen property – radios. Chapel St. in Melbourne is three miles long and all the way along, are shops selling electrical goods. Two thieves went to the first radio shop, broke the windows and took a few radio sets and sold them. The next weekend, they went to the second radio shop and did the same thing. They did this for several weeks.

The police were observing this pattern. One week, they staked out the next shop. When the two blokes walked up, they grabbed them.

Bill wasn't stealing the radios. These thieves told the police they were selling them to Bill Jones and to one of the people who worked for me, his wife's nephew. Bill took the radios to a shop called Standard Radio. The lift man there knew him. He sold them there. They traced the radios back to Bill. That's when they arrested him and where I came into it.

At the trial, the jury wouldn't convict Bill because of my evidence that the police had beaten him.

The lad who worked for me was also charged with Bill. When he was fourteen, he looked a young man.

The jury came back and asked, 'Can we convict one of these men without the other?'

The judge said, 'No.'

On the strength of my evidence they were both let off.

The war hadn't finished yet, so the fourteen year old joined the army and fought in Timor.

Bill's wife died only a few months ago. He was supposed to ring me when Val went. She'd had Alzheimer's for seven years. Bill rang and spoke to my wife. He was totally incoherent. He was so distraught, she knew immediately, without him having to say so, that Val had gone.

I rang up their daughter a few weeks later, to see how he was.

'Haven't you heard? Dad died a month ago.'

He died about two weeks after Val died. He visited her every day for all the years she was in a nursing home.

Tug Boats

When my father came home from New Guinea in 1944, I moved out of the kiosk into a flat with my mate Alf. With the old man home, my parents didn't need me there. Unlike many soldiers, Dad had seen nothing really traumatic, so he went on with life in much the same manner as in our earlier time in New Guinea. The difference was that now he was his own boss and had his own home, even though The Kiosk and The Pier were technically owned by the Victorian State Government. He had a long lease with them.

At the end of the war, the navy advertised a lot of boats. We bought the biggest one – the *Cerberus*. Every man in Victoria, who trained for the navy in Westernport, did their seamanship on her. Seventy feet long and sixty tons, she looked like a large, wooden fishing boat with the steering wheel up forward. She could do ten and a quarter knots with her Alan diesel.

Some of the boats that were sold were little steamers. Three of them came from the HMAS *Australia* – the original *Australia* from about 1910. There was a club in Sydney called SPUD. Those old fellows, steeped in steam, bought those three boats.

My father wrote to them and offered to tow their boats up to Sydney using the *Cerberus*. We were contracted to do one, so my father and I set off, accompanied by several of my drunken mates, who had no idea how to tie knots. When we arrived at Botany Bay, the club was happy with the job we'd done, so we were given the contract to tow the next vessel up.

On the way north with the second steamboat, we fell into strife. We were using a very heavy three inch diameter tow rope and it broke; it chafed through on the bow of the boat we were towing. We had two people on board the tow and we were off Warratah Bay, just past Wilson's Promontory. I was on the wheel and the waves were fairly large, so I stood off. I steamed around the tow and we tried to float a line down to her on a life buoy. A wave picked us up and our sixty-tonner surfed. The steamer was lying athwart ships and I saw it disappear under our bow. The two men on board were looking up with fear in their eyes. The bow of the

Cerberus whacked the steamboat and she fell back. My mates said the double-planked side went in, sprang back and then started leaking.

We needed to get another tow line across to the steam boat. We tried sending the heaving line across with a rocket. Three times, the rocket went towards the steam boat, but didn't take the line over to the crew. Eventually we managed to send a line aboard and then these fellows couldn't tie it on. Instead, they wrapped the line around a bollard and hung onto the end. That wasn't the main tow rope; that was just the heaving line. We nearly lost the boat, because they almost went adrift again. One of the crew on our boat put a ten shilling note in his pocket.

'If I have to swim ashore, I want some money with me,' he said.

We motored into Waratah Bay and anchored. We were very pleased to arrive into shelter, because it was cold. There were a couple of pinnacles of rock sticking up in the bay. We had about twelve men on board and my father instructed that anyone who woke in the night should check our position against the rocks to see that we hadn't drifted. About three o'clock in the morning, one of our crew let out a huge scream. Before he went to sleep, this lad had looked over the stern of these two boats and seen how far we were from the rocks. When he woke up, he'd looked over the stern again and he couldn't see the rocks. There was nothing to be seen; he was looking towards Tasmania, but we hadn't drifted. We'd just changed position with the tide. His yell woke up all of us.

In the morning, before we set off north again, I took some clout nails over to the steam boat and tacked up the side where I'd rammed her. When we came near Gabo Island lighthouse, I took the Aldus lamp out and sent the Morse calling signal, VE: "dot, dot, dot, dah; dot, dot, dot." I didn't get a reply and there was no sign of anyone. *God dammit, we pay these people to look after us.* We had no radio, so I kept this up, because I wanted to report our position.

I was watching with binoculars and as we continued to head north, a door opened about half way up the lighthouse. I saw someone come out with a ladder and a rope and lower the gear down to the rocks. Three men came down and set up a tripod with a lamp. Then they brought a little chair out and one sat down with a note book. They sent "dah dot," ready to receive your message.'

I sent back, "Greetings from the crew of the *Cerberus*." I couldn't expect any help from them. Fortunately, the steamboat didn't leak very much and we successfully delivered her to Botany Bay.

My mother had received no word of our position. The men at the lighthouse wrote a report to The Age Newspaper. The article said "Tug boat and picket boat in nightmare voyage up the east coast. Men in aft boat pumping furiously and lying exhausted on the deck." Mum read this story and became very anxious about us. The lighthouse men were paid a penny farthing a word for stories that they sent in, so they made up a big story.

After we'd done the three trips and delivered all of the boats into Botany Bay, we motored into Port Jackson, Sydney. There was a law that ships weren't supposed to come into the harbour during busy periods when the ferries were flying about. We didn't know that. The harbour master told us we could moor near the police station at Circular Quay. We looked like an official vessel; a bit like a small destroyer with a big flag out the back. We were going in and out of the quay any time we wanted to and the ferries had to stop for us. We wanted to organise for the *Cerberus* to be slipped and antifouled, because there was nowhere in Melbourne that could take her draft. Eventually it was all sorted and she was slipped at Berry's Bay Boatyard. When the work was finished, we returned to Melbourne.

Two Steam Tugs

In 1948, Dad and I bought two steam tugs, the *Hovell* and the *Hume*, named after the explorers. One had a Government contract to be worked out carrying mud dredged from the River Yarra to a barge. We had to tow the barge away and dump the mud. That contract lasted four months. We made a bit of money out of that, though not a hell of a lot. A few years later, we also bought another steam tug from the government – the ninety foot *Sprightly*.

My father wanted to pull the propeller off the *Hovell* in about 1948 or 1949. It would move the boat at nine knots. The prop was very big for a sixty foot boat; it rotated at 140 revolutions per minute. I had full diving gear, which I had bought new when I was working on the *Kakariki*. We hired two big bottles of air from CIG and early one morning, we went down to the wharf on the Yarra, where the *Hovell* was moored. I was in full diving gear and up to my waist in mud. I removed the safety clips that held the nut on the propeller. As I started to undo the nut, I finished the first bottle of air. We knocked off, because it was midday and went back to The Kiosk for lunch. Only my father was in attendance while I was under water. For the afternoon, we had the second bottle of air. On the Per was a young man we knew, called Elliott Brown. He asked if he could come with us to see me diving. He was a well-built lad with strong muscles. My father agreed. He came down and I put the suit on again, hooked up the fresh bottle and went down the ladder.

Years later, in 2007, Elliott wrote us a letter, describing what he observed that day.

'Col suited up, screwed in his face plate and got onto the ladder to descend. He picked up his tools and started to climb down. Very unlike Col, he slipped and dropped his tools. He was floating face down. Mr Kerby said he was looking for his tools, but I was not so sure and convinced Mr Kerby we should pull him out.

'Together, we pulled Col up until his helmet was just over the rail of the ship. Mr. Kerby removed his face plate and we lifted Col up with all his weights to hang over the ship's rail. This forced the air out of his lungs. When we lifted him onto the deck, the air rushed back into his lungs, making a strange sound. We removed his boots and brass, then we carried him to the car and drove to Prince Henry's Hospital in St Kilda Road.

'When we arrived in casualty, oxygen started to bring Col round. He saw the nurse with large scissors and kept repeating "Don't let them cut the suit".

'Mr Kerby brought the dive bottle to the hospital. The doctor smelt it and yelled, "Get it out of here."

'From that day, I think I considered Col to be indestructible – he seems to be in the process of proving it.'

Had Elliott Brown not been there, my father would have tied me up to the ladder so I wouldn't float away, left my helmet over my face, made certain I had plenty of air in the bottle and then gone off to get assistance to pull me out. Because Elliott was there, together, they were able to get me up the boarding ladder. Apart from my own weight, my diving gear weighed one hundred and sixty pounds. Because the young man was strong, they hauled me onto the deck, removed my helmet, put me into the car and drove me to the hospital. I came to in the hospital, covered head to foot in mud. People were walking around me with scissors, ready to cut my suit off. I sat up.

'Don't. Don't do that. What's happening?'

I saw a big white light over me in the casualty ward.

It turned out that the bottle that was supposed to contain air was 98% nitrogen. My father saw a solicitor about suing CIG. The solicitor said there was "no expectancy about life", so CIG couldn't be sued. My father went out to the factory and complained loudly to the management. The head of the company was very concerned and ordered an investigation. He discovered that the employees had been filling air bottles with nitrogen because it was cheaper. The manager hadn't known about it. To make oxygen, they freeze air and then bubble off the oxygen and capture it. What's left is nitrogen, which is largely waste. Most people used the air for inflating car tyres, so it didn't usually matter that they bottled the nitrogen and sold it as air, but it nearly cost me my life. It saved them work in the factory, but it wasn't supposed to be done. Without Elliott there, I wouldn't have survived.

I didn't do anything more about getting the prop off. My father left it on and after he died in 1957, we sold the boat with the prop still on. In 1958, I rang up Dean, a man I knew in Melbourne, who cut up anything old with steel in it to sell for scrap to Japan. He also had an antique shop.

'If I give you the *Hovell*, will you take it off my hands for scrap?'

'Is the steering wheel still on it?'

'Yes'

'All right, I'll take it.'

We towed the *Hovell* up the river and left it at his work shop. That was the end of it for us. He must have taken the steering wheel off to sell in his antique shop in Toorak. He probably made as much money for the steering wheel as he did for the scrap steel from the whole boat.

Boilerman

104

While we had those two steam tugs, we employed a qualified boiler man to work on them. While he was working for us, I decided I might as well study under him and get a boiler-man's certificate. I thought it might come in useful in the future.

The reference he gave me stated: "I have been employed by Mr Kerby for the past year and during that time, he has served under me..." and listed the time I had done. When I showed it to the Certification Board, they were mystified.

'Now just a minute! How do you explain this?

'That statement is perfectly correct. That is just how it was.'

I had recently saved a woman from drowning and it had been in the paper, so the Board was very lenient with me, though they went through all the right processes. Now that I had the certificate, I thought I ought to use it and consolidate what I had learned. Later on, I sat for a higher level certificate in steam.

Boiler Certificate, 1956 and Steam Engine Driver's Certificate,1970.

Candidate for Melbourne City Council.

Candidate for Melbourne City Council

In 1947/8, I decided to stand as a candidate in the Melbourne City elections. Once again, I was following in my father's footsteps.

There were two issues I campaigned for. I wanted cinemas to be allowed to open on Sundays and I wanted the old markets at the eastern side of the city pulled down. My opponent won handsomely, but eventually, both of those issues I stood for were implemented. When cinemas did open on Sundays, I realised that business at the Kiosk was slightly reduced.

Café Owner

I bought Judy's Café in 1948, after I sold the confectionary business. The café was in the same arcade as my photography business. I often went up there to drink coffee. I can't remember why I decided to buy the café, but not long afterwards, before I went to New Guinea, I sold it again.

The café held only fourteen seats. I thought that wasn't enough, so I altered it to make it hold another ten. I was using a star chisel to hammer holes in the concrete for attaching the tables, when I missed the chisel and hit my hand. I really paid for that with a broken bone.

Lady's Man

At this period of my life, I was into all sorts of things. Often, I had several businesses at one time. I learned how to fly and earned my pilot's licence. I was also interested in the Tivoli Theatre, doing some backstage work in the evenings. It was a good way to meet the girls. I met one or two of the dancers and enjoyed taking them out.

Jeannie McRae, I believed, was in love with me about this time. She was a nice girl and I enjoyed her company when we went out together, but for me, the relationship wasn't serious. I had a rather memorable evening in 1950 with Jeannie in Brisbane, on my return journey from Bulolo in New Guinea.

~

Not all of my girlfriends were dancers. I had a fairly serious relationship with Dorothy for quite a few months, but that didn't last. She married a policeman.

Col cruising about town in his sports car,
a 1930 Austin 7 Meteor.

One girl I knew at this time was Anne. During the war, she worked in a milk bar... a nice looking girl. She told me she was born in Scotland.

'I was very small,' she said.

'Babies usually are,' I replied.

She had married a Yank and she went with him to America. A few years later, she came back to Melbourne and I saw her.

'What does your husband do?

'He owns a motel.'

That was the first time I'd heard the word 'motel,' yet I understood what it was, though there were none in Australia at that time.

'Is he with you?'

'No.'

'Oh, good.'

I took her out that night. We went to the pictures as usual. We talked after the show. She didn't want to go home.

'You have to go home,' I said.

About two or three o'clock in the morning, I was still trying to get her to go home.

'I think I'll fly to Sydney,' she said.

I asked her, 'Where will you stay there?'

'I'll stay at the YWCA.'

'That's a good idea,' I said. 'Do you have any money?'

'Yes, I've enough to get to Sydney and stay a while.'

I was either tired or a bit stupid, because I didn't ask her anything more that I remember. I drove her out to Essendon, which was the only airport in those days.

After she'd gone, I was a little worried about Anne. *Nobody knows she's been out with me, so they can't say that I murdered her if she goes missing.*

Two days later, I received a phone call.

'It's Anne's mother here, Tony. Send her back.'

Anne called me Tony. I didn't know her mother at all, but apparently she'd gone through Anne's room and found this book with my name and phone number in it.

'She's not with me.'

She didn't believe me. 'Send her home, Tony.'

'She's gone to Sydney.'

I kept repeating that she had gone to Sydney and her mother kept saying, 'Send her home, Tony.'

Jesus, if she falls off the ferry into Sydney Harbour, I'll be in trouble. There would be a good chance I'd have to defend myself and say I didn't kill her.

She'd said she was going to stay at the YWCA, so I flew to Sydney to look for her. I wanted to drag her back. I went to the YWCA and told them her name.

'She was here, but she left last night. A young man called and picked her up.'

I've all Sydney to try to find her. I want to get her back to Melbourne. Where the hell do I start? Where is she going to get accommodation?

I bought The Sydney Morning Herald and looked up the Accommodation column. There were only three advertisements. I went to all three places. It cost me a fortune in cabs. There was a family in one. At the second one, several people were looking, but none of those was a young single woman or a young couple. The third one was at Manly. I went across to Manly by ferry.

I was in a café having a coffee when Anne passed in the street. She was staying at the address I was about to visit. In Melbourne, she had a solid American accent. I raced outside and grabbed her. She nearly dropped dead. Her accent went with it. She was speaking Australian, with a slight Scottish accent.

Apparently, she had rented this flat by herself, because she invited me up.

'No,' I said and dragged her with me back to Melbourne right then.

I took Anne back to her mother. It became a bit sordid, because I lent Anne a modest amount of money.

'This is just a loan.'

'Yes.'

Then I found out she was going back to the States without repaying my money. I felt resentful about that. It was a comfortable amount. I went to her mother's place.

'How about that loan?'

She had a brother who had a reputation for violence. I thought, *if this bloke comes out, he'll get a surprise.* I was in a collar and tie. For some reason, people who are dangerous think you can't fight if you're wearing a collar and tie.

He did come out and he said to his mother, 'It's all right Mum. You just stand aside.'

His attitude was that he was going to fix me. It was a little terrace house with a small garden in front. I had shut the gate behind me. I thought if he comes near me, he's going to get two feet right in the face. I was nonchalantly waiting at the door for him, but he didn't come out. His mother prevailed and sent him back inside. Anne repaid my money later.

The Tivoli

Working backstage with scenery and lighting at the Tivoli Theatre meant I was invited to staff parties. It was at one of these I first met Judy Lingard not long before I went up to New Guinea in 1950. She wasn't interested in me at all at that stage.

We met again when she was back in Melbourne for a different show. I had come back from New Guinea and we met in the street one night. Judy was with her best friend, Joan, and they wanted to get into a cinema. I also went to the pictures a lot and because I knew all the usherettes, I was able to get them seats.

It wasn't until after I'd been to England in 1951 that Judy and I began to see more of each other.

Judy Remembers meeting Col

Joan and I were at a big theatre party together and Col was there too. Joan was three years younger than me. She was sixteen and I was nineteen when I arrived in Melbourne.

I had started dancing when I was five and I was nineteen when I left home in Newcastle to go professional on the stage. My first job was in Melbourne with the Tivoli theatre. That was in 1950.

Joan was from Sydney. As teenagers, we often saw each other at the Eisteddfods in Sydney, when Joan's grandmother came with her. When we both arrived in Melbourne, we became very good friends and remain so to this day.

At the party, Col was emptying the dregs from beer glasses all into one glass and offering it to Joan to drink.

That bloody dreadful man. Look what he's doing, I thought. I was disgusted. I was a good girl then and I didn't usually swear, but I was furious with him for trying to give these slops to Joan. I felt very protective of my friend. That incident is the only memory I have of Col that year.

7 Showman

Slim and I heard there was a diving show at Luna Park in Melbourne. I'd sold the confectionary factory and wanted a new idea for a business. We went along to have a look. A fully dressed diver with a microphone was doing an act, but it was a very poor show. The water in the tank was dirty and he didn't demonstrate diving very well. His commentary was inadequate and he used very poor diction.

I knew we could do a much better show than that.

'How about it Slim? Shall we have a go? I'll build a tank and we'll take it around the show grounds.'

'Good idea. We could do a much better demo than that.'

I worked out very carefully how much it would cost, right to the last penny — twelve hundred pounds. After I'd spent four thousand pounds, we had it finished. What I'd designed was a tank eight feet high, five feet wide and four feet deep. It was steel, with glass at the front.

During the building, I was worried about the pressure of the water on the glass. This wasn't armour-plated or reinforced in any way. I couldn't get any figures on what pressure quarter inch thick glass would stand. When the tank was full of water, there would be four pounds pressure per square inch. I was jittery in case it broke. I went to a glazier in Melbourne, a very big place.

'What is the thickest glass you can sell me?'

'You can import one and a quarter inch from Pilkington's of England.'

Such glass was not available in Australia in 1949. I ordered two sheets because they were five feet by four feet, so I needed two sheets to cover the front of the tank. I had to put a steel belt across the front to seal it at the join. We screwed it all up and it never leaked a drop.

We had a van and a trailer on which we towed the diving tank. We thought it made sense to fill the tank when we arrived at each showground, but the first country showground we visited was rationing water because the area was in drought. To fill the tank to over seven feet, we needed eleven hundred gallons of water, which the fire station supplied. We had to guarantee we'd take the water back to them when we'd finished. When we returned, they pumped the water out and put it back into their tank.

Our very first public appearance was at a two-day show in Ballarat. Bill Dickson, a carpenter, did woodwork for me in a garage. He was interested in diving and wanted to go into partnership with the tank. I said no, even though he was a delightful man, because I was never keen on having partners, but he joined the team on tour.

We were very late in setting off for Ballarat. I was driving. On the way, there's a very steep section of road near Deer Park. Nancy, my girlfriend at that time, Bill and Slim were travelling in the back of the truck. From the cabin into the back of the van, there was a very narrow door. It was quite a job to get through between the back of the vehicle and the cabin. Slim was a tall man and it had taken him several minutes to climb into the back. I drove up the hill to Deer Park, but coming down, we were travelling too fast and the brakes were getting hot. I tried to change down gear. There was no synchromesh in the gear box. I missed the change. I kept trying. I was probably damaging the gear box as I tried to get into gear. I was thumping the gear lever so hard, it was slowing us up a little. My fingers were pulling on the hand-brake, my foot was stamping on the foot-brake, and the gears were grinding. The others came out from the back in about three seconds to see what was wrong. We whizzed down the hill and almost up to the top again before we managed to stop. We all jumped out and wiped the sweat off our faces before continuing.

By the time we arrived at the Ballarat showground, it was late on Saturday night, and most of the events were shutting up. We were shown the space that had been reserved for us. I had bought an enormous tent, which we had to rig. We three men took hold of the tent. Slim was at one end, Bill at the other end, with me in the middle. We walked across the show grounds carrying this very heavy tent. As we walked along, we came to a wide dip in the ground. I walked into the dip, losing my hold on the tent. I walked down into the hollow, walked about twelve feet and then came up the other side. The other two walked around it, taking the full weight of the tent. For some reason, we laughed and laughed over this. I think we were all high with the excitement of our adventure.

We put the tent up and placed the trailer with the tank inside the tent, then we retired for the night.

On Sunday morning, we bought a loaf of bread and I went off somewhere.

'We'll have breakfast,' the others said.

When I came back, they had left only one slice of bread. It wasn't even buttered. There was just a lump of dry bread left on the table. The three of them were sitting in the van when I came in. Someone pointed to the bread.

'There's your breakfast.'

'Is that all? I wouldn't have that.'

'Right.'

They fell upon it and it was gone. I finished up with nothing.

~

Slim or I would stand up in the tank, with a microphone. That day, Slim was our diver, Nancy manned the ticket box and Bill offered to be spruiker. I thought he sounded so confident, he must have done something like that when he'd been in the air force. We set up our ticket box outside the tent and placed the trailer by the open door of the tent, the glass front of the tank facing into the tent.

Slim, dressed in bathing trunks and ready to don the full diving suit, climbed up onto the platform. A crowd gathered around the trailer. Nancy was in our little ticket box, ready to sell the tickets. I found out later you have to point to the box and say, "The tickets are two shillings and you get them over here," so the customers will go over and spend their money, otherwise they don't pay.

I gave Bill the megaphone.

'There you are, go and do your stuff.'

'I can't do it. I've lost my confidence.'

'You bastard, I told you I can't do it.'

We didn't know what to do. Then I noticed a fellow across the way selling little balls of sawdust with paper over them, on elastic, like a yoyo. He was a real spivvy showman in a little hat with coloured bands. I went over to him.

'Can you spruik?'

'Yeah. What do you want?'

'Well, we don't have a spruiker.'

114

'What are you doing?'

'We're showing a fair dinkum diver in a glass tank.'

The man walked across to our tent. While we walked, I told him what we were doing. Slim and I had agreed that we wouldn't have any bullshit. We'd tell them like it is. The *Kakariki* was big news at the time and we said we'd worked on the *Kakariki* and we could cut steel under water. We had an oxy torch with us. A flame under water melting the steel and cutting it looks good.

He picked up the microphone

'Professor Nimbus has just flown in from the United States,' our spruiker began.

Slim was sitting on the platform, very modestly. I had the corselet ready for him. Slim blanched and then he blushed. I was embarrassed and upset too. I picked up the corselet, and instead of putting it carefully over Slim's head, I almost threw it at him, like hoopla, and it rattled over him, knocking his teeth.

'I won't be a professor for no bastard,' Slim protested to me as I was screwing him into the suit.

'Professor Nimbus can solder underwater. He can cut steel under water.'

'The bastard's crucifying me.'

'The diver will now give a free demonstration.' He turned to Slim. 'Demonstrate.'

Slim pulled his knife out and looked at the blade. That was his demonstration. He was wearing two diving weights and they were forty pounds each.

He tried to hand one to a bloke.

'Feel the weight of that, mate.'

'Not bloody likely.'

Slim was left holding the weight in his hand.

I slammed the helmet onto Slim's head. He wanted to hide, so he climbed into the tank. I didn't know what to do either, so I jumped off the platform and ran into the tent. People started crowding into the tent.

Now he was facing into the tent, Slim started off speaking into his microphone and we had a lead.

'The equipment you see me wearing here is a flexible, non-rigid diving suit.'

After just that one sentence, the amplifier went phut. We had about sixty people in the tent by then. I grabbed the megaphone and climbed up beside the tank. I didn't mind doing it by then and I continued the spruik.

'The record today is held by a British Naval diver.'

We didn't have any feedback to Slim, only a microphone out, so he couldn't hear what I was saying, but very soon, he realized the sound system wasn't working.

It cost me all told about eighty pounds to set up for that one show and we took only twenty pounds for the whole day. After that experience, we learned a lot and the show made money.

~

The next location was down at Traralgon, a town in Gippsland. We'd found out that you need to book your space ahead of time. You have to get there very early to choose your space close to where people are coming in, or somewhere else prominent. I thought we'd do something smart.

I had a pilot's licence by then. As soon as we packed up in Ballarat, I hired a Tiger Moth and flew down to Traralgon to book a good space. I landed in a paddock, which was against the Department of Civil Aviation rulings, except in an emergency.

There were a lot of cattle right up the other end of the paddock. Just as I was slowing down almost to a stop, about fifty cows started to gallop towards me. I thought they might try to eat the aircraft. I didn't know anything about farm animals. I'm a city slicker. I was taxiing at about thirty miles per hour to get away from these cows. I pulled up near the fence and I swung the Tiger Moth around. The animals crowded round inspecting the plane for about five minutes, while I sat inside wondering what to do. After satisfying their curiosity, they wondered off back to the other end of the paddock.

I went into town and saw a dithery old bloke, who was in charge of the agricultural section. I ordered a beaut spot and feeling very satisfied with myself, I flew back to Ballarat Aero Club, where I'd hired the plane. We drove down to Traralgon and when we arrived, I found some bloody woman had worked her feminine charms on the old bloke in charge and he'd given her our spot.

I'd had an amplifier built that was sixty watts. The regulation was that your amplifier was supposed to be no more than four and a half watts. I had put a sticker on it, saying four and a half watts. The amp was a beauty. I'd drown out the others.

'Hurry, hurry, hurry, the diving show is about to start!'

About four stall holders came along and queried the size of my amplifier. I showed them the tag saying four and a half watts.

'The speaker is a really good one,' I would add.

It was too. I over-ruled and drowned out everyone else when we started to spruik. We started to make money then. We went to all the country shows and we didn't do too badly. Just as importantly, we had lots of fun. After we'd finished doing our tour of the country show grounds, we sat the tank on St Kilda Pier outside the Kiosk.

I had a friend who had been down in a suit previously and he wanted to try it again. On the suit, there's a valve to keep the air in. We found that because the microphone was in the helmet, as the air came in, it made a noise over the mike. The valve would go "clack, clack," so I took the valve out, which was safe to do for diving in the tank, but would have been dangerous in deep water. Even in a depth of eight feet, if you lose your air supply, the suit squeezes you and nips your skin from the water pressure.

My friend was in the suit and I unscrewed the hose that came from the compressor, depriving him of air. The ladder was in there and all he had to do was walk up the ladder, but he panicked and started to punch the glass. He was out of air and being nipped all over. After about half a minute, I returned his air supply.

I had a girl called Mel work for me in the dark room of my photography business. She came down one time and I asked her if she wanted to have a go in the tank. She was keen. She was about eighteen, quite heavily built and strong enough to go down with the weight of the suit on. We were watching her when suddenly she spoke. Her voice came out over the amplifier. 'I've wet myself.'

We urged her to get out. She'd urinated copiously inside the suit, which is watertight. We had to wash it out well.

Col's mother, Ivy, beside the diving tank.

Her aunt also worked for me. She came down to the Kiosk one day.

'Mel had a go inside the suit. What's it like in the helmet?'

She was standing beside the counter in the shop, and we put The helmet on her head. It weighed sixty pounds.

'God, it's heavy,' she said.

She was standing there when some customers came in. I served them and they kept looking at Mel's aunt standing up beside the counter. She couldn't move. The customers didn't know what was going on. We kept that helmet on display in the Kiosk for many years.

Salvage Diving in New Guinea

Slim had worked for United Salvage once before. In 1950, they contacted him and asked if he wanted to dive on a gold dredge in Papua New Guinea. The boss, Captain Williams, wanted another diver as well, so Slim recommended me and I flew up there too. I was really keen to go back up there to see what changes had been caused by the Japanese invasion. A reliable photographer looked after my photographic business while I was away.

One of the Bulolo gold dredges, weighing 3,500 tons, had tipped over. Before the war, I'd worked on a different dredge at Bulolo. When the dredge was working, it dug up the mud and dropped it behind itself, thus moving the pond as the work proceeded. The whole area around Bulolo was covered with old tree trunks from an ancient forest. The timber was too heavy to float on the surface of the pond and too light to sink very deeply into the mud, so for the salvage exercise, we had to dive below the logs.

Salvage divers often have to work in mud and I have worked in mud as far down as thirty feet [nine metres]. Scuba divers are horrified when I tell them, because they dive only in clear water. The deeper one goes, the more difficult it becomes. Being slightly built is an advantage. A large diver has a smaller strength to bulk ratio than I have. Thirty feet down is about the limit to which we could go, because the density of the mud is thicker and buoyancy increases. I was the smallest diver, so I could get down further than the others. By strength to size ratio, I was also strongest. I received an extra ten shillings to a pound an hour because I could dive further down.

Whenever I worked deep, I put a shot line down that I could follow and went below the logs, deep into the mud. I carried my tools on a belt. Down deep, the mud was so thick, I could push the tools into it and they would stay there until I needed them. To remain in position, I had to find something like a girder to wrap my legs around. One day, I put my foot down and it touched a log. The log rolled and it gave me a hell of a fright. I thought the whole dredge was rolling.

When I climbed out, covered in mud, I would chase the natives around the deck. They would scream that a monster from the deep

119

was coming to get them. I looked like a tamberan – a devil or spirit – and the boys would run to the other end of the dredge, even though they knew it was really me.

Slim and New Guinean assistants on dredge, Bululo 1950.

We worked around the clock. The other three divers worked during the day and I did night duty. One time, I was on the bottom and Ernie was my attendant. We had a pump sucking muck out and I had to go down to clear a blockage. I went into the hole where the pump had sucked out all the mud and rocks. There were a lot of rocks like cricket balls. While I had one leg in the hole, all the rocks fell in on me and I was buried. Those boulders could have squashed me or knocked out my air pipe. To unpack them, I had to pick the rocks off me one at a time.

By tugging on the safety line, Ernie sent the signal, "Are you all right?" I was stuck in that hole for about one and a half hours. Eventually I pulled my leg out and I was able to surface. I had wondered why Ernie was so attentive that night. When I surfaced, I saw it was raining heavily. He was shivering and fed up with being out in the rain, but was still holding my air pipe and lifeline in his hands. That was my fourth brush with death and I was lucky to survive.

More Accidents

The boss wanted a line up a two inch wire, high up on the dredge. I climbed up about sixty feet, hand over hand and tied a bowline where there were some bulldog clips. I had to tie the knot one handed, which took me a while. I was coming back down when I realized I couldn't make it all the way. My arms were too tired. At this point, I was about twenty feet above the water. In the water alongside the dredge was a structure with many spikes, about a foot under water. I had to jump and I thought I wouldn't make it. I thought I would surely get spiked, but I couldn't hang on any longer. After letting go the wire, I kept my arms up straight above my head. I was very lucky. The spikes were about two feet apart and I went straight between them. I didn't expect to survive that.

When I surfaced, Billy Hodd, one of the other divers, laughed. The boss had been watching me.

'You should have seen the look you gave Billy Hodd when he laughed,' he said later.

One day, I had my sixth brush with death. I fell twelve feet off a girder in the rigging of the dredge. On the way down, I hit another girder across my back, just above the waist, then landed in the water. My kidneys were bruised and I started to pass blood in my urine.

From L to R: Slim, Col and two other divers.

~

Because of the accident, I returned to Melbourne for medical treatment. On the way down, the aircraft, a DC3, landed at Brisbane for refuelling. It was continuing the flight early next morning. I booked into the Temperance Hotel for the night. I was still passing a lot of blood. I went into the urinal and urinated almost pure blood. The fellow standing beside me couldn't get out fast enough.

Seeing Jeannie in Brisbane

The Tivoli dancers were performing at the Theatre Royal. The best looking girls in Melbourne danced for the Tivoli. A girl called Jeannie, whom I had taken out when she was in Melbourne, was dancing with the Tivoli in Brisbane. I thought I'd go to see her. I took a cab to the theatre. As I was walking up towards the stage door, I saw her ahead of me.

'Jeannie,' I called.

Her face lit up and she walked back towards me.

'Would you like to come out with me tonight?'

Instead of going to work that night, she came to the pictures with me. Later, we went to a café for supper. We were sitting in a cubicle and she was rattling on about a man up there who was madly in love with her.

'Yeah, yeah. What's his name?'

'Albie Farrow.'

At that moment, two men came in and sat down in another cubicle. One of them was looking at me quite fiercely. *What's wrong with this egg?* I wondered. Jeannie turned her head.

'Ooh, that's Albie.'

'Let's go then.'

We finished our coffee. As I was paying, the other two walked out. I noticed Albie was limping.

'What makes him limp?'

'He was hit by a bus.'

Outside, the street was pretty well deserted. Albie's car was about thirty feet down the street. Once he was inside, he wound the window down. His friend was round the front of the car. Albie was talking loudly and scornfully to him.

'Will you just look at it? Will you look at the poss? Look at the head on it.' [Poss is a theatrical term for a partial idiot.] 'Will you look at the head on it,' he said.

I didn't realise he was talking about me. I looked back up the street, only to find there was no one else there but me. That upset me. *What's wrong with this bastard?*

I walked back and just as I approached him, I saw him rummaging in the glove box. I grabbed him by the throat through the open window.

'Listen you, I've killed better bloody men than you,' and I squashed my thumb into his throat.

He pulled his hand swiftly out of the glove box and, in his hand, he had a Luger, a German pistol. He pointed it at me and it seemed to have the longest barrel.

I let him go quickly. I didn't like this turn of events.

'Now let's be reasonable,' I said.

He stepped out of the car and he came at me with the gun, digging me in the ribs. Next day, I had nine millimetre black washer-shapes all over me where the gun barrel had poked me.

'Who are you? Where do you come from?'

'I'm Colin Kerby, I come from Melbourne and I'm going back tomorrow, first thing.'

Jeannie was crying out to him.

'No, Albie! No, Albie.'

The fellow was following me up the road. At first I was backing up, then I turned and started to run. I didn't want to run too fast. I didn't want to look too much of a coward. When I came close to Jeannie, I grabbed her by the arm.

'Let's go.'

I nearly swept her off her feet. I should have left her with him. The doctor in New Guinea had told me not to exert myself.

'Whatever you do, don't exert yourself. Take it very easy. If you lose any more blood than you're losing now, you'll need a blood transfusion.'

'Yes Doctor.'

We rounded the corner of this long street, where Jeannie lived in an apartment house next to the Storey Bridge, right beside the river.

'How did you say his leg was damaged?'

'A bus ran onto the footpath and jammed him against a wall.'

I thought the bastard might come along in his car and jam me up against a wall. I rushed up to each telegraph pole, then sauntered past it, then raced up to the next pole and sauntered past that one. I thought that if he came round the corner, I'd hide behind a pole. It seemed a very long distance between them. Albie didn't come and I delivered Jeannie home and let her in the front gate.

'See you later,' said Jeannie.

Then I looked across the road, and I could see Albie in a lane, with his car lined up. I pointed it out to Jeannie and I went in and shut the gate.

'Is there a back way out of here?'

'Yes, you can go down the side of the building and the back gate is in the corner.'

I went round the side and the grass in the yard was nearly waist high. I reckoned I could hear him coming. I went up and down the fence like a fox terrier trying to get out, but I couldn't find the gate. I was in a lather of perspiration. *The bastard will shoot me here.*

The fence was six feet high, so I jumped over, sailed through the air and hit the ground, 'whump.' I didn't know the ground was a further six foot lower on the other side of the fence. I'd fallen nearly twelve feet down to the river's edge. If there'd been a telephone nearby, I'd have rung for an ambulance. Instead, I picked myself up, hurried to the corner and peered round looking for Albie. I thought that if he came down there, I'd have to swim the river to get away. Fortunately, he didn't come.

On the way back to the Temperance Hotel, I passed a Police Station. I started to get my courage back. *Who is this bastard chasing me around with a bloody gun?*

I went in and spoke to the cop at the desk.

'I took a girl out tonight and her boyfriend chased me with a Luger. He dug the barrel into me all over my chest.'

The copper picked up the phone.

'Car 78.'

When the car came in and the driver climbed out, he was six foot nine inches tall. I thought he was standing on the running board. He walked round the car to the footpath and he was still six foot nine inches.

'What's the score?'

I told them where Albie's car was. We drove up there and Albie was out of his car. He was looking through the gate into the apartments.

'That's him. That's the fellow.'

The cop drove up the road, did a 'U' turn and came back. I can't remember what sort of car it was, but the hinges were on the rear edge of the door. The driver approached, ran up onto the footpath. When the sergeant in the front seat opened the door, it jammed Albie in against the fence.

'Good evening, Sir. How are you? What have you there? You'd better give me the gun. What are you doing with this?'

'I'm a book-maker and I need this for my protection. I have a bad leg and I often carry large sums of money. That's fair enough, isn't it?'

'That might be so. What happened tonight?

125

'I was out and I saw a fellow with my girlfriend. He became offensive with me. He came up and grabbed me by the throat and said, "Listen, I've killed better bloody men than you".'

This constable beside me turned round and looked at me. I tried to appear innocent. 'Ooh, as if I would.'

'I think you'd better come back with us,' the sergeant said to Albie.

Looking out her window, Jeannie had seen the car there with a couple of men. She thought it was Albie's car and imagined they had me on the ground. She went for help from an army man, who lived in the same apartment block. She prevailed upon him to come out to protect me. The soldier came down carrying his army 45 Webley and Scott. Those guns are about the size of small cannon.

'Police here. Police here. Just a minute!' called the sergeant.

'I'm a resident.'

'Just give me that gun.'

Then the sergeant had two guns. Jeannie disappeared and I departed.

I don't know what they did with that young bloke. Nor do I know what happened to Albie's car or his mate. They took Albie down to the station and I walked back to the Temperance Hotel. I flew out early in the morning.

Jeannie told me later the police had asked who the fellow was with the rimless glasses? They were referring to me.

~

When I arrived in Melbourne, I saw the doctor, who sent me to have an intravenous pylogram. That's a painful procedure. To start with, they give you an enormous water enema to get your intestines clean.

'That's enough, that's enough,' I told the male attendant.

'Oh no, that's not enough. You have to take all that.'

He indicated the tank, which still had plenty of water in it.

'All that?'

The worst of it was they didn't have a toilet close by. After pumping all this water into me, I had to walk down the corridor to the toilet. The technician told me to put my pants on.

'Don't put your braces on. It'll take you too long to take them off.'

126

He was walking ahead of me to show me which door. 'Don't run,' he said. 'You might knock me over.' I just made it.

They put a dye into your blood to stain it. They strap two balls about as big as a fist, across your belly. That's the painful part. They wind these down so they put pressure on your ureters and the kidneys produce urine which can't go anywhere. Then they x-ray you to see where the blood is coming from. The doctor told me to rest for a few weeks while the kidneys healed. Otherwise, if I had haematuria again, I would need surgery. For once, I did as I was told and I had no further trouble with my kidneys.

~

For a long time my father had been making noises about brewing a low alcohol beer that could be sold in the Kiosk on Sundays. Before my 1950's trip to PNG, I ordered some books on brewing beer and took them with me. If I was bored in the evenings up there, I read up about beer making. It looked possible to make a low alcohol brew and I decided to look into this idea some more

~

A Deal with Luna Park

While I was in PNG in 1950, we had the diving tank on the St Kilda Pier. Eventually, after it had been there for eight months, we sold the tank to Luna Park in Sydney.

My truck was out of registration by that time. In those days, it was quite expensive to register a truck. *Bugger it, I'll try to get to Sydney without getting it registered*, I thought. The truck was going as part of the deal with the tanks and trailer. My first breakdown happened when I was still within sight of the Kiosk. Then I was booked several times on the way north.

The first night, I slept in the truck. The second night, I arrived in Albury, and I was starting to scratch. I hadn't had a shower for a couple of days and I was severely itchy. In Albury, I went to a pub. There were no motels in those days. Those pubs had communal bathrooms down the hall from the bedrooms. There were about three men in the bathroom, stripped and showering. I went in and stripped off and they all cleared out. I wondered what was wrong with them. Then I looked in the mirror and I had a colossal rash on me. I looked like a lobster. I didn't know what it was. The truck had broken down a couple of times along the way and I was dirty with grease too. I thought maybe the rash was because I was dirty or something. I'd never seen a rash like it.

I went up to the doctor's surgery. He wasn't in, but the nurse was. I showed her the rash and she was astounded.

'How do you feel?'

'I feel normal, but it's itchy.'

'That's a terrible rash.'

I told her where I was staying and she told me to come back in the morning. I didn't. In the morning I drove up to Holbrook, where I saw a doctor. I showed him the rash.

'You're suffering from Herpes Zoster, commonly called shingles.'

I was standing there in the greasy, dirty overalls.

'I thought only dirty people suffered from shingles,' I said.

'Shingles is very painful. It attacks a nerve,' said the doctor.

He told me some tale that I'd had chickenpox during my childhood and the virus stays in your body.

Just before I'd left Melbourne, my friend Alf, who was an athlete, took my head and clunked it each way. When I started to get shingles, I wondered if it was because Alf had pulled my head about. The rash started off at my neck, covering more than one nerve. Eventually it went away.

The person who had come to check out the diving tank in Melbourne was Jock Muir, the fellow who now makes anchor winches in Tasmania. He was in the deal with Luna Park. When I reached Sydney, I looked up those fellows from Luna Park and two men came to meet me. They'd already paid me half of the purchase price for the diving gear and truck and now they paid the balance.

They had a naval diver with them. When I had demonstrated the tank in Melbourne, I used the smaller compressor, because I wanted to keep the bigger one for spray painting. Their diver was huge, but he was pretty alert. I gave him the script and he learnt it overnight. I dressed him up and put him in the tank.

'It's a long time since I've been in one of these suits. They're heavy aren't they?'

'You'll get accustomed to it after a few dips.'

Every time he breathed in, the compressor ran faster. He could have done with the bigger compressor. He was a bit out of breath and unfit.

The suits come in small, medium and large. We had a medium suit, and you could adjust it to fit someone a bit larger. It's easier to use a bigger suit on a small man if you put a crutch strap on him. The suit has a couple of horns back and front and you make up a bridle, which you hook on these horns and run the strap under the crutch, so it helps hold the suit up. If your suit blows up, as mine did when I was working on the *Kakariki,* the helmet won't rise up on your head. The people at Luna Park were happy with everything and gave me my money.

We'd had some good times travelling around with the tank. However, by then, I was pleased to be rid of the truck. The last time I was booked, I was feeling very exasperated.

'If the police ask me for my licence again on this trip,' I said to the cop, 'I'll give it to them to keep.'

That embarrassed the traffic cop and he apologised to me. I never paid any of those fines imposed during the truck trip to Sydney, because soon after returning to Melbourne, I left for Europe. When the summons came to the Kiosk, the old man wrote back and told them I was in France. The fines were all scrubbed.

~

After the deal was done with Luna Park, I went off to look up Judy Lingard, who was, at that time, dancing with the Tivoli troupe at the Empire Theatre in Broadway, Sydney. I had met Judy and her friend Joan at a Tivoli party earlier in the year. A few months after that, we started going out together.

Judy: Col took me out for lunch. Talk about embarrassing. We were walking down Pitt Street and Col was still trying to get the grease off himself from working on the truck. He was walking along, rubbing cream into his hands and around his fingernails. He was also scratching at the rash from the shingles. I wasn't too happy to be escorted in public by someone in this state, but all the same, I was very happy to see him, because he was soon to leave for England and would be gone for months.

Part Four: The Nineteen Fifties

8 Beer, Sea Lions and Laundry

Brewing Beer

My father wanted to sell beer at the Kiosk on Sundays, when the public bars were closed. I read about brewing beer and alcohol content while I was up in Bulolo and looked into the regulations when I returned to Melbourne. If the alcohol content is below two percent, it is not considered beer and there's no excise on it. There are no restrictions on how much low alcohol beer you can make or where you can sell it.

I started experimenting with brewing beer. The trick is to make it just a fraction under two percent, but still make it palatable. I had never done alcohol determinations, so I went to a reputable analytical chemist in Melbourne called Heath and Associates. I told Mr Heath what I wanted to do. By reducing the quantities of malt and sugar in the beer before I fermented it, I reduced the amount of alcohol.

I had a flat in South Yarra, where I made the beer in the bath. I am a non-drinker. I have never tasted alcohol, so I gave samples to my mates or to my mother to try. My mother always said it was delightful, just because her son had made it. She finished up an alcoholic, but that happened later. We never had any indication of that until she was much older.

The chemist tested batch after batch. The alcohol content was gradually coming down. Finally he told me it was down to just under two percent. My mates assured me it tasted fine, so I brewed up three barrels each holding fifty-six gallons [225 litres] and took them down to the Kiosk. Also, I went to the chief of the Department of Customs and Excise in Melbourne, taking him a demi-john of the brew for his lab to test. I told him my plans.

'Mr Heath tells me the beer is under two percent. I've drawn off a gallon and poured it into two half gallon demi-johns. This is your sample. If Mr Heath tells me this beer is lower than two percent, I intend to sell it at St Kilda Pier on Sunday.'

'Okay, Mr Kerby. Leave it there.'

Mr Heath rang to tell me the beer was under two percent. I asked for that information in writing and on Friday, I received a letter of confirmation from Heath and Associates.

Col and his mother, Ivy Kerby.

We advertised on the radio and in the newspapers, so the word spread. My father wrote in several languages over the shop window: "Beer, 7d [seven pence] per glass." Dad said he'd sell it in the milk shake glasses, but I said we had to have the proper glasses, the seven ounce. We had to try to give the illusion of real beer. We bought all these glasses and cooled them down.

On Sunday morning, at ten o'clock, half the navy was hanging around outside waiting for us to open. My mother was away that day, so my father decanted two bottles and put them aside in the fridge for her. I told Dad that I'd lost my courage and I didn't want to sell the beer, but my father put a tea towel across his arm like a barman. He started selling the beer so quickly, he forgot to take payment for it.

By the time half of the first barrel had been sold, there was a sailor hanging onto the steel roof support in the middle of the Kiosk.

'Look out, look out, she's going. The Kiosk's going over.'

'He can't be drunk. It's just like lemonade. He reckons he's drunk,' I said to Dad, as I opened up the second barrel. We were in the beer selling business.

Noble Kerby serving beer on Sunday at the St Kilda Kiosk.

We sold the entire three casks. The old man even retrieved the two bottles out of the refrigerator and sold the contents of those as well. I thought I was going to be a millionaire. I couldn't believe how successful it was. I was going to buy the biggest bathtub available to make more beer.

~

Sometime during that Sunday afternoon, a copper came round and asked to see what we were selling. On Monday, and the rest of the week, headlines in the papers read, "Kerby's sell beer at St Kilda Pier on Sunday."

Nothing happened until about Wednesday. Two customs cars rolled up, with four men in each car. They came looking for my father.

'Have you any beer left?'

'No.'

'Not even a little bit?'

Dad picked up a glass jug with about half an inch in the bottom.

'How long's it been there?'

'Over the weekend.'

'No, that won't do. Where was this made?' And the old man didn't twig that there was a problem with the beer. 'Who made this stuff?'

'Col did; my son, Colin.'

'Where is he?'

'I don't know. He went out to buy hops and sugar and a big cooker to make more beer.'

Dad gave them my address in the city. Four of them came into my office.

'Did you make this?'

'Yes.'

I smelt a rat. I wasn't quite as gullible as my father.

'Where did you make it?'

I was going with a girl who lived in Coburg, the opposite direction from where I lived.

'I made it in the bath. It's a very nice bath.'

'Where?'

'Seventeen Centennial Avenue, Coburg.'

They jumped into their car and zoom, zoom, zoomed out there. While they were on their way, I phoned my girlfriend.

'I'm sending a few customs people out to your place. Tell them I made the beer in your bath.'

It turned out her bath was galvanized iron and not the most hygienic looking. The Customs officers arrived and found nothing. They came back to see me.

'What's all the fuss?' I asked them. ' Didn't my father show you the report from Heath's?' I asked.

'Yes.'

'So what's all this about?'

135

'Have you been back to see Mr Clark at the Department of Customs and Excise?'

'No.'

'We think you had better go down to see him.'

I went down to the Department of Customs and Excise and when I went in, Mr Clark was looking very hang dog in his office.

'Oh, Mr Kerby, how are you?'

'What's going on?'

'What did you say to me last week when you gave me that sample?'

'I told you I've brewed three barrels. I've taken a gallon off and halved it for testing. I gave you half and told you if it's below two percent proof spirit, I intend to sell it on Sunday.'

'Yes, that's what I thought you told me. I've nearly been sacked because of this business.'

'How's that?'

'I've had the minister on the phone to me all day yesterday and all day today.'

'Well what did your man make it?'

'Seven point two percent.'

'Well, can I ring up Mr Heath at Heath and Associates?'

'Yes.'

'May I use your phone?'

I rang.

'Mr Heath, I'm in the office of Mr Clark at the Department of Customs and Excise. He tells me that his analytical chemist made a reading of seven point two on that beer sample.'

I thought Heath would have said "Nonsense".

'Well, he knows more about alcoholic determinations than I do, so he would be more accurate.'

I nearly sank through the floor. Despondency washed over me and my previous elation was forgotten. Previous to this, I'd read *The Excise Act*. The Act said that for them to take us to court, they have to take three samples and seal them in the sight of the brewer or his agent.

'Mr Clark, where do we go from here?'

'You've got away with it. We can't do anything, because the samples weren't taken within your sight.'

'I gave you the sample and you didn't take it within my sight.'

'That's right, Mr Kerby.'

That information made me feel a little better. Now, I had to make the beer at two percent. It was pretty feeble. A couple of my mates tried it and were horrified.

'I swallowed it, I swallowed it,' cried one.

'Where can I spit it out?' asked the other.

~

The next Sunday, my father was selling beer I had made that week. Three Customs men came down to the Kiosk to take samples. When they took their gear out of the car, I spoke up.

'I'm the brewer. I have no agent. If you're going to take samples, I'm going out onto the Pier.'

'Oh no, you have to stop here while we take the samples.'

'No. There's nothing in the regulations that says I must stay here.'

They were so very bloody annoyed, they steamed. They didn't even take a sample.

After that, I wondered what I had to do to become a licensed brewer. I read the regulations again and decided it was worth my while to take out a licence, so that if the alcohol content did go over two percent, all I had to pay was the four and a half pence excise per gallon. I had to put up a five hundred pound bond to pay the excise when I applied for my licence. I also decided to go to England to study brewing, so I sold my photography business, because I planned to be away for many months.

~

For a few months, just before I went to England, I worked as a Boiler Attendant at the Melbourne Eye and Ear Hospital. Later on, I sat for a higher examination for attending to industrial steam engines. Much later in my life, those qualifications proved very useful.

Outside the hospital, there was a seventy year old paper 'boy'. I bought my newspaper from him every day. Soon afterwards, in 1951, I went to England to study brewing. One day, while I was walking down the Mall in London, there he was, selling papers. He looked up and saw me.

'Hello Col.'

137

'How the hell did you get here?' I asked.

I thought a paper boy would be penniless.

'Oh, I thought I'd do a bit of travelling. It is easier to sell papers here than it is outside the Eye and Ear Hospital in Melbourne.'

Voyage to Europe

When I sailed to Europe, I disembarked in Naples and went up to Austria to do some skiing first. In Melbourne, they had told me I wouldn't need a visa for Paris, but when I arrived in Basel in Switzerland, immigration wouldn't let me through to France because I didn't have a visa.

'How do I get a visa?'

'You go to the French Consul.'

'How much will that cost me?'

He told me a nominal amount. So I went to the French Consul and banged on the door. A maid came to the upstairs window and stuck her head out.

'Oui, Monsieur?'

I spoke in my best schoolboy French.

'Ouvrez la porte, s'il vous plait.'

She came down and opened the door. I was astonished. *This French really works.*

The Consul issued my visa, but the bastard charged me overtime. He stamped "Overtime, overtime, overtime" all over my passport. I went by train from Basel to Paris.

~

In Paris, I toured the sights and then went to the Moulin Rouge to see the dancers. I wanted to compare that famous dance hall with The Tivoli in Melbourne. I found that many of the dancers were Australian and just as good as those in Melbourne. I visited the dance halls in London too.

Next, I went across to England and up to Worcestershire, where I studied brewing. I arrived in Birmingham in November 1951. The elderly brewer who taught me told me he'd recently been sent to a new brewery nearby and the beer they were making was as bitter as gall. It turned out that the brewer was stirring the wort when the it had just finished its fermentation. The Wort is the fermenting agent – a yeast called *sacrimenti officii*. The brewer taught me that the cell

138

structure of the wort is very weak and if you stir it, you break the membrane, making the beer bitter. The enzymes get out and bugger it all up.

I went home after I had studied brewing for a couple of months and continued making beer for the Kiosk. I took out a brewing licence in case I accidentally took the alcohol content over 2% and I brewed beer for Dad to sell during weekends at the Kiosk right up until he died in 1957. Even though it was weak, the customers preferred to think they were drinking real beer on Sunday.

Dry Cleaning

I started a business with a dry cleaning depot, so I rented a whole building in the city centre of Melbourne, but I was using only the ground floor as the depot. I was the dry cleaning agent, collecting the dirty clothing. We took the clothes in and sent them out to a firm to be cleaned.

Soon after my return from Europe, my parents went to England for a holiday. I looked after the Kiosk and my parents' dogs while they were away. I also used Dad's Rolls Royce to deliver clothes to the dry cleaner.

In the Empire Arcade where earlier, I had my photography studio, there was plenty of wide, empty space. I had the idea of building a kiosk there for a second dry cleaning depot. I did a deal with the arcade owner and I erected a kiosk with a glass top. When Judy returned from touring in New Zealand, she helped me with the building, which we did at night after Judy had finished at the theatre. I didn't need much sleep and Judy could sleep in the mornings. I parked my father's Rolls Royce in the back lane while we worked.

~

One night, while I was in a hamburger shop in St Kilda, the owner had an argument with quite a fine looking man. The café owner, a little crippled man, was laying down the rules to this man.

'You was warned, you was, about creating a disturbance.'

Several nights later, I parked my dad's Rolls in the lane. I had my father's dog, Jinx, with me while I was working. I went up to the car to get something from it and found a fellow going through the glove box. It was the same fellow I'd seen miles away in the café at St

Kilda. I had a tussle with him and held on. The dog grabbed him by the trousers at the same time and I marched him into the Police Station just around the corner, where I wanted to charge him. The detective left the room for a few moments and the fellow tried to threaten me.

'Don't try to be so smart. You're well known in this city. You get round St Kilda hamburger places, threatening people there.'

He didn't know where to look. He had no idea I'd ever seen him before. He was charged and gaoled for seven days for digging into my glove box, even though I probably didn't have the car locked.

~

I started a third collection agency, located near the bus station at Princes Bridge. Every day, thousands of workers passed by there and left their dry cleaning with us, while they travelled on to work at the Holden car factory. I was on forty percent of the gross dry cleaning income, and I realised I wasn't gaining the profits I thought I should have.

I had become too busy to do my books but I realised gradually that something was wrong. After a couple of years, I sat down and looked at the figures. I was paying ten pounds a week for a girl to serve in each collection depot. The girls were costing me a further four pounds a week for insurance, holiday pay and sick pay. On top of those costs, I was using about twenty rolls of paper for wrapping garments. That cost another fifteen pounds every week. I worked it out and I saw at last that I couldn't make enough profit at forty percent. I decided to shut the depots. The next Monday, when Ken Perry, the drycleaner I supplied, came in to pick up the clothing, as he did every week, I told him I was finishing.

In the meantime, Benbow, whom I'd supplied originally and from whom Ken Perry had bought his dry cleaning business, had started a dry cleaning business in another suburb. When I told Ken I was closing the depots, he accused me of sending dry cleaning out to Benbow. We were standing in Flinders Street in the middle of Melbourne and he grabbed me. I thought he was going to send me to hospital.

'Hang on, hang on. I'll come out this afternoon and write it all out for you and see what you think.'

I went out to his place and I spoke to him as if he were a two year old. I wrote everything down.

'If you think there's anything wrong, we'll discuss it as we go.'

Then he made a mistake.

'If you were running that properly, you'd be making sixty pounds a week.'

'I tell you what, Ken: you pay me sixty pounds a week to collect for you and you take over the whole lot.'

He agreed at once.

'Right, right.'

'How long do you want the contract for?'

Five years.'

'It will kill you. Make it three years, then two by two if you still want it.'

'No. Make it five years.'

'Before you sign this contract, listen to me,' I said. 'You're going to come to me and say, "I can't make a go of it at that rate" and I'm going to say, "I told you so." If I were you, I wouldn't sign it.'

'I have to have that supply. I have to have those garments.'

So he signed it. I would go to him every fortnight and pick up my one hundred and twenty pounds for the two depots. I kept the third one – the kiosk I had built in the Empire Arcade. About a year went by before he protested.

'Colin, Col. Look, you'll have to reduce my rent. You've no idea of the costs of those collection depots.'

'Let me be the very first to say, I told you so. Too bad, you're bloody hooked.'

Judy and I used that money to eat out for lunches and dinners. I had no sympathy for him, because I had warned him so clearly.

Shirt Laundry

As well as the dry cleaning depots, I decided to try doing a six hour laundry service for shirts, using the first floor above the dry cleaning depot. It was an old building, with about ten layers of wallpaper. I installed an old household copper tub with a gas jet under it and my mother's little Hoover washing machine – a single tub with a wringer. Although there was a sink with a drain, I didn't have a tap in that room. We had to carry water up from the tap over

141

the gully trap in the back yard. For pressing the shirts, I bought a commercial iron called a Glad Iron.

Norman Parker was a mate from the Tivoli Theatre. He was a back stage technician, whom I'd met while I was working there. He offered to be my assistant in the shirt laundry during the day.

I paid Norm Swain to advertise "Six Hour Shirt Laundry" on the radio.

'Bring your shirts in at nine o'clock in the morning and get them back at four o'clock in the afternoon.'

The first morning, Norm Parker and I had a very long queue, which extended out of the building and down the main street of Melbourne. I thought I'd get four or five shirts in. To our amazement, we received twelve hundred shirts that first day, over a thousand by eight thirty in the morning.

In dry cleaning, you use a strip of paper like a streamer and staple it on to the garment. You write on it with a special pen that doesn't come off while it goes through the dry cleaning process. Naively, I thought it would be the same with washing shirts, so that was the system I used. I wrote a number on every shirt that came in, but I didn't realise that the paper would disintegrate in water. We were washing six shirts at a time. The copper boiled all day. After a few days, the steam started lifting the paper off the walls and it fell down in sheets.

We put the washed shirts into a basket and took them downstairs to the tap over the gully trap, for rinsing. By the time I returned them upstairs, all the name tags had disintegrated and we had to try to name the shirts all over again.

When the first shirts were dry, I tried the Glad automatic ironing machine I'd purchased. I placed the first shirt on the board and released the iron mechanism. It whizzed across the shirt front, taking off all the buttons. I placed the second shirt on the board. This time, the iron ripped off the pocket. Quickly, I learned I had to iron the shirts from the inside. It didn't take long to master the fast moving ironing machine and I had to buy only two replacement shirts.

That first afternoon, we had only three or four shirts with names on them. These shirts had been laundered previously at another laundry, where they had used the correct tape and named them in waterproof ink.

Norm was wearing a pair of shorts and nothing on top. He looked as though he'd just come from rowing in the galleys. I had made a big board of pigeon holes and only three shirts were folded up in those holes. A customer came in and gave Norm his tickets. Norm turned round to the three that were ready finished, and lo and behold, two of the three shirts belonged to this man. Norm put the shirts on the counter and pulled the paper off the roll to wrap them.

The man pointed to a spot on one.

'Oh look, you didn't get all the stain out. There's a stain there.'

Norm bellowed at him.

'What's wrong with you? Are you a poofter? A man oughta jump the counter and knock you right out.'

I was coming downstairs with a bundle of shirts to rinse. When I heard that argument develop, I turned round and walked back up.

'I just thought I'd point it out,' the customer said.

'Four and six,' said Norm.

We charged two and three-pence for each shirt. The customer paid the money and went, but I don't think he ever came back.

I had to tell Norm Swain to stop advertising. Norm Parker and I were very fatigued. We were overwhelmed with shirts and after a fortnight, we decided to quit.

I went to a big laundry where I sent my own clothes for washing and pleaded with them.

'I had this idea about doing a six hour shirt laundry, but it's become too much for me. Would you be able to help out?'

Fortunately, the owner was able to help me. Prior to this, he'd been doing the laundry for the Royal Melbourne hospital, but now they were doing their own in their newly built laundry that he'd designed for them. His own laundry had space and time to do the shirts for me. I took about three thousand shirts out to him and just about overwhelmed his business. We had a hell of a job to sort out all those unlabelled shirts and get out of our mess. His staff wrote in marking ink on each shirt. We were weeks behind, but eventually, with his help, we caught up and from then on, we were merely a depot for a six hour shirt service for this big laundry. At least I found a solution, because I couldn't have handled it otherwise.

After that, the laundry room became a party room. My mates and Judy's and my friends held parties there nearly every Saturday evening.

~

I was always looking for new business ventures. When the Queen visited Melbourne in 1954, I had the dry cleaning collection kiosk in the Empire Arcade. I decided I would make sandwiches there and sell them to the people coming into the city to see the Queen. My place was in the centre of the city and she'd be passing right by. I bought a hundred loaves of bread. We made sandwiches out of one loaf and then I realised I'd miss the Queen if I was busy with the sandwiches. We had ninety nine loaves of bread left over. I went to the Salvation Army and the man in charge was just walking out of his office.

'I have ninety-nine loaves of bread. Are they any good to you?'

'Yes, yes.'

'Where will I put it?'

'On my desk.'

He thought I'd said one loaf of bread. I went into his office to his desk, and he had a phone and some other items there. I took everything off his desk, putting it on the side and loaded his desk up with ninety-nine loaves of cut bread. As I was leaving, he returned.

'Bloody hell, what's all this?'

'You told me to put it on your desk.'

'You said one loaf.'

'No, I said ninety-nine.'

'Oh, all right, I'll handle it.'

So I left him with the ninety-nine loaves. That was a flop, that business. I was more interested in getting up a ladder. I had to see the Queen drive by.

Camera Stores

While I was collecting money from Ken Perry for the dry cleaning depot, I went to work for CT Lorenz Camera store. Soon Lorenz wanted me to take over management of one of his shops in Melbourne. He sent me to Sydney to train in management. After I had done that course, I ran the store in Melbourne for a year. In 1955, I moved on to work for Andrews Camera shop in Elizabeth Street, and enjoyed the work and camaraderie there.

Sea Lions on the Pier

During the mid-1950's, to draw more people to the Pier, my father wanted to put a shark on exhibit, using the hold of one of our boats for a tank. The *Sprightly* was a one hundred foot long [30m] steam tug. The vessel was tied alongside the Pier, where we pulled the boiler and the steam engine out and my father concreted the inside and filled the hull with sea water to make a viewing tank.

Dad was unable to obtain a shark, so he decided to get some sea lions. We weren't allowed to take sea lions from Victorian waters, because they were protected. The Department of Fisheries and Game suggested that we try for sea lions in South Australia for our side show.

We wrote to the South Australia Department of Fisheries and Game. They gave us permission to take ten sea lions at five shillings each and told us to catch them on the Page Islands in the Backstairs Passage, between the mainland and Kangaroo Island.

We drove over to Victor Harbour. While I was trying to find someone with a boat to take us out to the Page Islands, I met an old fisherman who had a big scar on his neck.

'Be very careful if you go out there. You see this scar. I received that about twenty or thirty years ago on the Page Islands. A big sea lion grabbed me and was dragging me into the surf when my mate ran up and hit it. I just managed to get away.'

He didn't say how big the sea lion was, but confident as ever, I wasn't too worried by his story.

We hired a boat from two fishermen, Nozzer and Harvey, whose business was in financial trouble. They'd even sold their ingots of lead ballast from inside the hull to help them survive. Although there was no ballast and the fishing boat was very unstable, we motored out to the Page Islands with these two fellows. My father stayed on board the boat, while I went ashore with the fishermen. These islands are nothing but huge rocks, with only a tiny beach, on which it's very dangerous to land.

The three of us, Nozzer, Harvey and I, brought nets to catch the sea lions, but we lost them in the surf as we clambered over the rocks to land. We managed to hold onto the chaff bags to put the sea lions into after we baled them up. Some of these sea lions were very big and bloody dangerous. We baled up one sea lion that weighed about as much as me, a little over ten stone or one hundred and sixty-five pounds [62 kg].

'You distract it and I'll dive on it' I said.

The fishermen weren't too happy about tackling the sea lions, because they are very muscular. This particular one flapped about and pooped everywhere. I flapped around with it and wouldn't let go from around its neck. Eventually, the other two men held the bag over its head and together, we put the sea lion in. Nozzer tied up the bag and the sea lion bit him through the hessian. When we returned to Victor Harbour, we had to take Nozzer to hospital to get the wound stitched.

We caught two large sea lions and three small ones – five in all. We had them on the Pier for two years. The little ones couldn't even swim at first. My father reared and trained them. He had a wonderful relationship with them. They would flop along the Pier after Dad and when they saw the feeding pump, they knew it was meal time.

We went to the market each morning to buy green whiting – a cheap fish – to feed them. We chopped the fish up in a blender and added milk. The pump was one for blowing up car tyres. Dad cut off the fitting for screwing onto the tyre valve. We sucked the fish mixture into the pump, then, with the end of the tube in the sea lion's mouth, one push of the plunger gave each animal about half a litre of fish and milk in twenty seconds. They loved the procedure.

Noble Kerby with two of his sea lions.

We charged a shilling per person to look at the sea lions. The customers could also pay to throw fish to the animals. My father's dog liked to go in swimming with them. Jinx was a big foxy and the sea lions objected when he ate their fish.

I can remember only three of the names we called the sea lions: Boofhead, Bingo and Cedric. Dad had trained Boofhead so that if he called out, "Boofhead, Boofhead," the sea lion would respond, "Oink oink".

One day I was sitting inside the Kiosk and my father was outside. A man walked in, paid his money to see the sea lions, then walked down the gangway to the boat. To give a demonstration, my father yelled out 'Boofhead, Boofhead.' This man turned round.

'Do you want to speak to me, Mr Kerby?'

My father was embarrassed and had to explain, because for once, Boofhead was reticent about performing. My father came inside, blushing.

~

The old man scrubbed out the sea lions' tank regularly. It was a very big task, because the hull was thirty-three metres long. Dad

147

would empty all the water, hose the tank and scrub it, then refill it with fresh water.

Occasionally, I stayed overnight at the Kiosk. I was there on my thirty-fifth birthday in November 1956. We were still asleep in the early morning when I felt the Kiosk get a decent jarring. You could easily feel such things, the Pier being on piles. It was about dawn on a Saturday morning and the weather was a little rough. I looked out my window. The *Sprightly* had flooded and sunk. The boat was on the bottom and we had to get it up. I woke my parents with the news.

For several days, my father denied he had forgotten to shut the valves. He admitted it about a week later. Two of the sea lions swam away, because the hatch was under water. The one we called Cedric came back to visit every year. We threw him a fish whenever we saw him, but I suspect a sportsman shot him eventually.

We were on a £1,000 bond to the Department of Ports and Harbours not to let a vessel sink at the Pier. I rang up the fire brigade and hired a big pump from them, called the "Tilly". They had a bigger pump, but they wouldn't let me have that one in case there was an emergency. They brought the pump down and I dived in my scuba gear to shut the port holes and the valves. The hatch was a little below water level at high tide. We had to wait for low tide to close the valves, pump out the rest of the water and then let her rise on the high tide. My mate, John Lucas, came down to help me overnight.

While we were waiting for the tide in the early hours of Sunday morning, we went to see a girl John knew. We asked her if she wanted to come to see the boat salvaged. She was enthusiastic, but her mother was suspicious about two fellows she'd never met before wanting to take her daughter out in the middle of the night, to watch a boat come up.

'Why don't you both come to watch?' said John.

'Yes Mum, come on. It will be fun.'

Her mother had the time of her life. She was into everything and damned near went swimming with the three sea lions, which were still in the tank.

I worked out the rate the pump would extract the water and how much water there was. By my reckoning, the *Sprightly* would start to float at 2.30 am. At twenty past two, the ladder down to the boat moved. *Gee, I'm pretty smart!* I thought.

The next morning, diving gear, hoses and the pump were still lying on the Pier. Word went around that the *Sprightly* had sunk, and on Monday morning, two inspectors from the Department of Ports and Harbours turned up.

'We believe the *Sprightly* sank,' said one.

'What makes you think that? You can see she's floating,' I said.

Nobody would admit that the boat had sunk. Two inspectors from the Fisheries and Games came down.

'I understand you're feeding the sea lions on undersized fish.'

'I don't know whether they're undersized or not, but we're buying them from the market,' said Dad.

These officers were behaving offensively to my father. I went outside and I caught just a slight whiff of beer. They were having a go at my father in no uncertain manner. He was pretty good in an argument, but he was losing this one. I weighed in.

'They're drunk. I can smell the beer.'

The inspectors rapidly departed from the Pier. Only ten days after this event occurred, the Olympics were due to start in Melbourne. We had to move the *Sprightly* away from the Pier for this very important occasion; the officials considered her unsightly at her location beside Melbourne's famous Pier. We agreed to tow the boat up the Yarra.

~

A year later, one of the sea lions, Bingo, died. He had been very sick and drooling. We needed to see a vet and phoned several, but none was willing to treat a sea lion. Eventually, a woman vet agreed to see us. We had to drive almost to Ringwood to see her. I sat down in the waiting room, holding a ninety-pound sea lion on my lap. Beside me was a woman with a canary in a cage.

The vet asked if the sea lion was hot and I told her I thought he had a bit of a temperature. Bingo was so sick he didn't care what happened. The vet suggested an antibiotic. She prepared a needle and syringe, then she felt around his flipper and jabbed the heavy gauge needle in. Bingo just about took off and roared. We took him home, but he didn't survive. We had just two of the sea lions left.

Standard Radio

I still had the dry cleaning depots and work in the camera store, when a friend persuaded me to try my hand at selling radiograms. Standard Radio was owned by Webb's. I went to work for Standard Radio as a salesman during 1956. It was while I was working there that I met my good mate John Lucas.

I did rather well as a salesman. One weekend, the regular salesman for the pianos was on leave. The boss asked me to stand in for him. I ended up selling two pianos that weekend. Normally, we sold only one every two or three weeks.

Standard Radio would take trade-ins to sell radiograms or pianos – sometimes these trade-ins were white goods: mainly refrigerators and washing machines. Webb's, who owned Standard Radio, sold the white goods to me and John Lucas. We re-sold these white goods at our kiosk in the Empire Arcade.

Another company owned by Webb's, LGE, wanted drivers to deliver for them. My father applied and was hired for the job. The old man bought a van and started doing deliveries. By then, John Lucas also worked in deliveries.

In December 1957, while Dad was out doing a delivery, he had a stroke. They called me and I raced him into hospital. The nurses put a pipe in his mouth for an airway. Despite the stroke, he was very alert and on the ball.

I was visiting him in hospital four days later, when a young lad came up with an electric razor, and before I knew what he was doing, he'd grabbed Dad by the chin and pulled his head around to shave him. Accidentally, he knocked the air pipe out of my father's mouth. I couldn't get that pipe back down my father's throat. I'd never had any experience of those things and didn't know the trick of it. The hospital had an oxygen bottle at the other end of the ward. I raced up and dragged this bottle back, but I couldn't undo it. They had done it up with a spanner. It was too late, much too late. Dad died in front of me. He had high blood pressure, and we didn't know. I was very distressed.

After my father's funeral, I met one of the fellows from the depot. He told me a story about my mate John and Dad. 'You know, six of us formed a delegation about this business of John Lucas calling your father "Pop Kerby." We took John aside and told him, "You don't call a man like Mr Kerby, "Pop." '

'That was very kind of you,' I said.

I was very cut up about my father's death and that I hadn't been able to prevent it. I felt guilty about it for a long, long time. He was only fifty-eight years old. If I'd known about CPR at that time, I reckon I could have saved him. I blamed myself for not stopping the lad from knocking the air tube from his mouth when he went to shave Dad. I also blamed myself for not getting oxygen to Dad in time. I was grieving and thoroughly miserable for the next couple of years. Dad had died, Judy was in Newcastle, although she came down for the funeral and promised to return. I wanted to leave Standard Radio to do something other than sell radiograms.

In the New Year of 1958, I needed a dramatic change in my life. I could no longer continue as I had been; I was too depressed after Dad's death to appear cheerful to customers and sell radiograms at Standard Radio. I made an agreement with Alan Mahoney, another radiogram salesman, and my mate, John Lucas, to build a light aircraft in John's garage. Alan and I both put in our notice to Standard Radio.

By the time Judy arrived back in Melbourne in March 1958, we had already started preparations for building the first plane.

Returning the Sea Lions

The sea lions had been my father's pets as well as a sideshow on the Pier. After the old man had his stroke, he asked me to return the sea lions to South Australia. I eventually managed to do this a few months after his funeral.

John Lucas and I built a cage and together with Judy, we drove them back to Victor Harbour. I enquired about Harvey and Nozzer, intending to hire their boat to take the sea lions out to the Page Islands. The old fisherman with the scar told me a tale about those young men.

'Harvey's dead. We think he's been murdered. He was out in Bass Strait fishing with a group and he fell overboard. The last they saw of him, he was swimming strongly in the moonlight. They said they tried to pick him up, but they couldn't pull him into the boat.'

'Nozzer's no longer here. He's gone too. We're convinced Harvey was murdered. I'm bloody glad Nozzer's gone, actually. He was a boxer once. When he was going to hit someone in the pub, he'd stand on their toes and they couldn't move back to get a swing. He'd stand on their feet and hook them.'

We hired another boat. Ashore on the Page Islands, the sea lions were all lined up on the tiny bit of beach and I wondered how they would receive our sea lions back. We were about eighty yards off the island. At first, I couldn't get the two sea lions out of the cage. The fisherman I was with gave me good advice.

'Take the little one out first, because the big one's protecting the little one.'

As soon as I put the little one into the water, the other sea lion dived in after him. When they surfaced, all the sea lions left the beach and came out to greet them. They swam around and welcomed them back home.

~

9 Romance

Col and Judy's romance was a stop start affair throughout the 1950's, culminating in their marriage in 1959.

Told by Judy

Joan and I walked out of the cinema. Our hopes of finding seats to see a film had been dashed.

'What now?' Joan asked.

'I don't know Joan. It seems a shame to spend our last free Saturday evening sitting at home. Once the show starts, we'll be on stage every Saturday night.'

'Hullo!' I heard a male voice from behind me. 'You girls look despondent. What can I do to help?'

'Hello Col,' chirped Joan. Do you remember Judy? We met at a Tivoli party a few months ago.'

'Yes, I remember.'

'Hello Col. I talked to you at that party too,' I said, remembering my poor opinion of him that night.

'Yes, you did. I always remember good looking girls.'

'We've just returned from a tour of New Zealand, dancing in "Tourist Trade".'

'I've just returned from overseas too. I spent a few months in New Guinea diving for a salvage team. A gold dredge tipped over up at Bulolo. Anyway, why such long faces on a Saturday night?'

New Guinea? I suppose that explains why he is carrying a jumper under his arm on a warm summer evening.

'We've tried all the cinemas and there are no seats available,' said Joan.

'Come with me then. I know all the usherettes. I'll see what I can do for you.'

We returned to the nearby cinema and within five minutes, Col had organised two seats for us.

That was my first real meeting with Col. He seemed nicer than I remembered, but I wasn't prepared to trust him.

In 1951, I toured both capital and regional cities of Australia. When I came back to rehearse for a different show, I met Col again.

'Hello Judy. You look well. In fact, you look exceptional. You are very good looking, you know.'

'Hello Col, how are you?' *You act so very smarmy. You are rather sure of yourself.*

'I'm well. I've been learning to brew beer for my father to sell in the Kiosk – you know, the St Kilda Pier Kiosk. My parents run it.'

'That's different. Do you live there with them?'

'No. I share a flat with my mate Alf. Where are you living?'

'Joan and I have rooms at the Clare Castle Hotel.'

'I might come and visit you some time; would you mind? I'd like to take you out on a date.'

'Thank you. That would be nice.' *I wonder if he really means that?*

Col did turn up at the hotel late one morning, accompanied by his friend, Alf Lazer. Joan and I had not been long out of bed and we were still wearing our dressing gowns. Col arranged to meet me after work that night and take me out for supper. I was reluctant, but agreed mainly because Alf was there and he seemed a nice man.

We finished work and were ready to leave the theatre at eleven o'clock. I was very nervous, because I hadn't had a real date before. I went out the rear exit from the theatre into Rainbow Alley. I couldn't see Col and Alf, so I ran back inside. When I peered out a second time, I saw them both and the three of us went out to supper.

Apparently, Alf had been in the car and had seen my earlier appearance at the stage door. Later, he told me he thought my silhouette looked like a crow, because I was wearing a black beret and a black coat. I laughed at the idea of myself as a crow.

Col was a perfect gentleman that evening and I began to lose my distrust of him. He recounted stories about his time in Bulolo, diving to recover the gold dredge. He also told stories about brewing beer and his difficulties trying to lower the alcohol level to just under two per cent, so that it could be sold in the Kiosk on Sundays. I found him entertaining and a very good story teller.

154

Joan Roberts and Judy Lingard in Perth.

'Would you like to come out for supper with us again?' Col asked when he escorted me home that night.

'Yes. Yes I would. Thank you for a lovely evening.'

Col arranged to meet me at the stage door again the next night after the show was finished. It soon became a regular arrangement. The three of us went out for supper nearly every night. We would go to Tony's on Wednesday for dinner, to The Savoy restaurant on a

Saturday night and Marr's restaurant in St Kilda was our choice on Sundays.

In 1951, I was on tour in Sydney. Col came up to deliver his diving tank to Luna Park. After he had completed his business, he took me out for lunch. I began to realise how much I liked him. I was so pleased to see him that day, even though he was scratching a rash and hadn't been able to scrub all the truck grease off his hands. That was the last time I saw him before he set off for England, to study brewing.

Alf Lazer and Col.

Col returned to Melbourne some months later, when I was also back there. I immediately became caught up in his life. At night, he was building a kiosk in the Empire Arcade to be used for a second dry cleaning depot. It was right outside a shop he had previously rented for his photography business. I would walk the two blocks from the Tivoli to the arcade at night after work, and we'd toil through the early hours of the morning, constructing that kiosk.

Col's mother had come from Lancashire and, in 1952, both his parents went off to England, leaving Col to look after their dogs and the business on the Pier. His father had a royal blue Rolls Royce. I felt very grand when Col picked me up in that car.

When the Empire Arcade kiosk was completed, we started work on a dining room in the St Kilda Kiosk on the Pier. We rebuilt that room from the piles up. The room measured 81 square feet and it was a huge job. We were putting in the last window when the ship from England, with Mr and Mrs Kerby aboard, berthed at Port Phillip Bay.

~

I travelled to New Zealand three times with different shows during the 1950's. We had performed "Tourist Trade" in 1951. Two years later, Joan and I danced in "The Tommy Trinder Show", which also toured New Zealand and all over Australia. Col flew to New Zealand to see me and took me out for lunch.

'Judy, I've missed you so much, I had to come to see you. I think I've fallen in love with you. How about you? Have you missed me?'

'It is so good to see you, Col. Yes, I have missed you.'

'I think we make a good team. How about we get married? Would you like to become engaged?'

'Yes. Yes, I think I am in love with you too. Yes, let's get engaged.'

I had always felt jealous when Col went out with other girls. I thought if we were engaged, he wouldn't do that anymore. Joan was thrilled about this development. We didn't have a ring though, so the engagement wasn't really official.

When the tour of New Zealand ended, the dance troupe returned to Melbourne to prepare for another show. Joan and I leased a flat in Mitford Street, St Kilda and Col continued courting me from there. This time, we made a happy foursome, because Joan started accompanying Alf whenever we went out.

~

My romance with Col was on and off, because I kept going on tour and Col had his trip to England. He was also sent to Sydney for management training for one of his jobs.

I toured Adelaide, Perth, Sydney and had another trip to New Zealand with the Tivoli company. The third trip took place in 1954. We were soon to leave with the show "Folies Bergère", when Joan pulled out and decided to go home to Sydney. Her grandmother was unwell. I was devastated by her departure. We had been so very close for four years. We had danced together, travelled together and shared accommodation ever since I had first arrived in

Melbourne, a young innocent about to embark on my career as a Tivoli dancer.

Despite the fact that my mate Joan re-joined the troupe on tour in Perth in 1955, I was still very unhappy. I had begun drinking quite a lot of brandy after each night's show, because I missed Col , but I was unsure of my future with him. During that time, I couldn't decide whether or not Col was right for me. He and I hadn't spoken much for some time and he was taking out other girls whenever I was away from Melbourne. I was also homesick for my parents. My father was quite ill that year. I wanted to be at home.

When the show ended in Perth, instead of continuing on tour to Sydney with the rest of the troupe, I resigned from my job and travelled by train across the Nullarbor back to Melbourne. Col and I decided to have a short holiday together before I travelled home to Newcastle.

'How about we hire a car and go on a trip together?' Col could see I was depressed and wanted to cheer me up. 'I'd like to have a look at Mildura. What do you think? Would you like to go there?'

We spent ten days driving up to Mildura, staying in motels. I put a ring on my left finger and we signed in as Mr and Mrs Kerby, so there would be no problem about our sharing a room. How different it is today, when no one cares if a single girl spends the night with a man.

Col took me to catch the overnight train to Sydney. Reluctantly, we parted at Spencer Street Station. I didn't know when I was going to see him again. While we were together, everything seemed right, but when we were apart, all my doubts resurfaced.

Eventually, my father recovered from his long illness, but I stayed on with my parents for another two years, working in Newcastle.

Col came up to Newcastle to see me, meet my parents and stay for a few days. I was overjoyed to see him, but after he left, I became very despondent again. I couldn't see how our relationship would work with me in Newcastle and him in Melbourne. It all seemed quite impossible.

I wrote to Col and told him I wanted to call off our relationship. After that letter, I didn't hear from him for a long time.

One night the phone rang and it was Col.

'Oh Col, how good it is to hear your voice.'

'I've been missing you too Judy,' he said. 'It is just as well your parents have an easily remembered phone number. I am at work and I was missing you so much, I thought I'd call you.'

'I have been so depressed, Col. Nothing seems right.'

'I've been very down too,' he replied. 'I'd love to see you again. Why don't you take a holiday and come down to Melbourne for a visit?'

I was ecstatic to hear his voice. After that phone call, I realised that Col was the man for me after all. I managed to take two weeks holiday from work and travelled down to Melbourne. We had ten days together during spring in 1957. It felt so right to be together with him.

Not very long after my return to Newcastle, Col phoned me again.

'Judy, it's my old man.' He was sobbing. 'My father's died. He died in my arms. I tried to save him Judy, but I couldn't do it. I didn't know how to save him.'

I knew Noble had suffered a stroke only a few days before, but that it hadn't affected his brain very much. Col had told me that although his dad was in hospital, he was very alert. Now he was dead.

I took leave from my job and flew down to Melbourne for Noble's funeral. While I was with Col those few days, I decided that I had to move back there. He was extremely upset about his father's death and kept blaming himself for it. I felt I should be there to support him in his grief.

Back in Newcastle, I told my parents my plans. My father was well again, but my parents were not keen for me to leave. However, I was twenty three years old and they didn't try to stop me. I gave notice at my work in David Jones when the Christmas rush had died down. I also informed the clubs where I had been dancing that I would no longer be available. By March, I was back in Melbourne with Col – for good.

Col: My parents left for a trip to England in 1952, a couple of months after I arrived back from Europe. While they were away, I ran the St Kilda Kiosk and looked after their dogs. My father had his workshop in the middle of the Kiosk. It was extremely messy and the floor was rotting. I thought he was a messier worker than I was, but Judy disagreed. She thought we were both equally untidy.

We moved Dad's workshop outside to a shed at the back of the Kiosk. Judy and I turned that nine square yard space into a dining room. It was a major building job. The floor was rotten and all we had were the piles. Despite the floor being open, we lost only one good hammer into the sea.

We had the room all stripped out when my parents boarded the ship in England to come home. We still had a hell of a lot of work to do, building and lining the new room. Judy would come down at night after the theatre to help. My parents' ship was already berthing in Port Phillip when we were finishing it off.

When my mother saw what we had done, she was delighted with the new room. My father was gracious about it, but when we next visited the Kiosk, we found he had moved Mum's piano in there, making the room very crowded. That annoyed me.

~

I missed Judy while she was away on tour, but not enough to prevent me from going out with other girls. I really enjoyed the company of pretty girls, but my relationship with Judy was special. I travelled up to Newcastle to stay with her for a few days. While Judy was out of earshot, Mrs Lingard spoke to me.

'You're quite the man about town, aren't you Col?'

Later, during that visit, she became more specific.

'Have you seduced Judy yet, Col?'

'Yes. Yes I have.'

'I'm sorry about that.'

'Oh, it was all right.' *Oops, I think that was the wrong thing to say.*

I was very upset when I received Judy's letter terminating our relationship. In fact, I was devastated. My friends, John, Norm and his girlfriend Beryl, took me off to Tasmania for a holiday to try to help me get over my deep disappointment. While we were down in Hobart, I decided to take John up flying. I hired a Chipmunk two seater. John really liked the experience of flying in a small plane.

That time on night shift, when I felt lonely and remembered Judy's phone number, was particularly important in our lives. If I hadn't phoned her that night, we might not have spent the next fifty-five years together. It was a really special time when she came for a holiday in 1957. She stayed for ten days, reluctant to go home again.

Things changed rather dramatically only a few weeks later, when my father had a stroke at work and later died in hospital.

Judy Continues: Alf and Col were renting a two bedroom flat in Dandenong Road in a mansion called Matlock. In March 1958, I hired a single room in the same house. I had to look for a job and found work selling kitchen knives door to door. Later, I sold 'Magic' makeup and became a team leader for them, making good money.

Col was still grieving for his father and very upset that he hadn't been able to save his life. He was really quite depressed, which made planning our wedding difficult.

I insisted on a church wedding, but all the ministers wanted to convert Col to Christianity. It took a year for us to find a church with a minister tolerant enough to marry us on our terms. Eventually, we decided upon the Unitarian Church opposite the Cathedral in central Melbourne. The preacher there was the only one who accepted that Col was an atheist. The Reverend Vincent Montgomery Keeling James married us on the 27th of June, 1959. Alf Lazer and Col's mother were our witnesses. It was a very small wedding, but John Lucas gate crashed with his partner, Pam. Joan was working in Sydney, so she couldn't come.

The wedding took place in the morning, with a professional photographer present. We were disappointed afterwards to find his photos were all out of focus. After the ceremony, we went to the St Kilda foreshore to take some more photos in 3D. Col went off to work and I returned to the Kiosk with Mrs Kerby Snr. That evening, Alf and John took Col and me to the Oriental Hotel for a celebration dinner.

Col and Judy on their wedding day, 27th June, 1959.

My parents didn't come down to Melbourne for the wedding, because I didn't tell them we were getting married. I rang my mother the following morning.

'I was married yesterday, Mum.' I burst into tears.

'That's nice dear. Who to?'

'Col Kerby.'

'I thought it might be him. Don't cry love. I'll call your father in from the garage.'

I was crying because I felt guilty for not having told them beforehand.

My parents came to visit us a year or so later and it was obvious my mother had trouble believing we really were married, because we couldn't find the marriage certificate to show her. By then, we had moved from Dandenong road to St Kilda and the certificate became lost in the move. I tried to show her the church where we'd been married and drove her into Central Melbourne. The church had gone; it had been demolished and all that remained was a car park. Later, Mum heard Preacher James on the radio. He impressed her and after that, she believed we really were married.

When we moved into the Kiosk as a married couple, Col's mother wouldn't accept me. After putting up with her odd behaviour for several months, I became so infuriated, I threw a pot of potatoes at her. On our first New Year' Eve at the kiosk, I left and walked for hours to get away from my mother-in-law.

After several months of friction, Mrs Kerby went to live with Hilda and Col and I took over the lease of the St Kilda Kiosk. Life in the Kiosk was much happier when it was just Col, me and our dogs. We lived there for nearly thirty – years from 1960 until 1987 and I ran the Kiosk shop for most of that time.

Col: After my father's death and before Judy and I were married, my mother was alone at the Kiosk. It was not suitable for a woman to be alone on the Pier at night, so I slept there for a while.

Then I found out my sister wanted to leave her husband.

'It would be better for you to move in with Mum, Hilda, and help her in the Kiosk. I don't like Mum being alone. If you moved in, it would solve her problem and your problem and I wouldn't have to sleep there.'

Hilda moved in, bringing her seventeen year old son with her, but did little to help our mother. After a few months, Hilda started having an affair with a local called Spiro, who would sleep with her at the Kiosk and walk through the shop and down the Pier on his way home in the morning.

Neither my mother nor the customers liked this behaviour. It was not acceptable in 1959. Hilda would come down in her dressing gown and with curlers in her hair on Saturday and Sunday mornings, the busiest time in the Kiosk. Mum was born in 1889, and such behaviour distressed her. Hilda rang me up, expecting that I would take her side. She was shocked when I didn't and very unhappy with me when I sided with our mother.

'You haven't been pulling your weight. On a hot day, the Kiosk can be very busy. Mum's getting on in years and you're not helping.'

'I thought you'd support me, not take Mum's side. You suggested I move into the Kiosk.'

'I did, but the condition was that you would help Mum.' I said.

In June 1959, after Judy and I were married, I insisted that Hilda go and we moved into the Kiosk. We helped Hilda find a flat where she could live with her son and helped finance setting her up there. Judy was able to help Mum in the Kiosk at peak times, but we were also busy at work.

Although Mum had previously been very good at keeping up with things, it soon became obvious to us that her alcoholism was becoming embarrassing at the Kiosk. Eventually, Judy could no longer cope with Mum and her unpredictable behaviour. Mum went to live with Hilda and Judy and I took over the lease of the Kiosk.

~

One day, I was serving in the Kiosk when a black man came in, wearing a Saville Row suit and tie. I looked at him for a while and I couldn't quite fathom whether perhaps he was African. I asked him where he was from.

'New Guinea.'

'I've worked in New Guinea, New Britain and New Ireland.'

'I'm from New Britain.'

His wife was with him and they were drinking my lemon squash.

'What part of New Britain?' I asked.

'Rabaul.'

Col when he took over the Kiosk lease.

'Oh, then you're a Toloy?'

'Yes, I'm a Toloy.'

'Which village were you born in?'

'A very small village between Rabaul and the North Coast.'

'Nordup?'

'Yes. You know Nordup?' This was a village of twenty huts. He spoke better English than I did, which quite irritated me.

'Yes. In the early thirties, I had a houseboy work for me from Nordup. His name was Larku and ...'

'Larku is still alive!' he told me.

'What house did you live in?'

'The one down near the creek.'

'There was a house down near the creek with a post and a hurricane lamp on it.'

'Yes, that was my house.'

I found it astonishing that within a few minutes conversation, I'd pinpointed exactly what house he'd grown up in.

'What are you doing here in Australia?'

'I'm a radio announcer. I speak Pidgin on the short wave Radio Australia programme.'

'What's Larku doing?

'Ooh, Larku is a good business man.'

'Yes, He always was. When you could hire a boy for eight shillings a month, he insisted I pay him ten shillings a month.'

'Larku has two trucks, which he runs down to the Warringu River and back, a service run. Do you know the Warringu?'

'Yes, I know that river. I swam across it once with a crocodile after me.'

~

10 Bee Aircraft

I loved to fly and earned my pilot's licence during 1945. Early in 1958, I saw Benson's advertisement for gyrocopter plans in a magazine. I wanted to build one for myself and maybe another to sell. I wrote away to Benson in America and soon after, the plans arrived. I was studying them in the shop [Standard Radio] one day. Alan, one of the salesmen, came up and looked over my shoulder.

'What's that?'

'I'm thinking of building a couple of these. How about going halves with me in the cost?'

I found Alan Mahoney annoying. He knew I had a pilot's licence and he had also been learning to fly. Every Monday morning, he would report his weekend flying experiences to me. That drove me mad, because I hadn't been out flying too. I thought that if I asked him to put some money up, I might frighten him away.

'If we're going to build aircraft, we'll need money to set up.'

'Count me in,' said Alan.

To my amazement, he pulled five hundred pounds out of his pocket and laid it on the counter in front of me. I knew it was probably money he had received as a deposit from a customer, but it was symbolic of his enthusiasm to take a share in this venture. Once Alan had paid over his own five hundred quid, we both resigned from Standard Radio. After that, we were in business together, building aircraft and fighting the Department of Civil Aviation.

As a business partner, Alan was terrific. Judy liked him too. That's how Alan and I started to make the first gyrocopters. My mate John Lucas decided to go in with us as a third partner and we made the first aircraft in his garage. Part-way through building it, the three of us decided to manufacture gyrocopters as a business. When Judy returned to live in Melbourne in March of 1958, we were already in the aircraft building business.

All aircraft in Australia were (and still are) controlled by the Department of Civil Aviation [the DCA]. Like most departments in Australia, they had many rules and restrictions. To understand these legal requirements, I obtained a set of the regulations pertaining to aircraft manufacture and read them very carefully. It was obvious that for an aircraft to be able to fly, it had to be tested to their specifications, but at your cost. It was quite a rigmarole to get it passed; almost impossible in fact.

I found the loophole right at the end of the regulations. It said "What has been said heretofore does not apply if the aircraft is tethered; not flown within five miles of an authorized landing ground; and not flown above 500 feet." I knew what they meant –

those model aircraft that kids fly on a string. I was elated. That was our way out!

Early gyrocopter.

We advertised in newspapers and every aviation magazine in Australia that we could access. Our advertisements said, "DCA permit this aircraft to be flown without registration and without the pilot being licensed in Australia." I didn't say it had to be tethered.

The following week after putting these advertisements out everywhere, I went in to see the DCA people. First, I contacted a Melbourne skywriter and asked who I should approach.

'You get away with a lot of stuff with DCA. Who's the best man to see?'

'Noel Scholes. He's very liberal.'

I went in to the DCA office and asked to see Mr Noel Scholes.

They took me to his office and I knocked on the door.

'Come in,' a voice bellowed out.

There was a RAAF man sitting behind the desk. He had a moustache about two feet long.

'Yes, yes?'

Col in flight in our first Gyrocopter.

I told him I had built a Benson Gyrocopter and that I wanted to get it type certificated.

He stood up behind his desk.

'You bloody what?'

I repeated my request.

'Are you the fellow who's been putting those ads in the papers?'

'Yes, that's right.'

'What do you mean, "DCA allow this to be flown without the pilot being registered or licensed."?'

'That's right. It's in Section 95A.'

'What does that say?'

'Tethered.'

He was standing up looking very aggressive. I thought for a moment that he was going to hook me. I stepped back a little from his desk.

'No one could fly that thing tethered,' he said.

I regained a bit of courage. I walked around beside him and tapped him on the shoulder.

'If a man can't fly that tethered, he's not worth his salt.'

They thought that would stop us. Soon, we were selling gyrocopters both powered and as gliders. When we sold them out of our showroom later, we gave the customers a ball of string and told them the plane must be tethered at take-off. If the string broke, of course, they had to find somewhere to land. Theoretically, they had to take off with the string attached, so the aircraft was tethered. I loved to find a way around regulations I thought were stupid and I happily embraced that loophole.

It took the DCA nine months to alter the law. When they did, the Director General wrote me a personal letter. *"This afternoon, we have passed a new regulation regarding section 95A. That is, aircraft flying tethered must not exceed three and a half pounds in weight."*

After the new regulation, people still bought aircraft from us. The entire exercise was a battle, mainly because there was nothing available in Australia for the building of aircraft other than bolts and some timber that was imported for repairs. The material we used was mainly aluminium. I had a fitter and turner make up a jig that I gave to the aluminium manufacturer. They used it to extrude aluminium to the size of beam we wanted. For the aluminium wheel hubs, I turned up the patterns to have them cast and we used ten inch wheelbarrow pneumatic tyres.

The biggest problem, other than the DCA, was the engines. Benson said motor bike engines were fine, but we found they wouldn't fly. I had an Ariel four square motor, which is 1000cc. I re-bored it to 1200cc, to take new pistons. I built a gearbox that reduced the motor from 10,000 revs down to 2,000. All these alterations cost us £400. The engine still wasn't entirely satisfactory, but it did fly to the extent that when we demonstrated it to the Police Commissioner, he became very keen to obtain a gyrocopter for the police to chase people in speed boats, who were exceeding the speed limit. The Police Commissioner being interested made it a bit better for us, because the DCA were there too. They were very sour faced about the police interest.

When we first started, John was supposed to look after the orders, but he was slow at paperwork, so Judy took over that role. He was a fabulous worker in other areas, but he was hopeless with the mail and orders. He was bored quickly and no good for the long haul. He became discouraged and eventually pulled out of the partnership. We bought his share, making Judy the third shareholder. The whole business was originally run by mail order to a Post Office box and we had been using John's garage to build the aircraft. Now, we moved to commercial premises in Huntingdale and named our business Bee Aircraft.

The lack of a good motor was a huge disadvantage. In America, a drone motor suitable for the gyrocopter was available, but Prime Minister Menzies and his government prohibited the importation of any motors to Australia, except those for wheelchairs. In the USA, the drone motors were used on radio controlled aircraft. It was a special motor also used by the army for target shooting practice. Not being able to obtain the correct motors made it very difficult for us. We tried a Volkswagen motor, but it was too heavy and didn't have enough power.

With the motor we installed, the aircraft weighed over 300 pounds. We sold the gyrocopters fully constructed or in kits. We sold twenty different kits of the plane in different stages of completion. We offered them with rotors and the fuselage in pieces, partly or fully assembled.

The backbone of the rotor was a two inch wide piece of mild steel, an eighth of an inch thick and ten feet [3m] long. It tapered from two inches wide at the hub to half an inch at the outer end. I tried all sorts of things to shape the steel, including cutting it with an oxy torch. I couldn't do it well enough to satisfy myself. My solution was to screw the blade onto a plank and simply cut it with a hacksaw. Every person who walked past stopped to spend five minutes sawing. That way, we cut one each day.

Alan ready to fly the Bee Aircraft.

The next day, Judy would work on it. She made one blade of a rotor a day. That's half a complete rotor. She placed the two sides of timber over the steel, screwed it together using about sixty screws and shaped the wood. Judy finished them extremely well. Finally, the finished rotors were test flown.

We received many mail enquiries for the planes. Judy sent out the forms describing the different options. There was so much mail to deal with, Judy thought that instead of using two fingers, she should learn to touch type, but she never had time to practice. She enrolled at a typing college and could touch type in class, but when she came back to the office, she used two fingers again, because it was faster. I would dictate the letters and Judy would type them.

We sold a number of aircraft to farmers to fly over their properties. They used them for mustering and other tasks. Many of them imported their own motors from the States after Menzies relaxed the import law. Those two-stroke motors weighed seventy pounds, were 600cc and they developed seventy two horsepower.

Alan Mahoney remained a partner and worked with us. Other staff included an aircraft engineer called Cecil Chawner, a man of about fifty five. Another Alan and a younger man, who was trained in making wooden propellers, worked together building the props. Eventually, we had a total of twenty on the staff.

~

We ran Bee Aircraft for almost four years, from 1958 until late 1961. In September of that year, we attended the Melbourne Agricultural Show, hiring a stand to promote Bee Aircraft. It went well, but I was getting sick of dealing with problems from the DCA, and with Customs over the importation of motors.

While we were at the show, there was a fellow at a stand in the same pavilion, who was in Alan's ear all the time. When we returned to work after the show, Alan approached me and asked to buy me out. Judy and I decided to sell out to Alan. I told him we agreed and discussed a price for him to buy everything, including all the manufacturing equipment, with the exception of my lathe, which I still have. Alan went into partnership with the fellow he'd met at the Melbourne Agricultural Show.

About two years after we sold Bee Aircraft to Alan and his new partner, Alan was flying a fox moth aircraft he'd bought – a four-seater with a small cabin. He was taking a customer to Ballarat. The man was negotiating to buy a gyrocopter and the two of them were going to see a chap about lessons on how to fly a two-seater. The weather was bad and Alan's son was upset about his father flying in those weather conditions.

'Dad, you shouldn't fly when you can't see.'

They flew the fox moth into a mountain in fog and both of them were burned to death in the crash. Ballarat lies 1800 feet above sea level and it was a day when the cloud base was down to 1000 feet. I read a small article in the newspaper about how a fellow in a fox moth had gone missing. I rang up Bee Aircraft and asked to speak to Alan.

'No, he's not here.'

'Is he dead?'

'We think he might be.'

When the cloud cleared, a farmer saw the burned out aircraft. Both men died in the crash. Alan would have been in his mid-thirties then. That was pretty much the end of Bee Aircraft.

~

There was a man called Anderson, who had borrowed some money from my father to buy a Cummings Diesel for his boat. Five years later, he still owed the money and I couldn't find out where he was. I knew his phone number, but whenever I rang, a woman said, 'He was here, but he's not here now.'

I knew the model of Cummings he had, so I rang up one day. I said, 'I have some spare parts for a Cummings 108B that I want to get rid of cheap. If you have a pen and paper, I'll read the part numbers out to you?'

She started to write down the parts and I gave her all sorts of parts and numbers. I sounded like the Post Office employee reading out a telegram.

'Would you like a copy of what I've told you?' I said casually, and she fell for it. She gave me the address.

In the meantime, Alan had moved the aircraft company from Huntingdale to another industrial suburb. Sometimes, I visited his new factory to see how he was going. One day about five or six factories away, I saw a ute with Anderson's name on it. He had a factory there making containers for household firewood storage, for the Housing Commission. After all my cunning to get his address, he was right there. I went up and saw him, but didn't really get my money back. Instead, he had a lovely little dinghy there, which I admired. It was beautifully made.

'I know I owe you some money,' Anderson said, 'but I'm not going too well. What if you take the dinghy?'

'Yeah, but what about your shirt too?' I said.

We took the dinghy and a gallon of monkey-bum pink paint, which Judy wanted to use for painting her car. We kept it until the paint can rusted through at the Kiosk and the pink paint spilt onto the floor.

I didn't want the dinghy, so I advertised it. A fellow came and I put him in the dinghy to demonstrate it to him, while his wife waited on the landing. The landing was about five feet up from the water. He wanted his wife to get in too. She stood at the edge of the landing and I said to her, 'Jump in.' She did. She leapt into space and landed on the gunwale. Her feet were inside the boat and her bum was outside the gunwale. Her head was slipping under water and she was blowing out, whoosh, whoosh. Her dress was up to her neck and the large bloomers she was wearing were fully exposed.

With great presence of mind, her husband calmly lifted up her feet and deposited them outside the dinghy. She came up still blowing.

'Swim round the back, darling,' he said, 'and come over the stern, just like we saw them do on television.'

She came in over the stern. Both of us had to get out of the way, she came in so fast. All through this, I was thinking, *there goes my money*, but they bought the dinghy.

Pets

When we sold Bee Aircraft, Judy was able to help Mum full time at the Kiosk. When it became obvious that Mum wasn't managing too well any more, she moved in with Hilda. We were much happier for just Judy, me and our pets to be living at the Kiosk. From 1962-1964, while Judy managed the Kiosk, I managed a lawn mower business in Hawthorne Road, selling and servicing Victa motor mowers.

Trouble and a Tempting Offer

Judy and I are very fond of animals, in particular, we love dogs and we kept several show dogs.

Judy and some friends took the pedigree dogs to shows and won awards. Usually Judy accompanied her friend, Barbara, to the dog shows. One day in 1964, Judy didn't go and Barbara set off for the show with another friend, Laurie, and her two children, plus dogs.

Judy holding one of her show dogs.

On the way, they had car trouble and they called for a tow truck. Laurie was riding in the tow truck and Barbara, the children and the dogs were still in the van. Rounding a corner, the van tipped over and caught fire. Barbara managed to get the children out of the vehicle and also most of the dogs. She had gone back in to get the last dog when the vehicle exploded. Barbara was burned to death. We went to bed early that night, because we were grieving for Barbara.

Later that same night, at about ten o'clock, there was another phone call – this time, from my friend, Dr Don Rabinov, who had studied physics with me.

When I went to England in 1951, Don was living in London, getting overseas medical experience and sitting for his FRCS [Fellow of the Royal College of Surgeons]. While in London, I stayed with him and his wife in their flat in Hampstead Heath.

Now, Don was asking me to contact Dr Sam Rose the next morning at Melbourne University Department of Physiology. They were involved in a research project at Melbourne University during the 1960's, and Don also had his own business as a surgeon. When he phoned, he told me things weren't going well in the research lab.

'We're researching cancer at Melbourne Uni, but it's not working properly. I've been wondering who I could get to keep everything working. I thought of you. I want someone to run the lab and sort out the problems. Will you go and see Sam Rose?'

'I don't know Don. It's not a very good time to ask me. What exactly would I be doing?'

'You'd be working for Sam Rose. You'd be Chief Medical Technician, running the laboratory. I know you could do it. Please ring Sam in the morning.'

Through Don, I'd met Dr Sam Rose previously. They'd gone to university together. I'd introduced Judy to Sam Rose once and she didn't like him much.

I went up to Melbourne University and had a chat with Sam. I decided I wouldn't work with him, because in my opinion, he was on drugs. His pupils were like pin pricks, so I thought he was on an opiate or something similar. After a few days thinking about it, I went back to tell Sam that I wouldn't work with him, but Sam had a very compelling personality.

'I'm just going to lunch. Will you come with me?' Over lunch, he persuaded me to take the job.

'I've done nothing with cancer,' he said to me. 'What if my mother became sick with cancer? What could I do to help her?'

Sam whetted my curiosity. He was a damned good salesman. He sold his ideas to the Americans to get research grants. He sold me on the idea of helping him run the laboratory and I became enthusiastic about the project.

When I accepted the job at Melbourne University, I gave up managing the lawn mower business. I was anxious about working with Sam, but at the same time, elated at the prospect of being involved in cutting edge medical research.

Part Five: Medical Research

11 Cancer Research

I started to work with Dr Sam Rose in 1964, running the cancer research laboratory at Melbourne University. This was the beginning of the most fulfilling period in my life. My job involved supervising the laboratory staff, making sure the experimental work was being done according to Sam's instructions and designing and building equipment for use in experiments. As well as myself, working in the lab were two PhD's and three female lab technicians, whom Sam had trained in surgery on rats.

We were researching a cancer called "Walker 256" that was peculiar to rats and I was breeding a thousand rats a week. We didn't use all of those animals in our research; many were passed on to be used in other university departments.

Sam realised that handling the rats and injecting them with a needle would in itself stress them. He wanted to inject experimental drugs into the rats without handling them, so that stress was eliminated as a factor. Sam was the first experimenter to use drug delivery tubes for this purpose. He became renowned as a world expert at putting tubes into animals.

To produce cancer in the rats, Sam would inoculate cancer cells on each side of the rat's jaw. Once the tumours developed, Sam would permanently install two tubes into each rat. The rat was put under anaesthetic while the tubes were fitted. The technicians would insert the tubes either side of the carotid artery on just one side of the rat's neck. They put the ends of the tubes into each rat using collars over which the girls inserted stitches, so that the tubes couldn't pull out. There was about a metre of tube coming up out of the cage and at the outer end, we fitted a syringe. At first the rat was upset by the tube, but soon became accustomed to it. Sam sealed the end of the tube closest to the rat with a wax stopper and then filled the tube with the experimental drug.

Sam had two cages made, connected by a tunnel that was fitted with a door. The rats lived in one cage and food was placed in the other. We embedded a photo-electric cell with an ultra-high frequency light into the roof of the adjoining tunnel. At set times, we opened the door, allowing the rat access to food. As it passed

180

through the tunnel, the light ray melted the wax stopper in the tube, allowing the drug to flow down the syringe and automatically release a dose into the rat.

We had drugs specially made for us – seven or eight of them with a short half-life. Through one tube, we delivered a drug that increased the permeability of the area around one tumour. The other tube would release the experimental drug into the same area. Because that drug had a very short half-life, it was delivered to only one side of the rat's body. It took seventeen seconds for the blood to circulate through the rat from one side of the jaw to the other and the half-life of the drug was only eight seconds. The active drug going into the blood on one side would lose its efficacy by the time it reached the control cancer on other side of the jaw.

This meant we had a treatment and a control within each rat. That was just one example of Sam Rose's brilliance. The Americans paid us to do this research in Melbourne. Later, Sam wrote a paper about his research.

~

When I took over the laboratory, some of the technicians were causing trouble. Jan and Bobby, both trained nurses, were employed there when I started. Most of the time, Jan worked on rat livers for another project. Bobby was doing only four operations per day, and wandering off for a couple of hours at a time. Mary and Anna were new employees that I put on for surgery. I wasn't happy with the number of rats they were operating on either; I reckoned they should be able to do ten in a day. If one had to go up the street on an errand, the other would go too, and they'd stay away for much longer than necessary. They were not doing a fair day's work. As head technician of the lab, it was my job to pull them into line.

I placed an advertisement in the paper stating: "Surgery on live rats in cancer research laboratory. Educational standard not required. Must be dexterous."

To test for dexterity, I timed the applicants picking fifty pins out of a bowl. I employed one girl, who worked pretty fast, but wasn't the fastest. She wasn't quite as bright as a couple of the other applicants, but I thought she wouldn't get bored as easily. I asked the other lab girls to teach Dora what to do. I told them not to tell her how many operations she needed to perform.

'I expect ten rat operations per day from you,' I told her.

Dora produced ten after three days. When she started to do ten, the other three smartened themselves up and, altogether, we were doing forty operations per day.

I still had trouble with Mary though. I found that she would just disappear. One day I went chasing her and I found her in a part of the university about two hundred yards away from our lab.

'Listen, if I find you not operating, I'll presume you've gone to the toilet. If you're not back within twenty minutes, I'm going to dock your pay.'

She wasn't there one day, and I rang up the paymaster and told him to dock her for the hour and a half she was missing. When she received her pay at the end of the week, she stood against the table looking at her pay sheet for an awfully long time. I couldn't stand it any longer.

'Is your pay a bit different?'

'Yes.'

'I docked you for an hour and half for when you were away on Tuesday.'

After that, Mary's daily work output improved.

Sam had taught the girls to insert the tubes into the rats and also to do anastomosing [joining up blood vessels]. They were very good at it. I'd already done surgery in New Guinea, so I was rubber necking to see how they were doing the anastomosing. When she saw my interest, Jan showed me how it was done. Rat veins are very small, so these girls were exceptionally good at joining blood vessels.

However, the girls were not so clever at making the tubes we needed to deliver the drugs. Judy started a business making them and Sam was most impressed with their quality.

'These are the best tubes I've ever seen,' he told me.

~

While I was at Melbourne University, I designed and built a centrifuge for washing blood. Until then, the technicians washed blood by hand to rid it of bacteria and viruses. We mixed a saline solution with the blood, spun it in a centrifuge, causing the clean blood cells to drop to the bottom, then we poured off the saline. This procedure had to be repeated five times; it was time

182

consuming and arduous. The machine I designed washed the blood automatically, allowing the clean red and white blood cells to be isolated from any impurities that might interfere with our research. I wrote a paper about this machine, which I presented at a conference in Melbourne in 1971.

I also built a centrifuge which we used to separate the white blood cells from the lymphatic fluid. White blood cells are used in the body's immune system. Both of these machines were very useful in cancer research.Ian Loder, another technician working with me, insisted I should patent these machines and sell them.

'Designing, building and patenting a machine is easy,' I told Ian. 'Selling something requires a special skill. You go out and see if you can sell my design.'

Ian went out and sold the centrifuge design to Varian Techtron, the Melbourne branch of a large American manufacturer of scientific instruments. We took out a provisional patent first. That gave us world-wide protection for a year. Later, Varian Techtron took patents on my behalf in Australia, the USA, Japan and eleven other countries. When manufactured, the centrifuge was stamped with the words "Made in Australia" and "Kerby Continuous Flow Centrifuge." Sam Rose became quite surly. He didn't like my success with these machines. He especially did not like my name on the machine.

~

Roy Wright was the Professor of Physiology at Melbourne University. He was knighted, so he became "Sir Roy." Roy Wright became more and more dissatisfied with Sam Rose and wanted rid of him from his department. Sam had personality problems. He was very good at selling himself and his projects to get finance for them, but he seldom finished anything. During 1967, Professor Wright dismissed Sam from Melbourne University and the next year, the whole project was shut down.

Sam went off to the USA, where he found work in Texas, at the Anderson Clinic in Galveston. He submitted a paper about the Melbourne cancer research while he was working at the Anderson Clinic, but it was published after he moved to work at the Salk Institute.

After the Melbourne University project was closed down, I applied to Monash University to work there as a senior laboratory technician, taking up my position in 1969. I also kept working on Sam's cancer research in a "garage" I built on the Pier, with Ian Loder as my assistant. It was, in fact, a workshop and laboratory, where we kept and operated on sheep. A mate from the Florey Institute instructed me on surgery with sheep. I would have a doctor from CSIRO come down to the Pier to do my post mortems

Before the garage was completed, one night we operated on a sheep in the Kiosk lounge room. We had a twelve year old girl visitor, who assisted with the anaesthetic. We wanted to insert a tube into the sheep's lungs. Ian intubated the sheep, then placed the end of the tube to his ear to listen for stomach noise, in case the tube was misplaced. It was. The sheep coughed and Ian received an earful of half -digested stomach contents.

At school, Lisa reported her holiday activity. The teacher wouldn't believe she had participated in operating on a sheep on St Kilda Pier.

At first, I was scratching for money to pay Ian a salary for his work. One day, Harry Rose, Sam's brother, and his friend Dick Ginter, a peanut farmer from New Guinea, came down to the Pier to see how our work there was progressing. They decided that Ian and I shouldn't have to worry about money. A couple of days later, they came back and took me to the local branch of Dick's bank, to open an account from which I could draw money as needed for our research. We drew on that account until Sam Rose moved to San Diego.

The Salk Institute

In 1969, Sam was invited to the Salk Institute in San Diego, California, to give a lecture about his research. Dr Jonas Salk, the founder of the institute, had developed the polio vaccine during the 1950's. Many well-known researchers came to his research institute to give presentations. Dr Salk paid Sam's fare and accommodation. Sam wove his spell over Salk while he gave his presentation and I was told later that Salk was on the edge of his seat during Sam's talk.

'I have a technician in Melbourne making this equipment now.'

He was referring to me and our work on centrifuges. The tense was what fascinated Dr Salk. Sam had said "*now*". It was going on now, and Jonas Salk wanted to be part of it. He investigated Sam, reading his thirty-nine published papers. He was very impressed. Sam was good at writing these papers. Dr Salk found he was happy with Sam Rose as a scientist and he invited Sam to work at the institute, to start cancer research there.

At that stage, Salk didn't know about Sam's personality weakness. Apart from not finishing his projects, he was a frustrated engineer. He cooked up all sorts of things that were spectacular from a showmanship point of view, but didn't necessarily add to his research.

Armand Hammer, a billionaire, had come to the Salk Institute and told Jonas Salk that he'd give the institute money to find the cure for cancer in his lifetime, so he'd get the kudos for having financed it. He told Dr Salk he could have five million dollars to get started.

After he heard Sam Rose talk, Dr Salk knew that he could get those funds immediately. He knew he wanted Sam there and that I was in Melbourne working on the research. Salk panicked. He also wanted me over from Melbourne. Just in case I cracked the cure for cancer first, Dr Salk wrote a letter to me saying he wanted to name the Kiosk garage "The Salk Institute of the Western Provinces."

Soon after Sam arrived to work at the Institute in early 1970, Jonas Salk opened the Salk Cancer Research Center. Dr Salk gave Sam money to send to me, so I could continue my work on sheep in the garage on the Pier. Salk told Sam he wanted me in San Diego too.

'I can't come. I'm a small cog in a big wheel, but I'm needed here,' I told Sam at first. I had been building a kidney preserving machine for Dr Gabriel Reisner and also working on liver transplant research at The Alfred Hospital.

Later, I changed my mind about going to America, because I was still a great admirer of Sam's work. I went on leave of absence from my job at Monash University from March until December 1970, flying to the USA to work as technician for Sam Rose and Jonas Salk and taking one of our continuous flow centrifuges with me. Ian

Smith, a young man I knew, worked at Monash in my place. Judy stayed behind in St Kilda, looking after the Kiosk and our many pets. It was a long separation and we missed each other a great deal.

~

At the Salk Institute, I met the billionaire Armand Hammer, who was financing our work. He was a remarkable man who, as a young adult, had trained in medicine, but never worked as a doctor. Once, he had been a friend of Lenin. When I met him, he was about seventy-five years old.

Armand Hammer, Sam Rose and Col Kerby.

'How did you make your first million, doctor?' I asked him.

'I found out how to make vitamins, Col, so I made vitamin pills for the sucker market. Before I finished medicine, I'd made my first million.'

That was going back nearly sixty years. He was an old man when I met him.

Armand Hammer owned an oil rig in the North Sea called Piper Alpha. On 6th July, 1988, it blew up and killed two hundred and sixty-five men. He was the sole owner. Ten days after the explosion and before the insurance money came through, he paid two years full salary to every family of those who died there. He was a very generous man.

Mexico

I'd been in San Diego only about four days when the secretary of the Salk Institute, Bessie, invited me on a trip to Mexico. Bessie was about fifty-five.

'We're going down to Mexico. We want to catch some little crayfish and to sleep on the beach. Would you like to come?'

'Yes, I would. I'd like to go.' Having come from Australia, I wasn't going to pass up an opportunity to visit Mexico.

The two older women, Bessie and her friend and Bessie's nephew Steve, who was eighteen or so, the other woman's daughter, a three legged Labrador and I went on the trip. They all wanted to sleep on the beach, so we drove onto the sand and bogged the car. I was the only one who, in my opinion, was sensible: I took a big sleeping pill with me. That way, I was the only one who had a good night's sleep on the sand. The others didn't.

Early in the morning, not long after daylight, I awoke to hear a woman speaking very rapid Spanish in a shrill voice. The others could speak Spanish. It turned out it was a local woman who lived in a cardboard hut on the beach, not far away from where we were camped. Our two women were arguing with her. She was claiming that their dog had killed her chicken. She wanted four dollars compensation

'Where is this chicken? Let's have a look at it,' I said.

She went away and came back with a seagull that had been dead for quite a time.

'This is a hold up, I said. 'This bird's a seagull that's been dead for months. I wouldn't pay her.'

She changed her tune then. The dog had entered her chicken coop and frightened all of her chickens. Bessie's friend decided she would go and have a look at the chickens.

'Go with her.' Bessie said to me.

I was still in my sleeping bag, so I pulled my trousers on, stood up and followed them. The dog came too. The woman went into the hen house and came back with a chook that was alive. She pulled the feathers back and showed me a rash.

'That's not a bite,' I said.

'Well, you're the scientist, what's wrong with it?' the American woman said.

'Christ, that's the first chook I've seen close-up in my life. How do I know?'

The Mexican woman had a daughter. She spoke to her daughter and the daughter went inside and came back with a single barrelled shotgun. She broke it open and put in a cartridge.

'You are a pain in the neck,' said Bessie's friend, starting to walk away.

'Don't walk away from her when she's holding a gun,' I told her.

We stood together.

'If she cocks that gun,' I whispered, 'I'll have to knock her out.'

The two of them kept arguing. In the meantime, the dog went back to the others and Steve opened the car door and shut the dog inside. The older Mexican woman took the gun and went up to the car. I kept right beside her.

'The dog can't get out. It's locked in,' I said.

She opened the door and the dog flew out. She made as though to cock the gun, but didn't actually do it. She put a cigarette in her mouth, so I struck a match for her, then I caught the dog and put him back into the car. If I'd had my wallet with me, I'd have given her four dollars.

'You're stupid,' Steve told her.

That made her annoyed.

'Buzz off, for Christ's sake. She has a gun!' I said.

Bessie came back and started to bargain with her.

'Dos?' [Two].

The Mexican woman agreed, so Bessie gave her two dollars and away she went.

~

We pushed the car out of the sand, off the beach and drove slowly along the foreshore. Another car was coming along the roadway behind us. The young girl was in the back seat.

'Oh no,' I heard her say.

The other car had locked its wheels. It swept sideways towards us, skidded past, bounced and landed on the median strip in the centre of the road. The others wanted to go on.

'No, pull up. The driver might be sick, or even dead,' I said.

Reluctantly, they pulled up and I ran back. A man stepped out of the car. Our teenage girl had been watching him. She told me later that the driver had seemed almost asleep at the wheel. Suddenly, he had seen us there.

'Are you all right?' I asked him.

He spoke quite good English to me. He said he was all right. He looked at his car. The wheels were either side of the median strip. I suggested I should get a tow truck for him, but a Mexican turned up, wearing a sombrero. He came over. They conversed in Spanish. On the way back to his car, he spoke to me.

'I'd advise you, Senor, not to stay. He's all right. Police will come. They will arrest you as a witness. I would advise you to go.'

I went back to the car and we left. The Yanks are petrified about the Mexicans. There's no habeas corpus in Mexico. The Mexican police can lock you up for two years without a charge.

~

Later, a painter at the Salk Institute told me about going to Mexico and sleeping on the beach. He woke up with a coyote standing over him. He roared at the coyote and it bit him on the face. He chased the coyote, killed it and cut off its head, which he took back with him. They tested the head at the institute; it was rabid and he'd been bitten. They gave him anti rabies vaccine, but he was sick for a year and they nursed him at the institute. If I'd heard that before I went with Bessie, I doubt I would have gone. In the States, people were supposed to have their dogs immunized against rabies, but not in Mexico.

~

Sometimes, I would drive from San Diego down to the Mexican border, leave my car on the US side and walk across to have coffee and donuts at Woolworths. It wasn't worthwhile taking your car in, because it took hours to get back through customs again. There were always long queues. If they decide to check out your car, they take everything out, then you have to load it all back in again.

It gets very hot in the south west USA and Mexico. I always wore only shorts, a singlet and shoes. I wore shoes, never sandals, in case I needed to run. I would walk around the back streets of Tijuana and being quite tanned, with my olive skin and black hair, I looked quite Spanish. The local shop keepers couldn't quite make me out. They

189

didn't know if I was a local or a tourist. Mostly, they didn't harass me.

One night, I was in a dark lane and a fellow approached me hesitantly. He must have decided I was a Yank.

'Do you want a girl?'

'How much?'

'Three dollars.'

'How much for two?' I asked

'Two girls, six dollars. Do you have a friend?' he asked.

'No. Two girls for me.' Although I hadn't seen anyone else in the lane, I said, 'A fellow further down the lane said his girls are two dollars.'

'My girls are better than his girls.'

'Well, I've to go back to work, so another time,' I said.

I told Bessie at work about the encounter. She said, 'You'd better watch yourself in situations like that. You'll get a knife in you.'

'No, I can run like hell. They'd be going to catch me.'

~

When I took a trip home, Sam came to see me off at the airport. We climbed into a taxicab and Sam started to talk cancer research to the cab driver. Sam explained his ideas and the driver became engrossed.

'If I took a little scratch of duco from a thousand cabs, and mixed it all up in a pot and put a little of it back on all the cabs, it would be something like the paint taken originally,' Sam explained. He was using duco as an analogy for antibodies. One line of Sam's research was looking to find a vaccination against a form of cancer. To immunise against a serious illness, we used mixed bacteria that had been killed and altered so they were not exactly the same as those we were fighting in the body, but were sufficiently similar to initiate the immune response.

We arrived at the airport after a twenty minute ride and the driver said, 'Then what happens to the antibody?' He was talking cancer research.

Jeese, Sam's good. Presumably, the driver had never before had any interest in cancer research, nor any passenger in his cab talk about it.

~

Jonas Salk went away on his honeymoon. When he returned, he interviewed Sam Rose and found he had made no progress towards finding a drug to conquer cancer of any variety. Instead, he had spent money on trying to duplicate my centrifuge. Sam really disliked the fact that I had patented the centrifuge in my name. Despite Sam's brilliance, Dr Salk dismissed him.

Dr Salk interviewed me the next day. He expressed his anger about Sam and showed me the receipts for Sam's expenditure.

'What do you make of all these items, Col?' Dr Salk asked, 'Do you think Sam is trying to build his own centrifuge?'

'Yes Dr Salk; that is what it looks like to me.'

'I'm putting Sam off the project, but I would like you to stay on for another six months and continue the work. Would you be prepared to do that?'

'I'm sorry, Dr Salk, I really must return to Melbourne. I went home recently for a short visit and I know my mother is dying. I would like to be with her for the last weeks of her life. My wife needs me at home too.'

We found a solution to the problem for Dr Salk. My friend and colleague, Ian Loder and his family moved to San Diego. Ian took over my job at the Salk Institute.

Jonas Salk: Photo he gave to Col.

Before I left San Diego, Jonas Salk gave me a signed photograph of himself and a wonderful reference. (See preface.)

~

Françoise Gilot, the woman Jonas Salk married, was once Picasso's partner. Paloma Picasso is the daughter of Françoise and Picasso and I met her at the Salks' home. We became friendly and when Paloma expressed an interest in learning to surf, I offered to teach her. I had learned to surf in New Guinea, when I was a teenager. Many of the young fellows up there surfed on those very long boards. I was no expert at surfing myself, but I did teach Paloma to stay up on the board in gentle waves. She was very happy with her achievement.

Transplant Preservation Machines

When my contract with the Salk Institute in San Diego was nearing its close, Professor Jim Watts, my boss at Monash University, wrote to me, requesting that, before returning to Australia, I go to San Francisco to see the Belzer Kidney Preserving Machine, to the East coast to visit a company in Chicago and also to see Dr Colibo in Washington DC. I agreed to go if he would supply money for petrol to drive there. He sent me $350 to cover my expenses.

I drove to a hospital in San Francisco, where I introduced myself to the Australian surgeon, Dr David Scott and to Dr Belzer, a kidney transplant surgeon, who had developed the Belzer Kidney Preserving Machine. My professor had asked me to look at it carefully, because if I found it satisfactory, he wanted me to build one for our department.

When I inspected the machine, I was not at all impressed. The machine was very large, very heavy, difficult to move and very expensive. Belzer priced his machine at AUD $22,000. In my opinion, it was designed very much like an agricultural machine. All up, it weighed just under half a tonne. It was built on a trolley and the refrigeration unit contained a sealed compressor that would have met the needs of a small butcher's shop – all for the purpose of cooling two human kidneys from the ambient temperature in a hospital room (24ºC) down to 8ºC.

As a kidney preserving unit has to be transported from the donor's hospital to the recipient's hospital, a fork lift was required at each hospital to handle the machine in and out of the transport units. In the case of air transport, money is a consideration.

Dr David Scott, who had been working with Belzer, was in raptures about this unit. Scott was due to return to Melbourne to work in our Monash Department of Surgery under Professor Jim Watts. He wanted Watts to buy one of the Belzer machines.

'Have you ever seen any other kidney preserving machines?' I asked him.

'No,' he told me.

After that I left, continuing on my journey to the Eastern states, as requested by Professor Watts. I visited one of our suppliers in Chicago, to discuss the design of the product they supplied to us.

Next, I drove down to the National Institutes of Health in Washington DC, to meet Dr Kollibo, who had developed a more efficient heart-lung machine than we had.

Our heart lung-machine was not good enough to keep a patient alive for more than a short period, which was usually long enough when we were doing a transplant operation. It was a different situation when we needed to keep the patient alive longer than thirty-six hours.

The force of the seat belt people are wearing in vehicle accidents can squeeze fat cells out of their tissues and into their blood vessels. Our heart-lung machine could separate out the fat cells and restore their blood, but it was a slow process and required several days of filtering. Dr Kollibo's heart-lung machine could quickly cope with oxygenating blood for many days. He had done a remarkable thing: he submerged a live sheep into a tank of saline, keeping the sheep's blood oxygenated using his heart-lung machine.

Kollibo used a seamstress to make a special filter for his machine. This involved using a very fine piece of gauze, like wedding veil material, which this very talented lady coated in an extremely thin layer of silicone, about .01 mm thick. His filter was much more efficient at cleaning the fat cells out of blood, than anything else we were aware of. Professor Jim Watts wanted me to examine this machine too and make something like it upon my return to Monash. I was very keen to continue building better machines for medical research.

My mother passed away within a couple of weeks of my return to Melbourne from the USA. Mum died of pancreatic cancer aged eighty, in December 1970, thirteen years after Dad's death. Although I grieved for my mother, my grief was not as deep as it had been for my father.

12 Kidney and Liver Transplants

Medical Research at Monash

Let's back track nearly two years here. When the cancer research at Melbourne University was shut down at the end of 1968, I applied to Monash University Department of Surgery and was accepted to work as senior technical officer under Professor Jim Watts. There were two major projects under way. One involved working to improve liver transplants in humans and the other involved kidney preservation and subsequent transplantation. I started in early 1969, assisting with liver transplants on pigs at The Alfred Hospital.

A few of us from the lab went over to Prince Henry's Hospital to set up a new Monash Department of Surgery research laboratory. Although the main hospital had been there for many years (it was previously called the Homeopathic Hospital), the Department of Surgery for Monash at Prince Henry's Hospital was a new building, just being erected. As the senior technical officer, I was given $150,000 to set up the research operating theatre for us and the university also built an animal house.

During the move to the new research laboratory, I injured my right knee. Four of us were shifting a very solid bench. The fellow at the same end as me tripped and fell over. I was worried that the end of the bench would fall on him and crush his head, so I took all the weight. In doing that, I tore ligaments in my knee. The university was very good about it and they put money away in a fund for me so that I could have an operation for knee reconstruction when I needed it. After forty years, I've finally decided not to put up with the pain any more. There's $24,000 sitting in an account waiting for me to use it.

I went to my GP recently and asked him about getting the operation done. I asked him how many of his patients had received knee jobs. He tapped at his computer, then told me fifty-one. I thought that seemed a reasonable sample, so I asked him to recommend a surgeon. He sent me off for x-rays. When the girl was doing them, I asked, 'Can you tell from the picture, how much pain a person would be having?'

'Yes.'

'How does my knee look?'

'It couldn't get any worse.'

'So I haven't been whinging without cause?'

'No.'

Unfortunately, when I had my quadruple heart by-pass in 2002, the doctors removed a vein from my right leg. Since my accident when I was nineteen, that leg has been without a femoral artery. The vascular supply to my leg is barely enough to enable a knee reconstruction to be performed. I suppose when I was in my early eighties, having the bypass operation, the doctors thought I wouldn't live all that many years longer and that it didn't matter from which leg they took the vein. It certainly matters to me now. I might be only a few months away from ninety, but I've plenty of life in me yet – possibly ten or more years.

~

At The Alfred Hospital, the surgeons and technicians taught me to do isolated liver perfusions and liver transplants. For this, we purchased live pigs from the abattoirs. We'd have two pigs and using proper surgical procedures, two teams operated simultaneously, taking the liver out of a pig. We'd transplant one liver into the other pig. The first pig would be humanely dispatched and its meat distributed to the staff. We put aside the spare liver for further research.

I built a heart-lung machine for the transplants. We kept alive the liver that would otherwise have been discarded by using the lung part of the machine to oxygenate the blood, which was then pumped through the liver. I would perform isolated perfusions with one of the PhD staff members. We tested the liver with various drugs to see what effect they had. Each drug was pumped through the liver and the academic wrote a paper about the effect it had. An increase in blood pressure going through the liver was the main indicator of the drug effect. If the blood pressure became too high, that drug was fundamentally bad for the liver.

Our department was aiming to be the first to make a successful liver transplant on a human being. We were very close when a doctor at the Austen Hospital in Melbourne made the first transplant. Although we were pleased to know it was achievable, we were disappointed not to be first. By this time, we had done more than one hundred and fifty liver transplants on pigs.

We passed on the knowledge gained from our research to young surgeons. Members of the team demonstrated surgical procedures and wrote papers for publication. As senior officer, my job included improving the equipment in instrumentation and anaesthetics.

Shortly after I arrived at Monash, a very interesting event occurred. A patient in The Alfred Hospital's maternity department experienced liver failure soon after giving birth. She was dying. A young nurse knew about the liver transplant research we were doing in the Surgical Research Department. She made the suggestion to her superior that we could temporarily use a pig's liver for this woman. The suggestion was passed on to the Head of Department, who authorised us to try.

We took a pig's liver and hooked it up to her blood via one of our heart-lung machines. After six hours, the woman came out of her moribund state and uttered a word. As the pig's liver cleaned her blood, the woman gradually recovered. After a few days, her own liver spontaneously began to work. That patient recovered fully and I later found out that a couple of years later,she successfully gave birth to another child. That experiment was not repeated for many years. About thirty years later, a similar event took place in the United States, to great acclaim in the media.

~

When I first arrived at the Monash laboratory, located in the Prince Alfred Hospital, I was like a black man in a white community, because I'd come over from Melbourne University. The conversation in the tea-room was always very stilted when I was about.

Just across the hallway, a surgeon was building something. Like a magnet to steel, I found myself dragged over to investigate what he was doing. The surgeon was Dr Gabby Reisner.

'What are you building?' I asked.

'A kidney-preserving machine.'

I questioned Dr Reisner about his machine.

'Are you working in stainless steel and glass?'

'Yes'

'Mmmm. I'm sorry to tell you those are not the best materials you could have chosen. Who instructed you?'

'Barnard[1]. He's written a paper about it.'

While I was employed at Melbourne University, I had pumped more body fluids – blood and lymph – than anyone else in the world. For someone like me, who'd done all these procedures before, I could see the instructions were quite inadequate. They were not detailed engineering directions.

At The Alfred Hospital, we had one theatre for use by the Department of Surgery, where I was employed as an assistant in our kidney transplant project. Using healthy dogs, we'd take a kidney out of a dog, put it in the kidney preserver in the cooler overnight or even for two days, then we'd put the kidney back into the same dog. The dog was still okay, because it had its other kidney. However, we'd then remove the other kidney and if the dog lived, we'd say that it had been a successful transplant. I thought the procedure was very sensible, because most of the dogs were still healthy after their ordeal.

If you want to do a kidney transplant on a human, you remove a kidney from a donor, alive or newly dead. The kidney has to be preserved until you can transplant it into the recipient. The mechanics of getting the kidney to a recipient in an operating theatre can be a problem.

Once you have the kidney, it must be preserved in something like a heart-lung machine, but with a method to keep it cool. It may have to be transported thousands of kilometres. Preparation of the recipient for a transplant is not always easy either. If your recipient has just had a big meal, you can't operate; nor can you operate

[1.] *Dr Christian Barnard, who performed the world's first heart transplant.*

immediately if the recipient is in a different state or country. We had to find a way of keeping the kidney alive. We needed an effective kidney-preserving machine.

Dr Reisner paid no attention to me. He ignored my advice and built his machine. In his paper, Dr Barnard stated, "You place a pump here." He didn't say what kind of pump. Gabby Reisner had a Sarens pump, a rotary pump, which was no good for this purpose, because it crushes the blood cells, leading to haemolysis. This was a serious problem.

Moreover, Reiner's Sarens pump would produce seven litres per minute at maximum speed and we needed to pump only two millilitres per minute to keep the organ alive. The pump had a variac, a mechanism which altered the speed of the motor. Gabby was hoping to slow the machine down sufficiently to pump two millilitres per minute. However, if there was any change in the flow of electricity, if someone turned on a heater in the next room or turned one off, it interfered with the flow of electricity to his pump. Sometimes the motor would stop or else it would speed up. I supposed Dr Reisner knew what he was doing. He went ahead and finished building the machine.

Dr Reisner was having considerable trouble with his Sarens pump. One day, I went into the theatre and, Dr Gabby Reisner, a fully qualified surgeon, gowned up and sterile, was sitting on the floor, looking very distressed. He was staring at a dog's kidney, which was greatly enlarged. The Sarens pump was far too erratic for the job demanded of it and it had been going too fast.

I left him there and went straight home to the Kiosk. In the garage at home, I had several pumps, which I had been using in the sheep experiments. Ian was working in our laboratory on the Pier.

'Do you need this pump? Can I take it?' I asked.

'No, I don't need it. You take it.'

I took the pump and Gabby was still on the floor when I returned.

'Gabby, have a look at this.'

I picked up a beaker, filled it with water and put in the hose for suction and the outlet in the sink

'What's that?'

'Have a look.'

I turned the pump on and one drop came out of the tube, then another drop and another – one millilitre, two millilitres. The maximum it would put out was about twenty millilitres per minute.

'That's the sort of pump I need.'

'That's what I've been trying to bloody well tell you. You can have a loan of this one for a few days.'

'You seem to know what's going on with this business of mine,' Gabby said to me a while later.

'Yeah, I do.'

'I'll make you a proposition. If you can build me a kidney preserving machine that works, we'll write a common paper. We'll publish the paper together.'

That was an extraordinary offer from a surgeon to a laboratory technician.

'Yes, All right, I'll do that.'

I built an effective kidney-preserving machine for Gabby and he kept his promise. With my kidney preserving machines and pumps, Gabby's experiments worked. He wrote the paper about the kidney-preserving machine, and while I was in the States the next year, he posted it over for me to check and sign. It was published the next year, 1971, in the Australia and New Zealand Annals of Surgery, with me as the second author, cited as Colin Kerby, Senior Technical Officer. Everyone said it wouldn't happen, but it did.

~

When I started at Monash, there was a pump in the basement, which no one had been able to make go satisfactorily. I worked on that machine for a long time and eventually I managed to get it pulsatile rather than working as a continuous pump. Dr Avni Sali came down to the theatre.

'How did you get that thing to work?'

'I went down on my knees facing Mecca and said three times, "Please make it work.".'

'If you did that, it wasn't worth two bob, because Mecca's not that way,' Avni retorted.

Avni was one of the first doctors trained at Monash. He was an Australian born Muslim of Albanian immigrant parents. He and I became extremely good friends. When I met him, he was fully qualified, but for having his FRACS [Fellow of the Royal College of Australian Surgeons]. He was working in the theatre getting experience and gained that surgery qualification very soon after I stopped working at Monash. Avni worked for the Department of Surgery, as did I, at the Prince Henry's Hospital.

Avni's Wedding

Avni invited Judy and me to his wedding, but he didn't invite his Professor, Jim Watts.

'You'll be going to Avni's wedding, won't you?' the office girls asked Professor Watts.

'No I'm not going.'

'Why not?'

'Because I wasn't bloody well invited.'

Avni is an unusual man. He is very straight down the line. He worked under our Professor, but didn't like him, although he was friendly with Philip Hunt, Professor's Watt's deputy and also with most of the other staff.

Avnis's was the only Muslim wedding Judy and I have been to. It was held in the University chapel, used by all religions. As we were waiting in the congregation, we heard a cry of someone shouting from a distance and it came gradually closer and closer. I thought it was part of the ceremony.

'Isn't that interesting,' I whispered to Judy. 'It's like someone advertising the marriage, rather like a town crier.'

As the sound came nearer, we made out the cry. The man was calling "Washing, washing." He was collecting washing from the students who lived in on-campus university accommodation.

~

All of this happened during the year before I took leave to fly to the United States to work at the Salk Institute. I returned from my time with Dr Jonas Salk just before Christmas 1970. On my return to Monash University in the New Year, I resumed my work in kidney and liver transplants under Professor Watts at the Alfred and Prince Henry's Hospitals. I reported to Professor Watts about the machines I had observed before I left the States.

'Don't allow Dr Scott to buy a Belzer kidney preserving machine,' I told him. 'It is an agricultural heap and is unnecessarily expensive. The Department of Surgery cannot afford to spend $22,000 on this kidney preserving machine.'

Early in the New Year, Dr Scott arrived at Monash with a Belzer machine. We had not bought it, but David Scott was to be the salesman for Belzer, to persuade our department to pay for it. Apart from the high purchase price, the Belzer machine was impractical, because it needed a crane and a large truck or low loader to move it.

Sometimes a suitable donor was thousands of kilometres away from the recipient, who would be too ill to travel. The kidney had to be kept alive and healthy in the machine until it was transplanted and receiving blood from the new recipient. Dr Scott and I didn't see 'eye to eye' about the usefulness of the Belzer machine. I had given Professor Watts a negative report on Dr Scott's work in the USA.

About the same time, we had a deceased female kidney donor. There was a matching recipient in New Zealand. The idea was to fly the donor kidney to New Zealand in the cumbersome Belzer machine. It turned out that when the donor kidneys were removed, they proved unsuitable for transplantation, because they each had two renal arteries, instead of one. Those kidneys were anatomical freaks and were no use to us, but it would have been an expensive exercise had those kidneys been usable.

The whole incident forcefully brought home to me the importance of being able to fly a donor kidney to the recipient quickly and easily. I realised that the ideal would be to have a kidney preservation unit that could be carried onto a commercial aircraft. The best way to do that was to build a unit small enough to fit into an aircraft seat and seat a courier next to it.

'I think I could make a kidney preserver to fit into an aircraft seat. What do you think if I made a much small version of the Belzer machine?' I asked Dr Scott. I went on to explain that I could use a twelve volt car battery and preservation could be maintained for fifteen hours. Transportation of a kidney in such a machine would cost only the price of two aircraft seats, one for the machine and one for the courier. That was a minimal cost compared with the problems associated with transporting the Belzer machine.

I spoke about this idea to a number of people in the department. Nobody condemned the idea. Some asked questions about how I intended to deal with certain problems.

I measured the width between the seats in various aircraft. Sixteen and a half inches [40cm] was the narrowest. I designed a kidney preserving machine that would fit into such an aircraft seat.

As an engineer, I wasn't impressed with the cam operated piston pump used in the Belzer machine. Although it did work, for pumping blood continuously, I preferred the rotary type motor used world-wide to circulate blood in by-pass and heart transplant operations. Dr Scott preferred the Belzer cam pump. He was very keen for me to manufacture the machine I proposed and at Dr Scott's request, I used the cam pump.

As well as continuing with the cancer research on the sheep in our laboratory on the Pier, I built the miniature kidney preserving machine at home during the evenings and my daytime work with liver and kidney transplants continued at Monash.

Just as I was near completion of the miniaturised kidney preserving machine, a commercial renal unit was preparing a display of manufacturers' goods related to kidney disease. I decided to enter my machine.

My kidney preserver had cost me just over $250 for the materials to make it. Reporters from The Age and The Melbourne Sun newspapers interviewed me on the opening day of the display and published the interview, in which I stated that the machine would be sold for $500. They also photographed a girl and me carrying the unit, to demonstrate its portability.

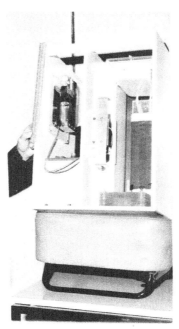

*Col's Miniaturised Kidney Preserving Machine
Capable of Fitting into an Aircraft Seat.*

Later that same year, 1971, the Ninth Annual Conference on Medical and Biological Research was held in Melbourne. I presented two papers at that conference, one about the continuous flow centrifuge I had developed and patented in Australia, USA, England, France and Italy; the other was about the blood washing centrifuge, which I had also patented. I had two hundred copies of each paper printed, to send out to people who were interested.

The annals of the conference published both my papers. I felt on top of the world. I loved my work and was excited about other projects I could work on. I had been seriously considering manufacturing an implantable artificial heart. I had huge experience in building pumps for both blood and lymph. The question of an artificial heart which could be implanted seemed wide open. I felt the next logical step in implantation was the production of an artificial heart and I believed that with my experience, I was the person most capable of designing such a heart.

My elation was not to last long. Towards the end of the year and after all my successes, I was sacked from my job. In my own time and with Dr Scott's approval, I'd rebuilt the Belzer machine so that it could be carried by one person and fit on an airline seat. The kidney-preserving machine I had built cost less than $300 for materials. I think Professor Watts was embarrassed that he had spent so much money on the big Belzer machine that didn't really serve its purpose and I suspect Dr Scott was jealous of my abilities and my successes.

Perhaps they also realised that I would patent my machine in my own name, the same as I had done with the continuous flow centrifuge and the blood washing machine.

I had been having so much success with my machines and with the papers we published, I could see myself going on with medical research for years. Now I had to leave the job I loved. I was given two weeks' notice, or I could take two weeks' pay in lieu.

I continued to work. I had projects I wanted to finish. I was furious with both Professor Watts and Dr David Scott for sacking me without warning and through no fault of mine. It is my understanding that Dr Scott told Professor Watts he would leave the department unless I was sacked. He claimed I had breached Belzer's patent. What he didn't understand is that a US patent does not cover Australia.

I was depressed to think that those fellows had enough power to kick me out when they were shown up for making mistakes. Even today, I still carry anger about my dismissal. Most doctors have very little expertise in technical developments, but they want the kudos of having their name on the machines developed by their technicians. I didn't go along with that practice. I patented my machines in my own name and was prepared to stand up and deliver papers about them.

At my appeal over the sacking, I was asked by the committee why I had chosen to continue working for the two weeks instead of just leaving and taking my pay. I explained that everyone was very busy and I had tasks to finish. They didn't seem to understand that. My being sacked in December 1971 brought an end to my medical research career.

My friend, Avni Sali, the Muslim doctor, was very annoyed and loudly outspoken about my dismissal. Much later on in his career, he became Professor of the Department of Surgery.

~

Only a month after I'd been sacked, the oven in the Kiosk exploded in Judy's face. I took Judy down to casualty at The Alfred Hospital. We had a friend staying with us who was accustomed to cooking with electricity. She had turned on the knob, but omitted to light the gas. Judy has a poor sense of smell and didn't smell the gas. When she went to light the oven, the gas exploded. Immediately, Judy was engulfed with flame. I have no idea how the synthetic frock she was wearing didn't melt to her body. Only the skin of her nose peeled off. I carried a bucket of water with ice in it with us in the car, while our guest drove us to hospital. Judy was very lucky not to have scars on her face and body after that event.

When the Surgical Department heard we were there, they came down to see if Judy was all right. I was friendly with most of them, except Professor Watts and Dr Scott. Although many of them were supportive, there was little they could do about my position, and I became very depressed. I didn't know what to do next. Judy suggested we return to building aircraft, but I had no interest in that.

Part Six: Industrial Engineering

13.. Boat Building and Engineering

Associate Professor Philip Hunt and Dr Avni Sali were very worried about me, probably with good cause. I was both murderous and suicidal. The Associate Professor at Monash considered that, with my personality, I was a suicide risk. He was right. I was thinking of double murder and suicide. I wanted to kill Professor Watts and Dr Scott, then myself.

During the fortnight's notice, while I stayed and worked, Philip Hunt mentioned this to one of my technicians. The technician came back to me.

'The Associate Prof thinks you're suicidal. In my opinion, he doesn't know what he's talking about.'

'Yes he does,' I replied.

Whether Avni Sali discussed my emotional state with Philip Hunt, I don't know, but I suspect he did. For years, I'd talked about building a boat and I had been toying with yacht design from when I was working at Melbourne University. Avni decided that the solution to my depression and being out of work was to build my boat. He jogged me into doing it and provided a large amount of practical assistance, which went a long way towards lifting my depression. I have enormous gratitude to Avni for the support he gave me at this time.

~

In 1969, before I went to The United States, we'd bought the steel and had it delivered to a place in Richmond. I had BHP Newcastle make it for me and they did the metallurgical testing to guarantee its grade: half inch Lloyd's A Grade mild steel for the hull and three sixteenth for the sides and deck. I didn't like the idea of sitting on a reef somewhere, grinding a hole through the hull. I wanted a strong hull.

After my return from the USA at the end of 1970, I had rented a state government owned bond-store warehouse on the banks of the Yarra, with the plan to build a boat. Because we were state government tenants at the Kiosk, we were able to take on another lease. We formed a sort of a club with four other keen sailors and they shared the cost of the rent and built their boats there.

Judy and I had talked about the design for a long time. Because the steel for the hull was half an inch thick, I couldn't bend it like I would the steel for the sides. I had to make a design I could use without bending the bottom sheets. I drew up a rather unorthodox design, then I took a piece of wood and made a model, one inch to the foot.

At Melbourne University, I had tank tested my model and continued playing with the design and testing it. I made up a spring scale with a pulley and a capstan, so that the resistance could be measured on the scale and took a reading. With a spoke shave, I shaved away the edges of the model to turn it into a conventional round hull. I did the test again, but the results of the original readings were better. Yachties hate the shape I ended up with, but it works.

A friend called Aub would come down to St Kilda Pier and talk to me about it.

'You have to build in wood and to a traditional design,' Aub insisted

'I disagree with that. There are so many different designs in ships and yachts. Most of them work. Besides, I'm not a carpenter, but I can weld steel.'

Aub was standing on the pier, smoking his pipe while I did this test for hull resistance in the sea on a very calm day. I showed him my test results.

'What do you think about those figures?'

'There's something not quite right.'

He was very surly. I became annoyed. I felt like punching him, but he would have punched me back.

'Christ, what's wrong with it?' I asked.

'Must have been a current.'

'It couldn't have been,' I said. 'I put some wood in the water, and it hasn't drifted away. It's still there.'

~

My design made the boat very easy to build. For the base of the hull, I had two pieces of steel 5'6" wide and 30 foot long, by ½" thick. To convert the bottom curve, I took my measurements directly onto the steel by measuring the offsets in inches on the wooden model and converting these inches to feet on the steel. I measured distances from the centre line, taking a measurement every foot [300mm], so I could mark the steel with a dob of paint where I wanted to cut. Next, I ran an oxy torch along my marks. That created the bottom of the hull and the off-cut was scrap. I welded the sheets down the centre line, in a 15º open vee.

I had some timber, about eight inches wide and three inches thick. After welding lugs onto the edges of the hull, I inserted those timbers into the lugs, so the timbers formed props on each side. The two sheets of steel for the sides of the hull were lighter. I could bend those. I clamped them onto the base at the front of the hull and, with a chain block across the stern, I pulled the steel into shape. While it was held in that position, I tack welded it all the way round.

The next step was to put in steel ribs. I welded them to the base, then tacked them to the sides. This process was the opposite of normal. Most people put the ribs on first and tack the sides to the ribs. When the structure was all tacked together, I could pull away the supporting timber. After that, I could weld the bottom and sides of the hull together.

We bashed hell out of the deck beams with a sledge hammer until I was satisfied the curve was right. We welded the beams into place and then laid two six foot wide sheets of steel on top for the deck, welding them up the centre. We had to handle it ourselves, because we didn't have any mechanical means of doing so.

Before we'd finished building our boat, we were given notice to quit the Bond store, so we finished building in a great hurry, working hard over long hours to get the hull, deck and keel finished.

Judy and I could not have built our boat in just six weeks, were it not for the Sali brothers. Avni Sali and two of his brothers, Hasset and Hismet, arrived late every afternoon and came every weekend to help. They couldn't weld, but they fetched, carried and held steel in place while I welded. Financially, their respective businesses suffered in the time they gave. They also supplied cash for equipment when I was unable to procure it. I never stopped being amazed as I watched a surgeon, a solicitor and a businessman in work clothes, sweating in the hot shed, at work using sledge hammers. Using a heavy, nine inch angle grinder, they smoothed all my welds, a particularly fatiguing procedure when working overhead. They all received small but painful injuries, as one does in industry. We still feel enormous gratitude for the support and friendship Judy and I received from them.

Professor Avni Sali

I managed to find twenty-two steel counterweights from lifts, which I placed into the keel. Those steel billets measured six inches by six inches by two feet. Around those, we stacked into the keel all the off-cuts from the building of the boat. We thought all that steel might be enough ballast. Only then did I weld the keel onto the hull, but later, we found the amount of ballast was insufficient and eventually, we added some lead.

When our yacht reached the stage of being prepared for painting, Judy sand blasted it with a half inch nozzle, which is pretty big. I filled the hopper with sand. The air blew Judy backwards to start with;. she repositioned herself and set to work. Her ability to take on practical tasks always fills me with admiration. We followed the sandblasting with four coats of paint.

Just before our lease on the bond store ran out, we were able to launch the boat. None of the fitting out had been done. We didn't even have the motor and prop installed. We hired a boat carrier to take her the quarter mile to the launch site on the Yarra. The man said he had to tie the boat on just the same as if he were taking the vessel five thousand miles. He spent two days tying her onto the loader, then he trundled her round the corner to the river bank and detached her.

Ooroo *at St Kilda Pier soon after launching, 1972.*

We pushed her into the water on 10th August 1972, just near where the Crown Casino is now. The launching went very smoothly. A friend, Henry, came down from Sydney with two bottles of champagne. He broke one over the bow, naming our vessel *Ooroo*, and Judy and some other friends drank the rest of the champagne. We towed *Ooroo* down the Yarra and tied her up in Port Phillip Bay, on the St Kilda Pier behind the Kiosk. I had rid myself of depression by the time *Ooroo* was launched, but after the launching, I didn't look at the boat again for almost five years.

Skilled Engineering

The income from the Kiosk wasn't enough for us to live on, so I needed to find other work. The day after the launching, I went to the contracting firm, Skilled Engineering. Most small firms had only one trained person for a particular position. If that technician went on holiday, the firm would go to a contractor for a temporary employee. I told them I had tickets in steam to attend to boilers and steam engines. I knew I'd be able to obtain shift work, so I could work in the daytime on the boat and at the Kiosk. I was very lucky that I could always and still can, go to sleep for ten minutes if I have some spare time. Afterwards, I wake up rested.

Skilled Engineering took me on and started sending me out to jobs a week later, on August 19th, 1972. After I had been attending boilers for a couple of years, I told the clerk who was looking after me, 'I've done fitting too. Is there any chance of my doing some fitting work?'

He asked about my experience.

'I did a thirty year apprenticeship with my father,' I told him.

Skilled Engineering sent me to all sorts of firms for fitting jobs. One of the many firms I worked for was Red Tulip. That felt odd, because many years earlier, they had wanted to go into partnership with me in my confectionary factory.

~

Insulwool, the factory that made 'rockwool', needed a fitter. To make the 'rockwool', they would crush volcanic rocks then heat them in a furnace until they became moulten. The moulten rock was poured into a centrifuge and spun until it turned into rock wool, similar to fairy floss. Glass fibres were mixed with the spun rock wool, to hold it together. This was baked in enormous ovens [40' tall by 35'wide] and it came out as a slab.

One day, Bill and I were delegated to repair one of the ovens. There was a 6'by 3' opening on the control floor near the top of the oven. I was using an oxy-torch to cut out some burnt steel where the door closed. A piece of red hot steel fell into the base of the oven and started a small fire.

Bill went upstairs to get a fire extinguisher and I lay on the floor with my head inside the oven, while I applied water from the hose. In case my glasses fell off, I placed them on the floor beside me. The hose broke, so I went to see if I could fix it. Seconds later, while I was standing near the tap, the whole oven flared. A tongue of blue flame and smoke roared twenty feet out of the door towards the stairs, just as Bill was coming down. He retreated to safety and we waited until the flame died and the smoke dispersed. All that remained of my glasses were two pieces of mangled wire. The lenses had disappeared. By seconds, once again I had escaped death.

When this incident was investigated, Management found that during shutdowns, the labourers were adding kerosene to the thick grease, which they applied to the oven walls after cleaning them. This made the grease easier to apply, but it also made it flammable.

~

Originally I went to Insulwool for only two days, but they kept me on much longer. They were doing a fairly big refurbishment of the plant.

'Would you be willing to be in charge of the refurbishment?' the boss asked me.

'I am here as a contractor,' I told him. 'You would have to ask the staff if they would accept me, a contractor, as foreman over them.'

The union called a meeting and it was agreed they would accept me temporarily as their foreman. I was paid more money for this role and so Skilled Engineering also received more money.

I learned much more about the plant then. The teeth on the rock crushing blades were wearing out every couple of weeks. I suggested to them they alter the blades by welding some hardened steel against the teeth. They agreed to alter it according to my suggestions. I bought a packet of hard facing material and welded it on. The teeth didn't wear out nearly so fast against the rocks and, after about a month, most of the hard facing was left and the other material was gone.

I also worked on their centrifuge, because they had continual breakdowns with it. Of course, they had no idea of the work I'd done with centrifuges. This one was water cooled and not very big – no more than half a metre in diameter. The seals for the cooling water would break down. It depended upon the fitter on duty as to how long fitting new seals kept all the employees off their duties. It could take twenty to thirty minutes to repair, depending on how quickly the fitter worked, his skills and a certain amount of luck.

Approximately twenty-eight people would be playing cards while they waited for the machine to be repaired. The plant operated twenty-four hours a day, seven days a week, so it was very expensive when this centrifuge kept breaking down. For that period of time, those workers did nothing productive. They were using steel washers for seals and the machine broke down three or four times each twenty-four hours and

'Why don't you use plastic or fibre washers?' I asked the chief engineer. 'They might give a little, making a better seal.'

'No, it wouldn't work,' he said.

This went on for many months. On my day off, Judy and I went to the city, where I decided to buy some plastic for washers. I paid $1.60 for a small piece of plastic. With my lathe, I turned up enough washers for the centrifuge. The next time it broke down, I put my plastic washers in. It worked for ten days without a breakdown. All the other fitters knew what I'd done, but the chief engineer didn't know. Lindsey, one of the fitters, was in the office one day when the production lists were out on the desk.

'Look at the production we've had,' he said, pointing to the lists.

'We haven't had a breakdown in over eight days,' said the engineer.

'I know why.'

'Why?' the engineer asked.

'You're not going to like this,' said Lindsey. 'You know that idea Col had about plastic washers? He put some in last week.'

I could see them talking through the window. I wondered what Lindsey was talking about.

Lindsey told me later that the chief engineer had asked him, 'How many people know about this?'

'Not many; only two or three,' he told the engineer.

The combination of these two repairs to equipment, which reduced frequent stoppages in production, was extremely embarrassing for the chief engineer.

'You've made me look a fool,' he said. 'I'm sacking you.'

'All right. Do you mind if I use your phone?'

Without waiting for his response, I picked up the receiver and dialled the number for Skilled Engineering.

'I'm finished here. Where should I report on Monday? Email White Goods? Yes, I'll be there at 7.00 am.' That took the wind out of the sails of the chief engineer. I stood up to go.

'I'd like to shake your hand,' he said to me.

'Don't be stupid. You've just sacked me.'

His outstretched hand trembled. After I left his office, I went to the Manager and complained about my dismissal. For the second time, I was dismissed because I could do something better than my boss. I felt very indignant and my anger with Professor Watts and Dr Scott resurfaced.

Lindsey worked there for many years and we stayed in touch with him. In the following eleven years, that machine never broke down. I saved them over three hundred thousand dollars every year. The washers cost me about forty cents each. I heard later that the engineer had moved on to another job.

Skilled Engineering continued to employ me. I started at Email the next week. To my surprise, immigrant women welders were employed at that company. Female welders are still rare in Australia.

~

Another job I was sent to was at Smorgen's. Socially, I knew one member of the Smorgen family. My acquaintance's brother, Sam, went to America, where he bought a small steel works, shipped it to Melbourne and I helped set it up there. I worked on the boilers for him. Sam Smorgen manufactured all sorts of things. He had an abattoir, a small-goods factory and also made paper. The factory operated twenty-four hours per day. One morning a woman rang up.

'My husband didn't come home from his 3-11pm shift last night. Is he working overtime?' she asked.

The office staff checked up. He wasn't there. The supervisor found he hadn't checked out from his shift. Eventually, they discovered him. He'd fallen into the enormous rollers and was rolled up with the paper. His body fluids were oozing out of the paper roll. The workers used a forklift to carry the roll into the paddock outside. They had a funeral service and a cremation ,right there, burning the whole thing, bones and all.

~

217

One of my friends nagged at me to get a full time job.

'You should get a proper job. There's no security in working as a contractor.'

I'd gone for a higher ticket in steam in 1975 and I wanted to use it, so I left Skilled Engineering for a time to work at Carbon Black. I started there in November, 1975. The company employed me to supervise their steam engines and boilers. These were shut down only for safety reasons, because the factory operated non-stop, seven days a week.

Carbon Black made thirty-seven different kinds of carbon and soot from heavy oil. A large amount of compressed air was needed to manufacture the various types of soot. (One type of soot was used in the manufacture of vehicle tyres.) Several steam turbines were required to drive the compressors, which burned the heavy oil, so producing the soot. A bi-product of this process was a flammable gas; this gas was mixed with town gas to fire the boilers producing the steam, which drove the turbines that drove the air compressors.

When I first entered the factory, I noticed the sign at the gate: "This is a very safety conscious establishment." It didn't take me long to find a number of unsafe practices. I wrote to the management about some of the conditions I saw, and they did make safety improvements. One of the obvious dangers was when a trap door dropped down and it came down to 5'6", which wasn't good for your head if you were under it. At Carbon Black, they paid for ideas that worked. I received eight payments for different safety improvements.

Carbon Black paid me good money, but I was sacked from there too! After a while I was put in charge of a nightshift. Sometimes, the gas from the town gas works next door fluctuated. If a turbine broke down or the air pressure dropped, we had to stop the boiler and not start it up again until the heating department gave us the all clear.

One morning, just after six o'clock, the air pressure dropped and I shut the boiler down. While I was waiting for my day shift colleague to come on duty, I was doing a round of the boiler house. Reno, the day shift supervisor, came in early. He clocked in at 6.15am and he started up the boiler. I received a hell of a fright and ran over to him.

'What's happened?'

'It's okay,' Reno said.

I thought he meant that he'd been told to start up. It was six thirty, so I clocked off.

I had three days off. When I came back, I couldn't find my card to clock in. I went to the security officer to ask about my card and he told me I'd been sacked, because the supervisor thought I'd started up the boiler.

'I didn't start it up,' I told him. 'Reno came in early, at 6.15. He started up.'

About a week later, I saw the Managing Director and a couple of other people in management and told them what had happened. One went away, looked at Reno's card and saw that he had checked in early that morning, just as I claimed. They reinstated me then.

I worked at Carbon Black for a total of eight months, but eventually, I became very tired of shift work, so I resigned in July 1976 and after that, I went back to Skilled Engineering.

Fitting out *Ooroo*

We started fitting out our yacht during the 1980's. Judy designed the interior. She even did the dovetailing. I'm proud of that. I bought her an electric jigsaw and she quickly mastered using it.

Judy: I went to Melbourne Technical College to learn wood work. There were ten lessons – two hours each week at night. Col took me in on the back of his motor bike. I was allowed to do only the first ten classes. This was prior to legislation against discrimination on the basis of sex and women weren't permitted to continue into the second term, so with my very limited knowledge, I had to do the best I could.

I didn't have any idea what wood to order, but I found some jettisoned timber in the sea. I rowed out about six hundred yards and tied a rope on it to tow it back. Col came down in time to help haul it out of the water onto the Pier.

Col: A friend came to me at the Kiosk to tell me that a catamaran, which had sailed from New Zealand, was being broken up, further up the Yarra. He said to come and collect some timber from it. He persisted for several days, and finally I went with him in his small truck. The material was much better than I had anticipated and I picked up a lot of spruce and Oregon, bringing home as much as his truck could carry.

We also inherited timber from Clem, who had worked backstage at the Tivoli theatre, making sets. The Tivoli had closed down and he still had lots of wood lying in his back yard. This meant Judy could look at it and see what she could do with it. I bought her a small circular saw. She became bloody good at using it.

Judy: I would have been hopeless if I'd had to order timber specially. I wouldn't have known what to order. I think now, that I built it all too heavily.

Col: Some of the timber we used was left over after the building of the animal house at Prince Henry's. The fellow who fitted out the surgical department put in too many drawers and shelves. We didn't need them all, so we took some of them out again.

'Where can we store all this stuff?' someone asked.

'I've an attic at the Kiosk. There's room there,' I told them.

We took it all down there over several days. When I was sacked, the timber was still there at the Kiosk and no one wanted it. Eventually, it went into our boat to make benches, the chart table and table top. For drawer fronts, we bought timber. We had a very big chart table, but later on, we cut that back in size and gave the rest of the timber to a friend. The drawer interiors were from salvaged timber. The fitting out took a few years.

Col: When we first built the deck, we had the hatch in the centre, but that meant Judy's galley was divided. When she started to design the interior, she realised she didn't like the hatch in that position. It was either going to divide her galley or else she'd have to have a very small galley. She didn't want either of those options, so we changed it, offsetting the hatch to the starboard side.

Judy: I made a mistake with the layout of the dinette. I didn't know enough about boat interior design. I had an L shaped dinette to start with, planning to be able to have six people sit down for dinner. For about three years, we had it like that, but, even with four people at the table, we kept hitting our knees on the storage cupboard beneath the table. I redesigned the dinette, with seats either side of the table. When I told Col of my plan, he suggested we wait until we reached Indonesia, where workmen could do it cheaply.

One day, Col changed his mind and said altering the saloon layout would be a good idea. While he was off the boat, I unscrewed and took out all the seating before he could change his mind. I moved the storage from under the table to under the settees. I am pleased I made the alterations, because we never sailed to Indonesia and I would have still been waiting.

Col and Judy on the Pier on their 25th Wedding Anniversary, 1984. The St Kilda Marina is in the background.

Melanoma

Judy spent a lot of time sun-bathing on the pier. On slow days during the sixties and seventies, she even went out between serving customers. During 1985, she developed a melanoma on the ribcage under her right breast. I noticed it and told her to see the doctor about it. She went to our GP, who told her not to worry. Eventually, I insisted she see a skin specialist. Judy went into the hospital clinic

221

and there were several doctors there. She showed the spot to one of them.

'You'd better show that man over there,' the doctor told her, indicating Dr Newton. Judy was in hospital the following morning to have the surgery.

Judy: Later, I was going back for check-ups, as you do. Again, there was a group of doctors there.

'I think there's something wrong here,' said Dr Newton. 'I think I can feel a lump.'

No one else could feel a lump and I couldn't feel it either.

'Nothing there, nothing there,' each one said.

We went to the GP, and he couldn't feel anything either.

Col: I took her down to my mate Don Rabinov. He couldn't feel a thing. Don sent Judy to Dr. Hope and he couldn't feel a lump.

Judy: Dr Newton was insistent. He operated and there was a lump there all right.

Newton was leaving Melbourne and going to England the following week, so I was extremely lucky he was there that week to find it. He removed all the lymph nodes in my right armpit, one of which proved to be malignant. They all thought I was a goner the second time.

Col: 'I was fairly philosophical about it. I was writing out an advertisement for a new cook!' Col told me.

Actually, we were very fortunate; after twenty-five years, Judy has had no further signs of melanoma.

~

For some time, we'd been talking of a big change in our lives. We planned to move on board *Ooroo,* and when we were ready, to set off on a world cruise. Once we were sure Judy's health was going to be okay, things started to come together. After Judy had finished fitting out *Ooroo*, she started dancing again with a group of ex-Tivoli friends. At first, she danced mainly for exercise and the company of her friends.

Judy: I didn't do any dancing between 1960 and about 1980, although I invited the old Tivoli crowd down to the Kiosk for frequent reunions. Only in the early 1980's did I go back to dancing classes with them. We went to Tony Bertussio's dance school in Melbourne and our group kept expanding. While we were still in Melbourne, I trained with them once a week. Tony was a big name in dancing. If someone wanted a dance troupe, they would come to him and he would send as many dancers as were needed. That was how I came to dance on television shows.

Judy with some of the Tivoli Girls at a reunion in the Kiosk

It was such a lot of fun; We all really loved it. Of course, we weren't as lithesome as we had been in our younger days and Joan wasn't with us. (She moved to New York with her husband, where she put on some shows and then she moved to Bermuda.)

I was dancing on television up until 1992, on the Don Lane Show and on other television shows. Even after we came up to Newcastle, I still went back and did another show in the State Theatre in Melbourne. In one of our performances, I had to make an entrance with Bert Newton. The producer altered the cue for our entrance, so I had to drag Bert by the sleeve to get him onto the stage. The spot lights were already on us. I was saying, "Come on Bert."

We did some filming too. One film in the mid 1980's was called "All the Rivers Run." Nancy Cato wrote the story about the Murray River. The director came to Tony and asked for four dancers. I was one of the four chosen.

223

For some years after we arrived at Lake Macquarie, I would fly down to Melbourne to dance with the Tivoli group on television shows. The Tivoli itself had closed down. It was converted to a cinema and later, it burned down.

Ooroo *moored beside the back of the St Kilda Kiosk, 1980's.*

Col: Sometime during the 1980's, we installed *Ooroo's* mast and rigging. I bought a second hand rig, which was a fairly good fit. We inserted the mast into a deck mounted tabernacle, arranging it so that the mast could be lowered if necessary. The shrouds didn't quite fit, so we added a few links of chain to the galvanised rigging wire. Gradually, we prepared *Ooroo* for the world voyage we were planning. We added navigation lights, radios and radar, back up compasses and other necessary equipment.

In the mid-eighties, we purchased a second hand 80 horse power Perkins diesel from a boat owner at Portsea. I pulled the motor out of the boat, reconditioned it and installed it in *Ooroo*. I managed to install the propeller shaft and the propeller without taking the boat out of the water.

Later, when *Ooroo* was slipped for antifouling at Sandringham, I cut open the keel and inserted several ingots of lead, weighing two tonnes. She was much better behaved under sail after we increased the ballast.

Col inserting a lead ingot into the yacht keel

Used Car Salesman

Between 1987-1989, the government renovated the Kiosk inside and out over a period of two years. It was a bicentennial project. We had to move into a flat which they rented for us in St Kilda for two years while the renovations took place. Before we relinquished the lease for the Kiosk and while they were refurbishing it, I sold second hand cars for six months.

The talk around town was that second-hand car salesmen were putting speedos back and selling dodgy cars. *I wonder if they really do this? If I become a car salesman for a time, I'll see if they really are cheats.* In Melbourne, Kevin Dennis had several big yards. I decided to try for a job at the nearest one and the manager employed me. I don't know how it stands in Victoria nowadays, but in NSW it is an offence to turn back the odometer. It wasn't an offence back then in Victoria. I'd be selling people a car and they'd come and say, 'Let's look at the speedo.'

'Don't look at the speedo.' I'd tell them. 'It was a second hand car when we bought it, so you can bet your life the previous owner has put it back and we've certainly put it back, so forget about the speedo. Look at the car.'

225

I earned comfortable money there.

One day, while I was in the showroom looking out onto the street, a taxi cut across another car and the driver became very upset because he'd had to brake suddenly. He pulled over and called out to the cab. The taxi driver stopped on the other side of the road and wound down his window. The first driver, a fellow in his early twenties, crossed the road towards the taxi. He was swearing very volubly and there were women and kids waiting at a nearby bus stop, who could hear him. He went up to the cab driver and punched him through the window of his car. He came back across the road, towards the showroom, still swearing loudly. I walked out onto the footpath and spoke to him. 'I say, old boy, it's not quite the thing to do to be swearing like this.'

I taught him a few words of the Australian vernacular and he came at me swinging a punch. Unbeknown to me, the fellow's father had climbed out of the front passenger seat and approached me from behind. I knocked the son's punch away, but as I did so, I saw a foot coming for my testicles from the other side. I grabbed the father's foot and dropped him onto his backside.

I discovered from their accents they were Italian, so I panicked. I thought at least one of them would have a knife. While I was dumping the father, the younger man came at me again with another punch. Despite being dressed in a suit, I dropped to the ground and rolled under a parked car. One of our salesmen saw what was happening and came running up. The Italians leapt into their car and drove away.

'Get their number, get their number,' I yelled to my colleague from under the car.

He recorded the registration plate number and I went into the office to ring the cops.

'We'll get him,' they said.

They did find the car and we ended up in court. The magistrate questioned me.

'What was he saying when he walked across the road?'

'Ah... it was pretty solid language.'

The court room was nearly deserted, but in one corner, there was a female newspaper reporter who I hadn't noticed until then.

'It was quite rough language. Could I write it down? '

'No, we're all accustomed to bad language in this place, even Mrs... over there.'

I started mumbling.

'We can't hear you. Speak up.'

I started to shout what the man had been saying. Suddenly, I felt liberated, so I became carried away.

'Steady on Mr Kerby. We get the picture.'

They fined the young man seventy-five dollars for both his language and for striking me. While I was getting rid of his father's foot, the son had swung at me again and knocked me down. They didn't charge the father, even though he'd kicked me and I had a bruise on my groin. Those two guys were very distressed at being fined seventy-five dollars.

Skilled Engineering Again

I soon grew bored with selling cars. I returned to work for Skilled Engineering and Judy continued her dancing classes. Not long afterwards, I had a car accident. At the time, my mate Alf was up in Sydney and I was looking after his place. His car was in his garage, so I decided to borrow it while mine was being repaired. I drove to the flat where we were living and parked the car on the road outside. It was a cream car, probably a Holden. I ensured the key both locked and unlocked the door, so that I wouldn't be held up in the morning, then I locked up the car and went inside.

I was working as a boiler attendant at a juice factory and the boiler had to be started for 6.00am. At 5.00 am, I went out in the dark and tried to unlock the car door. The key no longer seemed to work. I was shaking the door and knocking at it. I couldn't work it out.

Just then a police car came along and drew up beside me. I was dressed in a black boiler suit and, because it was cold, a black balaclava and black gloves. The two coppers asked me what I was doing. I explained that it was my mate's car and I was trying to get the door open. They asked if they could try, so I handed one of them the key. He tried the driver's door with no success. Then his mate took the key and tried the passenger door.

'This key doesn't fit this car.'

'Of course it does. I tested it last night before I went to bed.'

'What kind of car does your mate own? What's the number plate?'

'It's K something. KVY something, I think.' I looked behind me. 'I told you it was KVY. There it is,' and I pointed to Alf's car behind me. I had been trying to unlock the wrong car.

There was a hard hat on the back seat.

'Is that your hat?'

'No, that's Alf's hat.'

'There's a lot of difference between this car and that car,' said the suspicious cop.

'Listen, I can tell the difference between an MG and a Porsche. After that, if they've four wheels and they're painted cream, they all look the bloody same to me.'

In the meantime, I produced my licence and they took note of it.

'I have to get to work. I've a boiler to start up.'

Finally, they let me go. When I arrived at work, I told the story to one of the women and she became hysterical. She lay down and roared with laughter.

~

I worked for Skilled Engineering for sixteen years in Melbourne. Judy kept my daily roster in an exercise book. I started that book in 1972 and Judy kept it up to date. I worked for many different firms in Melbourne, including Australian Glass, Quaker Oats and Laminex.

Renovation of St Kilda Pier

The St Kilda Pier Kiosk was originally built in 1905. My father, Noble Kerby, first took out a lease on it in 1939, so my mother had a place to live and a small income while he was in the army during the Second World War. The State Government refurbished the exterior of the Kiosk in 1960 and Judy and I took over the lease that year. There was a renovation of the Pier, when it was concreted in 1969, after some youths had burned a large section of the wooden planking.

A major bi-centennial renovation of the Kiosk was completed between 1987 and 1989. I had been insistent that for the Pier and pavilion to remain safe from arson, it was necessary for someone to live at the Kiosk. Ports and Harbours didn't listen to me. Our home in the Kiosk was demolished in the refurbishment. Along with the upgrade, the Government built a restaurant onto the Kiosk.

When the renovations were almost finished, the state government stopped paying our rent for the flat. They talked about raising the Kiosk rent from forty dollars a week to twelve hundred. We couldn't make the business viable at that cost and we weren't interested in running a restaurant, especially when cars were forbidden on the Pier now.

The weather dictated how much business we received. People didn't walk the 500m to the Kiosk when it was too hot, too cold or too windy. Often, our least productive time was during a heat wave.

There were lots of letters from the public in support of us. People even wrote graffiti on the Kiosk walls, "Save Kerby's." Although the Kiosk had been leased by my family for fifty years and, even now, is still widely known as Kerby's Kiosk, we decided it was time to let the business go and we gave up our contract with the Victorian State Government.

I knew it would be only a matter of time before the new building burned down. The Kiosk was destroyed by fire in March 2003 and the state government rebuilt it because of popular support.

In 1990, Melbourne City Council erected a plaque commemorating our association with the St Kilda Pier.

THIS PLAQUE COMMEMORATES THE KERBY FAMILY'S
LONG ASSOCIATION WITH THE ST. KILDA PIER AND KIOSK.
MR. COLIN KERBY AND HIS WIFE JUDY
RAN THE KIOSK IN THE LAST THREE DECADES
AFTER SUCCEEDING HIS PARENTS,
NOBLE AND IVY KERBY, IN THE BUSINESS.
OVER THE YEARS MR. COLIN KERBY RESCUED
MANY PEOPLE FROM THE SEA AND RECEIVED
THE ORDER OF THE MEDAL OF AUSTRALIA IN 1984.
THE KIOSK WAS REFURBISHED IN 1988
AS A BICENTENNIAL PROJECT.

UNVEILED BY
COUNCILLOR JOHN T. BRODERICK
MAYOR OF ST. KILDA
13TH MARCH 1990

We transferred directly from the flat onto *Ooroo,* which we had moved into the marina at the end of the Pier. She has been our home ever since. Once we were living on board, it was only a matter of time before we set off to sail the world.

14 Life Saving, Rescue and Salvage

Life Saving

Over the years on the Pier, my father and I saved many hundreds of people from drowning and rescued many people from their boats. During my father's day, before we knew about mouth to mouth resuscitation, we would rush the victims to the hospital. But you know, mouth to mouth resuscitation was known in Biblical times. 'He breathed life into him.' I read that in the Bible before I became an atheist.

My father and I had a technique at The Alfred Hospital for when we brought in drowning cases. As we walked into the Emergency Department, we'd call out 'Drowning case!' The staff would run out straight away with a stretcher to pick up the victim from our vehicle.

One day, a friend of mine and his girlfriend had a car smash. It came over the radio that she was in hospital and needed a blood transfusion. I went to the hospital to see if my blood would be suitable for her, because I am group O. I walked into the emergency Department to ask where I should go to give blood. Two of the attendants called out 'Drowning case' and ran out with a stretcher. I had to run out after them to say there was no drowning victim.

~

On New Year's Eve, 1943, my mother and I were serving in the Kiosk. It was a beautiful calm night. A boy came in and told us, 'A man just jumped off the end of the pier.' At that time, the Pier continued for about a hundred yards past the kiosk.

I went outside and spoke to one of the fisherman. He took his boat out to look, while I went back to serving customers. At three o'clock in the morning, this voice came out of the sea, 'Help'.

I launched our life boat and found someone to help me. We used a spot light, but to start with, we couldn't see anyone in the water. Eventually, we came across this fellow at the end of the Pier. He couldn't swim, so he was lying back in the water, with his knees up. His face was a mass of blood where the sea lice had been biting him and it looked as though his legs were growing out of his head. I

231

couldn't see his body. We got him around to the back of the boat and hauled him aboard. We motored over to the landing close to the Kiosk and eventually got him up the boards. He was a big man, about 14 stone, but beautifully proportioned and well-muscled. It was about thirty feet from the landing to the Kiosk. I managed to get him up the steps and we staggered up to my mother at the Kiosk. He was very weak, having been in the water for over three hours. Mum fed him a cup of sweet tea from a spoon. He told her that in the last few minutes, life became very precious.

Another time, a woman came up the Pier and was going to jump in. 'I dare not go home,' she told my mother.

'It might not be quite as bad as you think,' my mother told her. Later she changed her mind about jumping.

Mum could tell which people were planning to jump. She saw this fellow coming up the Pier one day and rang our local detective, Peacock. 'I think this fellow is up to no good,' she told him.

'What makes you think that?' the detective asked.

'I think you ought to come down and talk to him,' she insisted.

When the detective talked to him, he realized the man had been wanted by the police for about two years for house breaking and other criminal activity.

'Mrs Kerby, if you are ever again suspicious about anyone on the Pier, just call me,' Peacock told her later. 'I've been promoted on the basis of catching that man.'

Another time, a young girl walked up the Pier. She thought she was going to fail her exams. Judy talked her out of jumping. Later, she came back and gave Judy a handkerchief for her help. She was one of the very few who thanked us for saving them. Most didn't.

A fellow called Nelson lived on his boat. One night, he saw this round thing floating by. He thought it was a buoy. He tried to lift it up, but it was the head of a drowned man. We went down and removed the body from the water and called the police. In his pocket, the police found a letter stating that he must never work again. It was dated that same day. His wife came down looking for him.

Judy was driving down the Pier when she saw an old woman sitting there and thought she looked odd. She stopped the car and talked to her.

'You're not going to commit suicide, are you?'

'Of course not,' she said.

Judy thought she'd phone from the box at the end of the pier, but before she had driven that far, the old woman jumped and she was starting to float out to sea. The police came asking if she'd been wearing rings. Apparently she had been wearing expensive rings and they weren't to be found. She was eighty-two or eighty-three years old and she took her false teeth out before she jumped.

Another time, a fellow came down, jumped in, then hung onto a pile and yelled. When I arrived in the dinghy, I couldn't pull him off the pile. He wouldn't let go. We put a rope around him and pulled him off with the boat.

One night, we saw a man out fishing. Later we looked, and there was only his fishing rod there. We looked, but we couldn't find him. Some days later, someone else found him. His body was on the bottom quite a long way out. I rang the police and they sent their divers to retrieve the body. There was a landing beside the morgue, which was almost level with the sea. It was awash at high tide. I watched as they carried him out on the stretcher and at least a gallon of water gushed out of him, drenching the man behind. His mother also suicided by jumping off the Pier.

A group of three young fellows came onto the Pier one day. Two of them jumped into the water, but they couldn't swim. They were clinging to a pile.

With great urgency, one called to his mate still up on the Pier, 'Sing out "Help". We're in deep trouble down here.'

I was nearby, so I went down and pulled them over to the landing.

Another time, a young lad disappeared, leaving his fishing gear on the Pier. We went looking for him, but couldn't find him. Two days later, a man went walking by where *Ooroo* was tied up. The kid was prone on the bottom, in the shadow of *Ooroo*. He hadn't risen and the man could see his body lying there.

A few weeks later, his mother came down and tried to suicide. We saw her crawling across the Pier one night. We managed to stop her and took her to the police station, but she tried again later and succeeded. The police came and told us she had drowned.

Another woman jumped in front of our van when we were driving down the Pier. We grabbed her and after we had a fight with her, we managed to lock her in the back of the van and drove to the police station. She was fighting and screaming all the time. When the police opened the door of the van, they said, 'Come on, get out.'

She wouldn't move, so they grabbed her by a leg each and pulled. She was sitting down on the floor and they tried to drag her out.

'Let her legs go. Let her stand up.' Judy said. 'Let her legs go. Let her stand up.'

Reluctantly, the cops let her go and the woman stood up and walked out of the van.

The Royal Humane Society awarded me with a bronze medallion for bravery in 1983. In October of the same year, I was presented with the Tattersall's Award for Enterprise and Achievement. Judy and I were travelling in the USA when I received the phone call asking if I would accept the Order of Australia Medal [OAM] in 1984. I was surprised and humbled by that, but I had to wait until the next year, when we were back in Australia, to receive the medal from the Governor of Victoria, Sir Brian Murray, at Government House. All of these awards were for saving lives and rescuing people and boats.

Oddly, when I was presented with the Tattersall's Award, there was a very big turnout of people, including the local MP and his entourage and it made bigger headlines than the awarding of the OAM or the Bronze Medallion for Bravery from the Royal Humane Society. We never kept a record of the people we rescued. There would have been hundreds – maybe five hundred just during the time Judy and I lived at the Kiosk. We'd be called upon about once a month. Once, we rescued four people in one day.

Col and Judy with the Tattersall's Award for
Enterprise and Achievement

Boat Rescues

We frequently went out to rescue people in trouble on their boats. There were no flares in those days to send up if you got into trouble. You used a metal bucket, put some fuel in it and a rag, then lit it. We were on good terms with the police and, because they had no boat, we would do some of their work for them. When a boat went missing, they would ring us up and we'd go out in *Ooroo* to find the boat and tow it in. There was no payment involved. Of course, all this added to my kudos later when I was awarded my OAM. The State Governor mentioned that I'd salvaged many boats and saved many lives.

There were often several people in a boat that was in trouble. On one occasion, we rescued eight people off a sinking boat. My father and I rowed out in two dinghies and we each made two trips to shore to get them all to safety. It was winter. The last one I tried to take off the submerged boat had his hands gripping the rigging. He wouldn't let go and I had to prise his fingers off the wire, one at a time. He screamed with the pain.

Judy Congratulates Col on the receipt of his
Order of Australia Medal

We went out to rescue two lads on sail boards. The wind turned with a storm out of the north, and they were in strife out in Port Philip Bay. One dropped his sail and paddled hard for the nearest shore, where he phoned to alert the police that his mate was in trouble. Before we could reach him, the other boy followed his friend's actions and dropped his sail. He also paddled safely to shore, which was no mean feat with wind gusts up to eighty knots across the water.

One night, we found two fellows stealing a boat. Apart from those at the marina, there were always lots of boats tied up to the Pier. I went out and spoke to these fellows, but they sank that boat. I called the police, who came and arrested them. They were charged and I had to give evidence in court.

In those days, there were no helicopters and there were no police boats. The authorities used to rely on us a lot. Now, there's a new marina built at St Kilda and the police have rescue boats moored there.

The Order of Australia Medal

Animal Rescue

Sometimes people would throw unwanted puppies and cats into the sea. I saved many of these animals from drowning and we kept some of them. As well, sometimes, people gave us dogs they'd rescued or found. We had no restrictions on our pets on the Pier and dogs were a big part of our private lives. We both love them. We also kept some of the cats we rescued: Bill Cat, Sykes, Mummy Puss – they were all ones we rescued out of the sea after people had thrown them off the Pier. Bill Cat had a huge abscess on the side of his face. Mummy Puss was very pregnant. Mankind can be so cruel. Animals feel pain the same as we do. I hate even to see a fisherman hold his fish up by the hook in its mouth.

Another Kind of Rescue

When we took over the Kiosk, there were no toilets on the Pier. It was okay for the blokes, but sometimes women were in strife when they needed a toilet. We couldn't let them use the toilet in the Kiosk, because sometimes on a summer Sunday, there would be hundreds of people on the Pier.

I was becoming tired of asking the authorities to provide public toilets. Late one afternoon, I caught sight of a woman who was obviously desperate. She was searching for somewhere on the rocks where she could unobtrusively relieve herself. In a flash of inspiration, I grabbed a camera and using a long lens, took some shots of her urinating.

The next morning, I went along to the Premier's office, where once again I bemoaned the fact there were no public toilets on the Pier. This time, I pulled out the photos I'd taken and showed them to the Premier. He was shocked.

'That's terrible!' he said. 'We can't have this happening. I'll get on to it.'

Before very long, a group of workmen appeared on the Pier and a toilet block was constructed. Judy and I volunteered to keep the toilets clean. I cleaned the men's and Judy cleaned the women's.

Sometimes in winter, Fishermen would light a driftwood fire in the gents to try to keep themselves warm. They could watch their rod at the same time. Often a hobo would sleep in the building, keeping out of the wind. The fires endangered the building.

I put up a notice: *Free transport will be provided to The Alfred Hospital for anyone found damaging these toilets.*

The police received a complaint and the sergeant came to visit me. I showed him my notice.

'I completely agree,' he said. After wards, there were no more fires.

Laying Moorings

Once the motor was in *Ooroo*, we could use her for salvage and also for laying moorings. We put down private moorings in the vicinity of the Kiosk. In Port Phillip, because of the severity of the winds from both north-east and south-west, you have to put two moorings down, linking them with chain.

We used large railway wheels, which we picked up on a trailer from the railway yards at Newport. With the wheels on board *Ooroo*, we'd steam up to the marker buoy, drop the first wheel, then swing back and drop the second one. *Ooroo* was good for that job. We put a swivel in the middle of the chain to attach the mooring line. Laying moorings provided a comfortable profit for us.

Salvage

The Department of Public Works would ring us up to tell us where a boat had drifted ashore. Rather than rescue, this work was salvage.

'Do you want to do anything about it?' they'd ask on the phone. We did, because they didn't want to.

A forty-two foot steel yacht went ashore on a beach. We consulted a solicitor about the law regarding salvage. He told us that when you have salvaged a boat, the receiver of wrecks takes charge of the vessel and, if the owner is unknown, he puts it up for auction. If it sells for sufficient money, then you get paid for the salvage. Otherwise, you can keep the vessel and use it, but it's never yours. You can sell it, but the money must be put into a trust account for the owner. You can use the vessel, but if the owner turns up, he can claim it back. I suppose eventually, the money goes to internal revenue. In practice, you can't go off shore or leave the country in the boat. You can only use it in local waters.

When I went into the library and obtained a copy of the *Navigation Act (1912)* to read for myself, I found the Act stated much as the solicitor had told us. It also said there was an exception if the boat was wrecked in a boat harbour, which this yacht was, so we went ahead and salvaged it.

We hired an amphibious tractor for eight hours, at $1.80 per minute. After that time, there was a big penalty. We tried to drag the forty-two foot steel yacht bow first off the sand and into deeper water, but that didn't work. She was lying on her side, on the beach, parallel to the shore. Somebody had taken the transducer for the depth sounder out of the hull and I had to block up the hole left by its removal. For six hours we tried to pull that boat out of the sand. Then we tried to pull her out sideways. In half an hour, with a shovel, I moved six tons of sand from under the hull. Finally, we dragged the boat the length of the sand bar with the tractor, and anchored it in deeper water.

We went looking for the owner.

'The owner's backpacking around the world,' a young woman told us.

'What's backpacking?' This was 1981, and I'd never heard the term.

On the boat, we had found a wet suit and other gear with the name Clarke on it. At this time, Terry Clarke was a criminal in Melbourne. His story is told in the TV drama, 'Underbelly'. We also found an Arnott's biscuit tin chock full of marijuana. We told the solicitor about this. He said we should be careful or we might find ourselves dead and thrown into a quarry. Clarke was renowned for getting rid of bodies into a quarry. We were a bit worried about it, so I put the marijuana down the toilet and later told my mates about it. They were very bloody annoyed with me.

Later on, the owners actually turned up. It wasn't Terry Clarke's boat at all.

'We don't want her anymore,' said the young couple. 'Could you sell the boat for us?'

'How much do you want for it?'

'$15,000.'

The yacht was fully rigged, so we thought it shouldn't be too hard to sell.

That night, we went out to dinner with friends – a vet and his physiotherapist wife. We told them the story of this boat. The next morning, they came round to our place.

'Gerry's been looking for a hobby,' said Gerry's wife. 'He was thinking about homing pigeons, but we think we might buy the yacht.'

Gerry had a photographic memory and he had completed four degrees, but he knew nothing about boats or the sea. He'd never had anything to do with boats in his life. Nevertheless, Gerry bought the yacht. We took $2000 to cover our salvage costs and gave the owners the rest of the money.

Gerry kept that boat for four years. I sailed with him on an ocean race from Melbourne to Devonport. We drifted across the line backwards in Tasmania, being placed 156th out of 157 competitors.

There was a catamaran on the rocks behind the Kiosk. We salvaged it and tied it up against the St Kilda Pier. Later, We decided we would tow the catamaran across the bay to Williamstown with *Ooroo*. Just before we left the Pier, a teenage lad came along.

'What are you doing?' he asked.

'We're going to tow this boat over to Williamstown.'

'Can I come with you?' he asked.

'Can you swim?'

'Yes.'

'All right, you can come,' I said.

We started off with Judy at the wheel, but the cat started to sink in the middle of the channel. She was still attached to the tow line. A big ship came steaming down the channel towards us. The catamaran was acting as an anchor and Judy couldn't steer because of the weight we were towing. We were proceeding at cruising revolutions.

'Put the throttle on full,' I advised Judy.

She pushed up the throttle and we just made it out of the way of the ship. Once we were clear, I told the boy to get over the back and start bailing water out the cat. He went into the water and boarded the catamaran, but he couldn't keep up with the water, so he swam back to *Ooroo*. We went full bore across the bay and took the cat to a pier at Williamstown. When we arrived, a helpful man, fully dressed in a suit, jumped into the water-logged vessel and used a bucket to help us bail the water out until she was floating again.

Rescues and salvage added some adventure to our lives. We missed that when we moved onto *Ooroo* and put her in the St Kilda Marina.

Col falls off the Marmong Marina wharf, 11 August, 2010

Many years later, long after we'd moved from St Kilda to Marmong at Lake Macquarie, I was the one who needed to be rescued. The wind was blowing fairly hard. I had a trolley to take back to its compound, so I climbed onto my pushbike and dragged the trolley behind me.

'You'll fall in the water,' Judy said.

'No I won't.'

241

I rode up the wharf, holding my keys in the same hand as I was holding the handle bar; the other hand was pulling the trolley. I didn't tie the trolley to the bike. I rode about twenty yards, then turned the corner and went down the pier about 80 metres.

I dropped my keys, became confused and the next thing, I let the trolley go. Suddenly, everything went green. The keys fell in the water along with me, but the float worked, so I didn't lose the keys. The bike went in with me and the trolley stayed on the wharf.

It was bloody cold in the water. I swam about fifteen feet to a space where I thought I could climb out. The marina is fourteen inches high – I measured it later. There was no way I could pull myself up. It gave me the shock of my life to find I couldn't pull myself out. All I did was cut my leg on an oyster on the float under the wharf. I tried several times to pull myself up onto the pier, but I just couldn't do it.

I looked at my watch to see if that was still working and it was. I had to decide what to do. Judy was about 100 metres away. I called, 'Judy, Judy.' She couldn't hear me.

Lloyd's boat was not far away, so I called to Lloyd, a friend of many years. He didn't hear me either. I was in the water nearly twenty minutes. In the end, I thought I'd swim back to our boat and I could bang on the side, but first I thought I'd try the old fashioned "Help!" I told myself I would call ten times and if no one came, I'd have to swim.

I called 'Help' eight times. *Bloody hell, I'm going to have to swim*, I thought. *No, I said I'd give it ten times, so I'll call twice more.*

I did and a woman came out of a nearby boat that I thought was empty.

'Ahh, there's a man in the sea.' She ran back in and called to Russell on *Panache*. 'Russell, there's a man in the water.'

'Who is it?' asked Russell.

'Col,' I called out.

'What are you doing in the water?' asked Russell.

They came down and took one arm each and pulled me out.

'I'm pleased you're light,' the woman said.

My glasses were still on. I didn't lose those. Fortunately too, I had taken my hearing aid out before I set off, because I thought it might rain. They're a thousand bucks each now and you can't get them wet.

I said I was all right to go back to *Ooroo*, but they wouldn't let me and escorted me back to the boat. I had hypothermia all right. I stripped my wet clothes off in the cockpit and then I had a hot shower and stayed under the water until I warmed up.

Next day, I took a grapnel down and with one throw, I snared the bike and retrieved it.

I never thought I would have to be rescued from the sea. After rescuing so many people in the past, I found it somewhat humiliating to be rescued myself. Following this incident, the marina owners presented me with a lifejacket. I always wear it when I am riding my bike down the marina pier.

Part Seven: Travelling

15 Sailing Away

What a memorable Christmas we had in 1990! That Christmas morning, it just seemed right that we should set off. At Portsea, we ate cheese sandwiches for Christmas dinner. Eighteen years after we had launched *Ooroo*, we sailed out of Port Philip Bay into the end of a big storm from up north, with high winds and seas. It was the tail end of Cyclone Joy.

Right up until our departure, I continued working for Skilled Engineering and we lived aboard at the St Kilda Pier marina. For many years, we had been planning and preparing for our world voyage, but we'd always said we wouldn't go during the northern cyclone season. What did we do – we left while a big Cyclone was up north.

It was bloody rough out there in Bass Strait. We went out the heads and along the coast to Westernport. The town of Flinders is right at the entrance to Westernport. We anchored there and had quite a pleasant night until, at two o'clock in the morning, our keel touched the bottom and started bumping. We had a 65lb CQR anchor out, so we hadn't dragged, but I'd forgotten that the tides are fairly large at Westernport.

We jumped out of bed. Judy started the engine and I pulled in the anchor. When the anchor came up, a large lump of sea grass was wound around it. We had put all our torches in a special place so we'd know where they were. Of course, we couldn't remember where that was and were unable to find them. We had anchored among all the commercial fishing boats and other craft. Without any light, we crept out of the anchorage, trying to dodge the moored craft. As well as the CQR, we have a 25lb Herreschoff anchor and an Admiralty anchor. I put the Admiralty anchor down in much deeper water and it held while the wind blew like hell from the north-west.

Early next morning, we decided to go up to Hastings to shelter from the wind. We were approaching Cowes Pier on our port [left] side. That was the naval depot, where my father and I had bought thirteen boats after the war. I remembered these places from back then and kept on motoring towards Hastings, thinking I'd turn into Han's Inlet. When we neared there, I wasn't game to turn, because the seas were so high, I was scared a wave might hit the hull broadside and roll us over.

'We'd better put on our life jackets. It won't save our lives, but it'll give the coroner something to look at,' I said to Judy.

We motored up to Sandy Creek and tied up to a pier there. Only an hour later, the wind turned and came in from the south-west. We could see our boat's paint on the pile, so we untied and moved to the other side of the pier, where we were fine and we were able to relax. I couldn't believe that only half an hour beforehand, it had seemed we were battling for our lives

The next day we motored on to Hastings. Judy was steering.

'See that pile up there. Pass it to starboard,' I told her.

Then for some reason, I took over the wheel. I passed the pile to port and we ran aground. We managed to pull ourselves off and we tied *Ooroo* in a berth at the Hastings marina.

Soon, we were down the street in a café drinking cappuccino. What a contrast.

~

Leaving *Ooroo* in the marina at Hastings, we returned to Melbourne for our car, loaded it up with belongings from our storage lock-up in St Kilda and drove up to Newcastle. The Daihatsu van's brakes failed as we drove down Macquarie Pass, north of Kiama. It was rather scary, but we managed to dodge other vehicles and stay on the road, eventually arriving safely in Newcastle. We stored our belongings and the car at Judy's mother's place.

When we returned to Hastings, we stayed in the marina for more than three weeks, waiting for the weather to moderate, after which we made another attempt to leave. As we approached the channel exit from Westernport, a tanker was coming in, blowing his horn at us. Torrential rain had made him invisible to us. We turned around and came back in again. We weren't going to mix it with a bloody great tanker and the seas outside looked too big. The rain began falling so heavily, we couldn't see the land. Back at Westernport, we tied up to a buoy. The tide was going out and the wind was against the tide, making the seas almost rectangular.

I called up on the local marine radio station to ask where we could go. A woman told us to go to Cowes Pier to tie up. We set off and the north-westerly came in stronger. We were looking at Cowes

Pier and the seas were breaking over it. She didn't know much. Just before I turned the radio off, a voice came on that reeked of experience.

'Christ almighty, she's sending them over to Cowes wharf in a north-westerly!'

We returned to Hastings. That was when we met Ashley Coulson, who'd built an eight foot yacht (the length of a dinghy). His boat was on a trailer in the boatyard there. Ashley was a first class seaman, who had sailed to New Zealand in that tiny boat, taking forty-five days to arrive and over seventy-five days to return. Dick Smith awarded him an explorer's medal.

Nowadays, Ashley Coulson is serving three life sentences in Pentridge for killing three people in Melbourne. Of course, we didn't know he had the potential to murder when we met him and his older partner, Jan. They were also waiting for the weather, so they could set sail to Tasmania in Jan's thirty-eight foot yacht, *Gulliver*.

We listened for weather forecasts and finally one was for calm to moderate seas.

'This is it,' we said and both yachts set off.

We sailed in company with Gulliver from Hastings up to Refuge Cove on the eastern side of Wilson's Promontory. We rounded the Promontory and went in to Refuge Cove.

While *Ooroo* and *Gulliver* were anchored there, no other yachts or people were there. We had Jan and Ashley on board *Ooroo* for dinner and we were very friendly with them, enjoying their company. Several days later, *Gulliver* departed to sail around Tasmania, and we sailed on up the east coast.

A couple of years later, Ashley Coulson was arrested for murder. Two girls living in a flat in Melbourne needed another flat mate, so they put an ad in the paper for a male or female to share expenses with them. One of the girls asked her relative, a young man, to come to act as a sort of chaperone while they did interviews. Ashley Coulson, with whom we'd kept company in Refuge Cove, went there armed with a sawn off .22 rifle, bailed them up, tied them up with electrical tape. He undressed one of the girls and shot all three of them in the head, yet he left no clues for the police to lead them to the perpetrator.

Ooroo *anchored at Refuge Cove, Wilson's Promontory,1991.*

About six weeks after he'd committed the murders, Coulson was in St Kilda Rd, near the Prince Henry's Hospital in Melbourne. He approached a couple who had just climbed into their car and, while pointing his gun at them, asked for money. After a struggle with Coulson, the couple ran. Two security guards saw Coulson with the gun and chased him. He shot one guard in the thigh. The other overpowered him. When the police did a ballistics test on his weapon, they found it was the same gun that had shot the other three people. Coulson was convicted of the murders in 1995 and sentenced to serve three life sentences. Having seen the news of his conviction on television, I thought I'd write to him in prison.

'Is it any good my writing to you?' I asked in my letter.

'I'm pretty busy,' he replied, 'so I don't know if I could write back very often.' I don't know what he'd be so busy doing in prison.

~

After setting off from Refuge for Eden, we struck bad weather again. Visibility was poor and our fluxgate compass and our Sat Nav both broke down. In our stress, we forgot about the three spare compasses on board. I had been sixty-four hours without sleep, standing up at the wheel, when I started to hallucinate. A woman called Rosalie was originally supposed to come with us up the coast.

I hallucinated that she was with us. I turned around and I 'saw' Rosalie in the cockpit, sitting on a sail. I went down and told Judy.

'Good. She can do some work,' said Judy.

We had been steering in seventy-two knots of wind and in fairly steep seas. They weren't dangerously steep, but steep enough for us as novice sailors. We didn't really know where we were. At daylight on our second day out, we couldn't see Australia. I turned back and when we found the coast, it was already getting late in the day. We came into the Welshpool area, in the corner on the eastern side of the Prom. Although it is safe enough once you're in, there's a sandbar and it isn't all that easy to enter.

I called up Melbourne Coast Guard on the radio and told the fellow who answered my call that if he could get a pilot to come out and lead us in, I'd cross his palm with gold. He said to try putting out an APB [all points broadcast]. A marvellous young woman answered my call. She asked for our position. I told her where we were.

'Steam due north. What speed can you do?'

'Six knots.'

'Steam due north for one hour. You'll come to a red buoy. If you like, you can tie up to that buoy. I'll contact the fishing fleet coming in to Port Albert and get them to lead you in.'

After steaming north for one hour, we found the red buoy. After another half hour, the fishing fleet turned up and we followed them in to Port Albert. There are massive sand bars both at the entrance and in the channel. We tied up in the harbour and no sooner were we in our bunk than there was knocking on the side of the hull. We were in a fishing boat's berth and we had to get up and move to another spot on the pier. Port Albert has a fourteen foot tidal range, so it isn't easy to tie up safely. When we woke up, I looked at *Ooroo* hanging on her mooring ropes. *We should climb over the sides and antifoul her!* Instead, we eased her back into the sea and adjusted our mooring lines.

From Port Albert, Judy caught a bus to Adelaide, taking the Sat Nav to be fixed there and the fluxgate compass to go for repairs in Melbourne. When both instruments had been fixed, Judy returned with them to the boat. It was strange they should both have gone "phut" the same day, because they were on different electrical circuits.

~

When the weather was clear, we set off again, stopping at Eden, then continuing north. We were listening to weather reports and getting better at knowing when it was okay to be at sea. We had no problems at all sailing to Lake Macquarie from Eden. The boat behaved well and the instruments kept working as they should. We pulled in to Lake Macquarie to buy fresh bread and to visit Judy's Mum. Twenty-one years later, we are still here.

Lake Macquarie

I had visited Marmong Marina on our recent visit to Newcastle, so I knew we wanted to tie up there. When we were outside the lake, approaching Moon Island, I called up the Coast Guard. They came out and led us into the Swansea channel. After we were over the bar and through the Swansea Bridge, where the Pacific Highway crosses the Swansea Channel, the Coast Guard stayed with us. The channel was too shallow for us to get through to the lake, so the Coast Guard boat took a mast-top halyard from us. They leaned the boat over sideways and pulled us across the very shallow area of the "drop-over". Once we were into the deeper water of the lake, we motored north-west to Marmong Point. Initially, we thought we'd buy fresh provisions, visit Judy's mum, then continue on our voyage.

It was Judy's mum that kept us here and we found we liked living at Marmong. We decided to stay while she still lived. To start with, we moved in with Mrs Lingard, but after a while, that became a strain and we moved back onto *Ooroo*. After we'd been at Lake Macquarie for about two years, Mrs Lingard had a stroke. One of her neighbours noticed she hadn't seen her about for a day. The neighbour knocked on the door and Mrs Lingard was still in bed, unable to get up. The neighbour called an ambulance. My mother-in-law lived for about another four years after that stroke.

~

Life at Marmong Marina has been very enjoyable over the years and we've made good friends with people staying on their boats. The members of one family in particular have become very special to us – more like family members than friends. When we arrived in Lake Macquarie, Paul Kelson had recently launched his forty-five foot steel ketch, *Revival* and he and his wife Helen came to live at the Marina. First, Jacob was born and three years later, Amelia. We have watched those children grow up into wonderful young adults; they are like grandchildren to us and the whole family is very much part of our lives.

Near Disaster

A decade or more ago, we had *Ooroo* out of the water for antifouling, when there was a wind storm. The pressure of the wind on *Ooroo* made the cradle collapse and our boat fell, damaging several other boats. The mast broke and the rigging was strained in the accident. Luckily, it happened at night and no one was in the boat yard at the time, but it was a great shock to have our home tossed onto her side like that. We received money from our insurance to help repair the damage.

Back to Work

I returned to work again for Skilled Engineering, which had a branch in Newcastle. Even though Skilled Engineering in Melbourne knew how old I was, I took ten years off my age when I went to work for the Newcastle branch. I was 71 and I told them I was 61. I worked at a number of places around Newcastle and the Hunter Valley. It was nearly all fitting and turning jobs and I stayed for ten years.

They sent a group of about ten of us to BHP. When we arrived there, the foreman asked, 'Anybody familiar with scraping bearings?'

Two of us answered that we'd scraped bearings before.

'Do you have any scrapers with you?'

I had one in my toolbox, but the other fellow was an American and he didn't have tools with him. It was usual to take your tool box with you. They found him a scraper.

A couple of bearings in the rolling mill required scraping. I'd scraped bearings in cars and diesel engines, crankshafts etc. The biggest crankshaft bearing I'd scraped previously was about four or five inches in diameter. These bearings were enormous. There was a gear wheel that was twelve feet in diameter [3m] and the shaft was just under three feet diameter [800mm]. Inside the crankcase, I could reach only the top half of the bearing.

Col and workmate scraping a rolling mill bearing

We put a blue dye onto the bearing, then we turned the crankshaft. The areas where the blue was scraped off indicated the high points on the bearing. These are what we had to scrape until the bearing surface was reasonably smooth. To do the scraping, one usually picks the shaft up. This one must have weighed four or five tons.

'How do we get to pick up the shaft?' I asked the foreman.

'You'll have a crane driver on the gantry.' He replied. 'He'll pick it up for you and come along when you want him.'

I became so fast doing this scraping that the other workers wanted to watch me. Of course, it didn't have to be as accurate as on a bearing from a small crankshaft.

~

Col when he worked for Skilled Engineering, Newcastle.

Once, a team of us flew up to Queensland to help with the fitting out of a new power station. We were at Williamstown airport, waiting for our flight. I wanted a coffee and I asked the others if anyone else wanted one. None of them did. As I started off to the cafeteria, I looked back and saw the team supervisor had called the group into a huddle and he was talking to them. Later on, when the supervisor was out of earshot, I asked the others what he had said to them.

'Now listen, while we are in Queensland, if anyone asks Col's age, you are to say he is fifty-eight. For Christ's sake don't tell them he's sixty-one.' That's what he told them to say. I had a good laugh about that, because I was actually seventy-one.

~

At Pasminco, I had to be tested for lead contamination. I'm not sure if they also tested us for zinc. Usually, the nurse on site would take the blood. There were some blokes there who were so fat, she couldn't put the needle deep enough to find the vein. In those cases, they called in a doctor.

~

I worked in the mines too. One time, I was working on a conveyor belt at the Wombo mine in the Hunter Valley when the Director and another fellow came down to inspect a problem.

'Did you put those slugs up there?' one of them asked me.

'Yes.'

'How did you get them in there?'

'I climbed over the top.'

'Did you use a ladder or something?'

'No, I just climbed over the top.'

'They weigh twenty-five kilos. How did you get them in?'

'See that bit of a port hole. I put the slugs outside of that, then I climbed over and took them in through the port hole and bolted them on.'

'What did you stand on when you were in there?'

Underneath, there were two crushers for crushing up the coal. They weren't in operation at the time. This was all new equipment. I explained that there was an inch thick piece of rubber stuck on the one wall. That was there so that when the coal poured in, it would hit the rubber rather than wear the steel out. I told him that I put both my boots onto that.

He thought for a while. You could see dollar signs appearing in his eyes – insurance, damages and so on. Then he said, 'I'll send somebody up to give you a hand.'

He gave me all the ticklish jobs after that.

~

At Forgacs Engineering, which has the floating dock in Newcastle Harbour, a team of us were employed to remove big ship propellers. Many of these measured six metres in diameter. We also pulled out prop shafts, which we reconditioned, and replaced bearings.

~

Another job was on Kooragang Island in the Hunter River, near the Stockton Bridge. Incitec Pivot manufactures 600 tonnes of explosives a day there. We weren't allowed to enter the works until we received a security pass. There was a lot of dangerous machinery and they wanted to keep a record of where we were going in the factory, so they could pick up our remains. When we arrived at work, we had to wait in the tea room for the security clerk.

Three of us were drinking coffee this particular morning, because the clerk who issued the passes hadn't come into his office next door. I was checking about every five minutes to see if he had come in, so we could get our passes signed. He wasn't there and his office was still locked. After clocking in at 7.30 am, we waited close to an hour. One of the big chiefs came down and roared at us. 'What are you doing in here drinking coffee? We don't pay you to drink coffee.'

'There's nobody in the office to sign our security passes.'

'He's there now,' he said.

He left, so I went to the office, but it was still locked.

'Hey! You're a bloody liar. He's not here,' I shouted after the boss, as he walked down the corridor.

He turned back. 'You're off the area,' he told me.

I went back to the tea room. 'I'm off the area. I've just been sacked.'

'If you've been sacked for being here, we'll get the sack too,' said John. 'We'll go and see what the union says.'

Just then, a team came down to start work. A clerk came along and gave us our passes.

'I've received a pass. It looks like I'm not sacked,' I commented.

We went off and did the job we had been allocated and the rest of the team were on the floor above. When I finished my job, I went up top. They were pulling pipe couplings to pieces.

'What's doing? How are you going?' I asked. 'What's to be done?'

'This has to be taken off. And that one and that one.'

'I'll do these while you lot are working over there.'

I undid the first coupling and the pipe was full of nitric acid. It poured all over me, especially my hands. I did a very quick 100 yards to the tap to rinse the acid off, but I was still burned. While I was washing my hands, one of the foremen came over to have a look.

'You'd better get up to the first aid room. There's a nurse up there.'

I went to the first aid post. A sign said: "If nobody is in First Aid, go to the Security Doorman." I did that and told him I'd been burnt

255

with acid. My skin was blistering. He was non-plussed. He wasn't a first aid man. I went back to washing my hands under every tap on the way back to the rest room. I came out to check on the First Aid station again. Two people were approaching, a man and a woman.

'Are you the fellow who burnt his hands?'

'Yeah.'

'We're from Work Care. The Security man reported an accident to us. What happened?' I told him. 'They gave you the wrong information.'

The nurse finally turned up and she bandaged me. While I was being treated in the First Aid room, the fellow who'd sacked me came along. 'You were burnt?'

I told him how it happened.

'Bloody hell!'

He came down and sacked the bloke who had misinformed me that the pipe to be undone had been cleared. It was a two inch diameter [50mm] pipe and the acid had gushed out. I stopped it as fast as I could.

Neither the boss nor I mentioned our altercation earlier that day, when he had told me to get off the area. At a general meeting of all contractors at three o'clock the same afternoon, the chief executive came down.

'We had an accident this morning.' He went over what had happened to me. 'Because Colin is one of the older fitters, he works on the old principle that if you run out of work, you go and help your mates – unlike the rest of you modern men.'

~

Incitec had a machine that weighed 1,200 tonnes. It was an enormous thing. To get it out, they had to bring a heavy duty crane up from Adelaide. They'd had the crane up only two months before and they'd sent it back to Adelaide. Twelve semi-trailers were required, just to carry the counter-balances. The crane driver wasn't allowed to drive a truck. He came solely to drive the crane.

Suddenly, they needed the crane again, because some of the riggers had scratched though a surface on a huge machine. Incitec needed to replace that very heavy piece of machinery, but they also needed to keep it going for the six months it would take to bring a replacement machine from the United States.

I was the oldest fitter there and they thought I would be the most knowledgeable man to repair it. I had to hand-machine the damaged surface to smooth it. After that, this machine had to be bolted together in a manner which would withstand twelve hundred pounds per square inch of pressure. They asked me to fabricate bolts specially for it. I bolted it together in a special way, using extra bolts, because there wasn't enough space to weld it. I did the repair in what I thought was a very smart way.

Ten years later, Incitec rang me to ask how I had put those bolts in. They had ordered the replacement machine, but only ten years later did they need to replace the one I had fixed. They were pulling the old machine to bits and they couldn't get the bolts out. I told them it wasn't possible to pull them out. They probably had to cut that machine apart, but they could only use cutting tools if there was a general shut down. Sparks are a problem when there is so much explosive material about.

I felt a surge of satisfaction about my engineering skills, when I learnt that a temporary repair had lasted for ten years.

~

Judy bought me a ticket to New Guinea for my eightieth birthday. When I returned from the trip, I returned to work at a job on the *Kanimbula*. We were working long shifts; twelve hour days, seven days a week.

Later, I went to my doctor for a check-up. He sent me for a cardiograph, which showed an urgent need for a by-pass operation. I went straight to hospital. A week after the quadruple bypass, I was up and about again, feeling very fit. Before long, I was back working long hours again.

Retirement
I retired from Skilled Engineering late in 2002, after more than ten years of working in the Newcastle/Hunter Valley region. At that time, my aim was to ready *Ooroo* for sea and continue sailing north.

Having been on the marina for so many years, all sorts of equipment and machinery on the boat needed checking and repairs. It seemed that no sooner had I fixed one problem, than another appeared. After I had overhauled the engine, the fridge and freezer needed a major overhaul. I built special ladders for climbing back on

257

board if one of us fell overboard. It went on like this for several years.

~

Friends suggested we go sailing in small steps, because apart from putting *Ooroo* up on the hard stand for antifouling, it was a few years since she had left her berth. One day last year, we "took the plunge" and set off to sail on Lake Macquarie from Marmong to Pulbah Island, south of Wangi Wangi Point.

To our dismay, the boat went aground on a sandbar near the island. We needed to stop the boat drifting further onto the sandbar. Judy climbed onto the boarding ladder and, hanging by one arm, reached with her foot to hold the dinghy in close to the hull, while I placed the anchor into it. Her arm tired and she nearly fell overboard, but I managed to rescue her, hauling her back into the cockpit. I rowed out and set the anchor.

Soon, Helen and Paul Kelson arrived to assist, and used *Revival's* powerful yacht engine to drag *Ooroo* back into deeper water. A little chastened, Judy and I motored back to Marmong Marina, where we carefully tucked ourselves into our berth. Except that it wasn't our berth; it was our friends' berth 'next door'. We had a good laugh at ourselves over that.

16 Travels at Home and Abroad

Judy and Col have travelled widely in Australia, America and Europe. The story of their travels together is told mostly by Judy.

Judy: We were driving through a Melbourne suburb one day in 1984, when Col saw a sandwich board outside a travel agency advertising a cheap fare to the USA. On the spur of the moment Col decided that we should fly there. We stopped and went in to ask details about the flights.

'Write the cheque,' he told me.

'We can't go. We have a business to run and about twenty animals to look after,' I protested.

'Does the aircraft have more than one engine?' Col asked the agent.

'It's Qantas.'

'All right, we'll go,' he said. 'Just write the cheque, Judy.'

I wrote the cheque. Soon, we had organised somebody to look after the Kiosk and farmed out the animals to our friends. We flew over to the USA for three months. The lass we asked to look after the Kiosk was very pregnant when we left. I worried about her all the time because our ice-cream fridge was quite deep. I was concerned that as her pregnancy advanced, she would injure herself reaching for the ice-cream.

We flew from Melbourne to San Francisco, staying with friends for three days. During that time, we bought a seven seater station wagon for transport. Ironically, the person we bought it from was coming to live in Melbourne and we visited her after we returned home. We kept that car until the last day of our stay. We finished our journey in New York at Joan's home. Col went to the local garage and sold the car to the man there and Joan ordered a taxi to drive us to the airport.

After we bought that car in San Francisco, we drove through town. First, the indicators failed and then something else failed. Col wasn't very happy to have these failures right in the middle of the city and driving on the right hand side of the road for the first time in fourteen years. We wondered what else could go wrong.

Heading south out of San Francisco, the car conked out. Someone towed us off the main road to a motel. We had broken a timing chain. The garage didn't do an adequate job of fixing it. They put in a new timing chain, but the push rods were all bent, so the engine was still sick. It wouldn't idle and it wouldn't accelerate properly. We drove onto a freeway, where the traffic travels at speed. We were trying to get south to Los Angeles. Col was driving and I was navigating. We chugged as far as Anaheim, where Disneyland is. There, we pulled into a motel and booked in. The management wouldn't let Col work on the car in the motel car park, so he set off on foot to find somewhere suitable. Not far away, there was a big tool shop with a good sized car park. We spent $15 buying a kit of tools to strip the motor. Right near there, on public land beside the road, we were able to park the car and work on it.

It was strange to us in California that shops kept very little stock. Everything was ordered from catalogues. On the first of January every year, every business in California must pay 15% tax on the value of all the stock on the premises, so they keep as little as possible on hand. Whatever you order is flown in very promptly.

To pick up these tools we'd ordered, we had to catch a bus. We found we had to have the exact money for our fares. They don't give change. You put your money into a perspex container. The driver looks at it and pushes a button if you have paid enough. Because we were tourists and didn't know the system, the bus driver gave us a free trip. We met the same driver coming back. For our return trip, we had the right change.

Col worked for three days, pulling the motor to bits. It was a V8, with two heads, four cylinders each head and sixteen push rods. After the second day, a security guard came by with a spray can, hand cuffs and a pistol attached to his belt.

'What are you doing?' he asked. 'I've seen you here with all these bits for two days.'

'It costs $600 to strip the motor and grind the valves, so we thought we'd do it ourselves,' said Col.

'But you can't do that in the gutter. You need a competent mechanic and a full workshop.'

'Yes, and we have neither.'

261

The fellow went away shaking his head. The guy in the tool shop was more understanding.

'Anything you want to borrow, just come in and ask.'

This was happening in late October, coming up to Halloween. Across the road was an enormous paddock. I don't know how many acres it would have been, but it was full of yellow pumpkins for Halloween. People came to buy a pumpkin and wandered around the paddock, looking for the one that suited them. Some were very strange shapes.

'What do people do with the pumpkin they hollow out of the shell?' I asked the sales lady. 'Do they make pumpkin scones?'

'Oh no, they never cook. They're very lazy,' said the sales lady. 'They just spend their time on the beaches.'

After Col had stripped the engine, he ground the valves himself using grinding paste. We bought new push rods and installed those. Next, we had to fit the valves. On the valves, you have a valve stem spring. Each stem has a pair of collets to retain the valve spring. Col was pushing these collets down with a screw driver on each side and I was holding them in. You have to be careful not to catch your fingers. One of Col's screwdrivers slipped and the spring came up and knocked the collets out of my hand into the grass. We went through the grass very carefully until we found those two collets again and fixed that spring in place. Eventually, Col finished fixing the car. Once the engine was back in, we did ninety miles an hour. The car went beautifully for the rest of our journey to Tijuana in Mexico, across the States and it eventually took us to New York.

~

I'd heard Col's tales about his exploits in Mexico in 1970, so I feared we might have our car stolen there. This time, we were going down the coast, further south than Tijuana,. First, we went to a market. It was so filthy, I couldn't stand it. I needed a toilet and that was something else again! It was quite disgusting.

We had to have something to eat, so in trepidation, we went to a café for a meal. They brought out some milk for Col's coffee and there was a fly swimming in it. We complained about that and they took it away. Next, they brought our food: Col had burritos and I had fish. To my astonishment, it was the most exquisite fish I have ever eaten.

After we'd finished, we decided that we wouldn't follow the same route back into the States. We would rather take an inland route. We became lost going that way and ended up at the border on dirt roads, where there was no crossing. We had to return to Tijuana to cross the border.

~

Originally we had planned to stay in the USA for only six weeks, but we stayed for three months altogether and we needed more money for those extra six weeks. Some years previously, Col had been given some shares. We went to see a solicitor to organise their sale. It was Halloween that day – an event so much bigger in America than I had ever imagined. Adults on the street were dressed up in black capes and masks of all kinds. Even the solicitor's receptionist was wearing a plastic pig snout.

Col: In 1970, I took the five year old daughter of friends trick or treating. I thought I would just go with her until she tired, but I was astonished. She just kept on going. She never stopped. She wanted her sack full of lollies.

~

Judy: In those three months, we did a lot of travelling and sightseeing. We set off down the coast, camping most nights. We had a mattress in the back of the car and if the motels cost more than $15 per night, we slept in the car at camping grounds, which were very cheap.

At one camping ground, when we booked in, we were told, "In the event of an atomic explosion, please follow the instructions of the ranger." That astonished us.

We had no set route plan. We'd go to a place and talk to the locals or other tourists. Someone would say, "Have you been to ...?" We would go and explore that place if it sounded interesting. For example, someone asked, "Have you been to Bryce Canyon?"

'No.'

'Well, it's in that direction.'

We took advice like this right across the States and came across some lovely places. Bryce Canyon, near Zion National Park, (in the south-west corner of Utah) was one of the most spectacular.However, Bryce was the only place on the whole trip where there was no accommodation and no showers. It was freezing at night in the camping ground. A box with a lock on it protected your food from the bears overnight. Little squirrels came begging for food. When we gave them some, they would run away to hide it. When they returned for more, blue jays flew down and raided the squirrel's storage hole.

We were so cold in the morning, we decided to walk down into the canyon. We both wore layers and layers of clothing, but as the sun rose higher, we were stripping them off. By mid-morning, Col was down to his singlet. The canyon was glorious – quite stunning.

The Grand Canyon is another awe inspiring place we explored. From there, the road led south to the Carlsbad Caverns in New Mexico. We walked down a very rough track to the first cavern. It opened up into an area as big as a football field. At the bottom, we found the lift, so we went back up the easy way to have lunch in the caves' shopping area. Normally, ten thousand bats live in the caverns. They fly out about 6.00pm, but by October, they have migrated to Mexico, so we missed seeing them.

'Are you going across Interstate 10?' someone asked us.

'Where's that?'

'It goes across Texas. It's well worth seeing.'

So, after we left the Carlsbad Caverns, we went across Texas, even though previously, we had decided that we weren't interested in crossing all that desert. We discovered that it was lovely and worth the decision to travel by that route.

After crossing Texas, we drove down to New Orleans in Louisiana. In New Orleans, we walked all the streets of the central city, where bands played on every corner. We tried all the food specialties of the region and we loved it. We both enjoy travelling and sampling ethnic foods, but most of all, we love sightseeing and taking photographs of the wonders of the world.

From New Orleans, we went back through the Bayeux, because I wanted to see the alligators, but they were hibernating. We had also hoped to take a trip up the Mississippi River on the Natchez paddle steamer. Thinking it would go through areas with the big, old, southern, antebellum homes along the waterfront, we made enquiries, but we were told the channel only passed industrial areas, so we didn't do that trip.

We stayed in Kosciusko, Mississippi with Bessie, who had been the receptionist at The Salk Institute, and her husband Dale. Bessie showed us around the cotton fields that her family had owned in the past and the big old family home. They owned slaves back then.

'Where did the slaves sleep?' Col asked, looking for the remains of slave quarters.

'In the house.'

We'd booked into a motel before we made contact with Bessie and Dale, but they insisted we sleep at their home. Southern hospitality ruled. What we didn't realise was that they had only two bedrooms, their own and Bessie's ninety-six year old mother slept in the other. They put us in their bedroom while they went off to her sister's place somewhere close by and left us there. They came back in the morning to make breakfast. We were very embarrassed when we found out. We stayed a few days with them, before heading off to Tennessee.

It rained heavily while we were in Tennessee. We went to the Grand Oprey Land Hotel, where all the big country and western shows are held, but we didn't see any of them.

After the south, we drove north through Virginia, the Appellations and the Blue Ridge Mountains, stopping off at Washington DC to visit Dr Kollibo again, at the National Institutes of Health. Col wanted to see how he was progressing with his centrifuges. He asked Col, 'Are you the fellow using the centrifuge for a door stop?'

Col had told him about this when Kollibo attended the bio-medical conference in Melbourne in 1971. The two of them talked for a while about the technical aspects of building centrifuges.

From Washington DC, we drove up to New York to see Joan for a few days. By then, we were keen to go home, but Joan didn't want us to leave.

'Stay for Christmas, stay for Christmas,' she pleaded.

We did fly home from New York and when we returned home, Lisa and her husband were sad about us coming back so soon. Lisa's baby had been born by that stage. They enjoyed being on the Pier, they loved the Kiosk and everyone on the Pier loved Lisa. She was very happy doing the job and didn't want us to come back. Had we

265

realised that, we could have stayed longer and had Christmas with Joan in New York.

Col: Years before we went on our holiday in the States, I had built a telescope for the public by welding a circular base onto a six inch pipe on one end and the telescope to the other end. I put a money-slot in the pipe and installed the telescope on the Pier outside the Kiosk. We charged a shilling initially to use the telescope and when the coin dropped down the pipe, it hit a micro switch, starting a timer connected to a 12 volt current which was connected to an indicator. Do you remember the little Morris Minors in the 1940's and 1950's that had those little orange indicators which stuck out from the door post? I found one of those and used it to lift a flap over the front of the telescope. When two minutes was up, the flap dropped back into place. I cut a door further down the pipe to collect the takings from the box which held the money.

Occasionally, I raided the money in the telescope pipe for change for the Kiosk. I had told Lisa about this. After a while, she had the idea of putting money into the pipe for safekeeping at night. Two young fellows came onto the Pier one day looking for the telescope. When they moved on, Lisa found that they had bashed the little door open and taken all the money. She rang the coppers and when the police came down, they mistook a marina about two miles away for St Kilda Pier. In the meantime, the two young fellows disappeared. Eventually the police realised they were in the wrong spot. When I came back, she told me all about it. We lost a fair bit of money in that robbery. It had been a good season that year.

We made eighty thousand dollars over twenty-four years from that telescope. One day, a man came from the Department of Taxation.

'The Taxation Department!' I exclaimed. 'You're just trying to frighten shit out of me. What do you want?'

'I want to look at your books.'

'When do you want to come to do that?'

'I'm here now. Let's do it now.'

'No, no. That's no good. I'm a businessman. You have to make an appointment to see me. You make an appointment and you can come and look at my books to your heart's content.'

He made an appointment for a fortnight hence. When he came back, the first thing he concentrated on was the telescope.

'What about that telescope? How much do you charge for that?'

'Twenty cents. That's all to do with me.' I said.' The money from that goes straight into my pocket and I spend it. That doesn't go into my revenue.'

'Ah well, you do a lot of good around the Pier. I'll let that go. I won't tell my boss,' he said.

Hong Kong and SE Asia

Judy: After the States, we made a trip to Hong Kong (1987) and later had a holiday in Thailand (1988). We're not shoppers, just sight seers and nomads. We did have to buy a lens for a friend's camera. She wanted a lens like I had and went over it very carefully before we gave it to her. It had to fit her camera of course, and it did, but we were afraid she was going to say it wasn't what she wanted.

~

When we arrived in Bangkok, two Thai men came up to us and offered to escort us and show us the sights. We agreed. They gave us a fabulous tour of the city, taking us across the river to show us gold encrusted temples that visitors don't normally see. On the way back, they stopped the boat in the middle of the river and started arguing with us about how much they wanted to be paid. It seems the older one had been impressed by me. Eventually, the older man said something in Thai and you could tell it was something like, "Let them go. They're nice people." The young man reluctantly agreed and they took us back to our side of the river. We did pay them quite well, but it was definitely a nasty feeling out in the middle of the river.

Later, we flew inland up to Chang Mai. That is a wonderful place; very beautiful and interesting. We went to see the silver workers and to see jewellery being made, also fabrics and paintings. They paint everything – umbrellas, silks … We also saw wood carvers working on the most magnificent carvings; tables and clocks and all sorts of things. We had two guides; one was the actual guide and the other was the driver, who owned the vehicle. They would drive us to one cottage industry and leave us to wander and look at our own pace. There was no time limit. When we were finished, they would take us on to the next place of interest.

When we arrived back at the hotel, they wanted only six Baht, which was about two dollars fifty. Col gave them twenty Baht and they panicked at first, because they thought we wanted change and they didn't have it. The guide was so happy to be given so much money that he asked us if he could take us somewhere else the next day. We agreed. He was there at eight o'clock the next morning, but his driver wasn't. He'd become drunk celebrating his unexpectedly large payment and he couldn't get up in the morning.

'You wait. I go find another driver,' the guide said.

In a very short time, he was back with another driver. They took us up to the caves and to witness elephants working in the forest. Col objected to the fee requested for seeing the caves. That was a twenty minute walk through the caves with the guide carrying a hurricane lamp. For that, he wanted fifteen baht. We asked him why he was charging so much.

'For the lamp.'

When we refused to pay what he asked, he threatened to call the police.

'Do that. I'd like to talk to the police,' Col said.

In the end, we gave him what we thought was reasonable and we left.

From Chang Mai, we flew up to Chang Rai, on the border with Burma. We were allowed to put our foot over the border into Burma. The market near the border sold beautiful Thai craft.

A limo took us out to The Golden Triangle. For that, we had a female guide, who spoke very good English. She also arranged for us to go up the Mekong River. The fellows in the powered long boat had machine guns with them. Up there, we rode on an elephant through the jungle to tribal villages. We were astounded at how carefully the elephants trod. If they get bogged, they die. We were on the elephants for two hours and during that time, there wasn't one second when we were still enough to take a photograph.

~

We went to Bali in 1998, with Joan. We hired limousines to go sightseeing everywhere on the island. There are numerous markets in Bali. I love markets, but we stopped at only one or two on that visit.

Our World Trip

The next trip was around the world. That was in 1999 with Joan. We flew to Italy first, but Joan was quite ill when we arrived and stayed in bed for some days. Col and I wandered all over Rome and Joan arose from her sick bed on our last day, to visit the Vatican with us.

Col had his pocket picked in Rome. He saw a gypsy woman walking beside us, but didn't feel anything when she took his wallet. We had walked a few hundred metres when a boy ran up to us.

'You dropped your wallet, Senor.'

Col's wallet contained only Australian money and it also had his name inside. I always carry the money. Even his bankcard was still there. They couldn't use Australian currency or an Australian Bankcard in Italy, but it was a good lesson. We became more protective of wallets and purses after that.

When we reached Barcelona, Joan was still sick; again, Col and I went on long walks. One day, we both heard something go plop right behind us. There were two young men involved. One came rushing up.

'Oh dear, you have mud over you. I have water and a cloth to clean the mud off.' Col looked up and the young fellow's mate had dropped the mud on us, so Col kept his hand on his wallet the whole time. He wiped me down and the young fellow wiped Col down before they realised no cash was forthcoming.

We hired a car in Barcelona to drive through Spain. We became lost every day, but the local people were very kind. The countryside was beautiful and there were olive groves wherever you looked. . All the villages had very narrow streets and lanes that were difficult to negotiate with the car. We stayed in a fourteenth century castle in a village called Sequenza to the west of Barcelona. It was magnificent

In another palace at Ubeda, a woman recognised Col. Joan and I were off exploring the palace and Col was walking across the ground floor. This woman was on the first floor, looking over the balcony.

As he walked past, she said, 'Kerby?'

269

Col looked up and said, 'Yes.'

'You're a little piece of history,' she said, then she turned round and went into her room. Col didn't see her again and never found out who she was or exactly what she meant.

We drove round the southern coast of Spain and joined the long queue waiting to cross to the island of Gibraltar. They drive very fast in Spain.

Almost every taverna we stopped at had filthy floors. I don't know how hygienic the food was. We would send Col in first to check out every café and restaurant. They throw their cigarette butts, serviettes, everything onto the floor.

Col learned to say 'No hablo Espangnol.'

On one occasion when we were lost, he approached a man in a car, and said those words to the driver.

'I want to go here,' Col said, taking out his map and pointing.

'Will English do?' The driver came from Birmingham.

We went into an Irish café at Malaga on the Mediterranean coast. That place was clean, but we were still nervous, because these were tough Irishmen. From there, we drove up to Cordova and on to the Portuguese border, where we left the car with the hire company.

We had to walk across the border to the train station. The train was supposed to leave at a certain time. We waited and waited. There was no one else on the platform and no sign of this train. We sat there waiting for over an hour, unaware there was a one hour time zone difference between Spain and Portugal.

~

Col had already been to Paris in 1950 and I didn't want to go to there, so from Lisbon, we flew to Heathrow. We hired a car and first, we went west nor' west of London to the Cotswolds. That area was wonderful and we stayed at a delightful hotel. The villages had quaint names such as Lower Slaughter and Stowe on the Wold. It was beautiful, with cobbled streets and thatched houses.

We drove to Stonehenge, where we walked all around. Col had been there back in 1951 with Don Rabinov. They bought an air pistol for seven pounds and ten shillings.

'You could get a colt for six pounds ten back then,' said Col. 'We put up twenty two-shilling pieces, stood back about ten feet and took pot shots at them.'

I couldn't believe it. These stones had stood there for over three thousand years and Col and Don had to take pot shots at them.

By 1999, the area was very well patrolled. We were wandering along the designated walking paths and Joan called out, 'Not as good as The Devil's Marbles!'

After driving south through Stratford on Avon and the old city of Bath, with its narrow paved streets, our route took us west along the coast road. We loved the pretty villages near Plymouth and just to the north, we came to the home of Sir Frances Drake. The cellar of that house was particularly interesting. We saw dozens of suits of armour and many ancient weapons.

After that, we took Joan back to Gatwick Airport and she flew off to Bermuda. She had a house there and some business she needed to sort out.

Col and I stayed another week in the UK, during which we drove up to Scotland. It was twenty four-degrees in Edinburgh.

'All the Scotsmen took their kilts off, they thought it was so hot,' Col said. He loves to pull peoples' legs.

We visited Hadrian's Wall, walking along part of it. The wall and the forts were built over a thousand years ago; the Romans put those rocks there and the ruins still exist today.

When we were due to leave England, we dropped the car off at Gatwick. We were to fly to Bermuda to join up with Joan again and we were sitting in the airport lounge.

Where's my wallet?' Col suddenly asked. 'My wallet's missing. It must be in the car.'

Fortunately, we had enough time before our plane departed, so we raced back to the car hire depot. The wallet was still in the car. Col has a habit of forgetting how often he mislays it.

~

We had two wonderful weeks in Bermuda, staying in Joan's house, which looks out over the water. It is a stunningly beautiful island. The weather was hot and steamy, but fresh water is scarce. Under Joan's house, she has huge water tanks and electric pumps to bring the water into the house.

From Bermuda, we flew to California, hired a car and drove down the Pacific coast to Mexico. From there, we went up to Las Vegas and spent three days visiting theatre friends from Melbourne, Valda and her husband, who was a producer at the MGM Casino. We went to some spectacular shows. Siegfried and Roy were animal trainers. Their show involved bringing white tigers onto the stage. They coordinated circus acts with a magic and illusion show. Another memorable show was "The Sinking of the Titanic."

'I was looking under my seat for my life jacket,' said Col. 'That's how realistic it was.'

I always dressed up in high heels and make up, but everyone in Los Vegas gets around in thongs and jeans. People carried little bags of money from one casino to the other, or even from one machine to another. Sometimes, if they left a machine to get some more change or go to the toilet, they placed a notice on the machine to warn anyone else from using it.

New Guinea

For Col's eightieth birthday, I promised I would buy him a trip back to Rabaul, because I doubted we were ever going to be able to sail there. He waited until the cyclone season was nearly over and flew there in early 2002.

Col: When I came to New Guinea in 1950, I didn't visit the island of New Britain, just Bulolo on the main island. It was strange and a little sad to return to Rabaul after so many years. Twenty thousand Japanese had been in Rabaul harbour and on the island during the 1940's and I hadn't been there since 1941–sixty one years ago. I enquired about my native friends, but nobody knew about them. I went to their villages. Toviat and Tingari had crewed on the *Tilbora* and I was very keen on seeing these mates, but they were both dead. I was bitterly disappointed to find everyone gone.

I saw an old man at a market.

'Who comes from Nordop? Is Larku alive?

'No, He finished. He dead.' That man was about the only person there who spoke Pidgin to me. Most of them spoke English by that stage.

Toviat's son offered to show me his father's grave, but I refused. I was too upset that he had died before I was able to return.

I also went down to have a look at the wharf. Nobody knew anything about the *Tilbora* or what had happened to her.

There had been another big volcanic eruption in 1987, which buried the old town. I looked for Chinatown, which was about three quarters of a mile square. I couldn't find it. It had just disappeared under ash and silt. Nor could I find the solid brick building Mark Kung's owned for his business.

I walked up to the Rapindik Hospital, where I had worked for two years. The steps of the hospital were all that was left. I found our water tanks for the laboratory. The ash seemed to have passed over those structures.

Kokapo is now the main town in the area. The name has been modified to Cocopo.

'What's this 'Cocopo?' I asked.

Apparently the authorities thought that Kokapo was a bit suggestive. What a lot of bloody nonsense. It was Kokapo from two hundred years before the Germans came and now the authorities wanted to put a collar and tie on it.

America Again 2006

Judy: On our final trip overseas to date, we returned to America. This time we went up to Canada twice. We flew into San Francisco again and hired a car for three days while we looked for a vehicle to buy. Actually, we wanted to buy a campervan, but the only campers available were as big as a house. We didn't want one of those. We wanted something like a Kombi or a Toyota Hi Ace van. In the end, we spent about $5,000 buying quite a nice station wagon and instead of camping, we stayed at motels – about seventy-nine in all. Most were very good. They also have nice motels in Canada.

On the way north, we stopped off at an aircraft museum in Oregon, to see the Spruce Goose. It is a great big seaplane, built by Howard Hughes. It flew only once, I think, for about sixteen miles. The museum was fantastic. They had a gyrocopter on display, similar to the Bee Aircraft we manufactured during the 1960's.

Col: They had a B29 there. Because of my accent, the fellow in charge took it upon himself to presume I was English and an RAAF man.

'Have you done any time in one of these?'

'Oh yes, in several squadrons.' I told him, hoping he wouldn't ask which ones. Of course, the B29's did fly over New Guinea, but only very late in the war, long after I'd gone back to Melbourne.

Judy: Also in Oregon, we drove through The Avenue of Giants, which is the avenue of enormous redwood trees. They are, by far, the biggest trees either of us have ever seen. A house has been carved out of one fallen redwood. That house has full head room. That gives you some idea of the girth of one of those trees.

In Canada, we drove around Vancouver and went over to Vancouver Island. At Kelowna, we stopped to visit some friends who had lived in Australia. Back in the late sixties, when he was quite young, the man worked for Col at The Alfred Hospital. We took them out for a meal one night, then returned to our motel after we'd dropped them off. The next morning, we went to McDonald's for breakfast. Fifteen minutes after we'd driven off, I looked for my camera case, but couldn't see it.

'Where's my camera case Col?'

He'd left the cameras and our passports in the McCafé. We went straight back, but of course they'd gone. They were never returned to us. Three thousand dollars' worth of cameras had gone, including our rare stereoscopic one. Worse still, our passports were stolen. We had to have passports to get back into the USA.

We went on, but I was so distressed about losing those passports and cameras that I couldn't enjoy what we were seeing. We decided to go back to the border and see what would happen.

When we arrived at Border Control, the woman there was fantastic. Apparently the problem is that students go into Canada, sell their passport for about ten thousand dollars each, then come back and claim it has been stolen or lost. At that time, an Australian passport didn't have the magnetic strip implanted into it. They accepted our explanation and believed we were genuine, mainly because I was so upset. They let us through without passports. We had to drive immediately to Denver, Colorado, where there was an

Australian Consul. On the way, we saw a sign for Glacier National Park, so we diverted there first. It was a magnificent area.

When we arrived at Denver, the Consul was totally hopeless. All he did was have photos taken of us. He told us that when we reached Los Angeles, we could pick up new passports. Believing him, we just enjoyed the rest of our trip. We went up to Mount Rushmore in South Dakota, where Col bought me a good digital camera. This renewed my enthusiasm for our holiday.

In Yellowstone in Wyoming, we saw our first bears. We also witnessed the giant geyser, Old Faithful. After passing through several more national parks, we arrived in Los Angeles.

The Australian ambassador in LA gave us two full passports, but they were tenable for only nine months. That was plenty of time to finish our touring.

From Los Angeles, we drove east across southern California and into Arizona, where we visited the OK Corral of Wyatt Earp and Doc Holiday fame in the town of Tombstone. From there, we went on to Chiricahua, noted for its photogenic scenery.

At El Passo, we were advised to visit a magnificent canyon in Mexico. About sixty kilometres south of the border, we were stopped for Immigration. They wanted us to pay $50 each to become immigrants, just to go in as tourists. We couldn't be bothered with that. We'd seen lots of impressive canyons already in the States, so we turned round and crossed back into New Mexico.

At Albuquerque, in New Mexico, we saw the annual hot air balloon festival. That was beautiful. Many hundreds of balloons were flying; all different shapes and motifs. It was a spectacle we'd hate to have missed.

We love the States. There's always something different to see there. Mesa Verde in Colorado has fascinating old Indian ruins from the 12th century. We'd been there on a previous trip, but enjoyed seeing the ruins again.

We travelled up through the Colorado Rockies. It was August, so snow was dripping off the trees in picturesque fashion. After visiting Aspen, the top skiing village in the United States, we turned west into the Mormon state of Utah and drove to Salt Lake City. I told Col he was welcome to get a second wife there, so long as she was a good housekeeper. If she did all the housekeeping, I would be happy. He didn't take the opportunity.

Having several months more on our visas, we decided to return to Canada to enjoy some of the places we had missed the first time. Up there, autumn leaves were in abundance. At the ski resort of Banff, we rode up the mountain to overlook the township in all its glorious colour. The highway north to Jasper is called the Ice-field Highway. We stopped frequently to photograph glaciers and snow covered mountains, which were reflected in mirror-still lakes.

Unaware that it was possible to return to the west coast via Whistler, we retraced our route back to the border, then travelled on a different route down through Idaho, next to the beautiful Snake River, where the salmon return to spawn every year. It was a fabulous trip.

When we arrived back in San Francisco, we still had money in the bank and we weren't ready to go home. We wondered where we could go. We'd been north several times; we'd been east through Death Valley and into Yosemite National Park, a majestic area, and south to Mexico as well. There was really nowhere in that area that we hadn't been. If we'd had any brains, in two days, we could have been in Alaska. We just didn't think of it. We still haven't been there and we are still kicking ourselves about that.

We flew home from San Francisco. Our American holiday lasted for three months and since then, we haven't been overseas.

Travels in Australia

Years ago, we went for a car trip into outback Australia. On a rough road, flying stones knocked a hole in our petrol tank. Col climbed under the car and plugged the hole with a paste made from soap, water and dust. We had heard the idea from Jack Absalom on television. We weren't sure that it would work, but the hole remained sealed for the rest of our trip and for thousands of kilometres more.

More recently, we've been to Lightning Ridge in north-west New South Wales.

A couple of years ago, we took our car down to Tasmania, where we drove two and a half thousand kilometres around the island. The west coast was very interesting, but the roads were awful – narrow

276

and rough. I went walking quite a bit, but Col was restricted by his knee. It was too painful by then for him to walk far into the gorges with me.

We've never done a tour of New Zealand together. I went on tours with three different shows during the fifties, when I was dancing for the Tivoli Theatre company, and Col came over in 1953 to propose to me. I went to Rotorua back then too. Princess Rangi lived in Rotorua and we met her there. Later, she came to Melbourne and she came to see us at the Tivoli.

Alaska, that's the place I would really like to go to – or China. Maybe we could go when Col's had his knee replacement. Perhaps we could go for his ninetieth birthday, during the northern spring.

Col and Judy in 2010

Epilogue

Col retired in 2002, about eight months after he turned eighty-one. Nine years on, he is still fit, alert and capable, except for his wonky knee, which causes him considerable pain. He is waiting to have a knee replacement.

In the meantime, Col and Judy continue to live on *Ooroo*. Judy turned eighty this year. Her friend Joan, who lives in Sydney, hosted a surprise birthday party in Newcastle for her.

The lives of this active couple have not changed very much over the ten years we have known them. They keep up to date with current events and 283ocializi with other people living at the marina. Judy loves to cook, entertain, do puzzles and read. Col delights in telling his wonderful stories. They frequently drive to Sydney to visit Joan and also to Melbourne, keeping in touch with friends there.

When they are not 283ocializing, Col is maintaining his boat. He keeps the refrigeration and mechanical parts in good working condition, and always has a mechanical project on the go. Every few years, Judy repaints the interior of the boat, including emptying all the drawers, sanding and painting them. Once a year, they have the boat taken out of the water onto the marina hardstand, where they antifoul the hull and check through-hull fittings.

There comes a time, however, when telling stories about the adventures in your life, becomes the adventure itself. We are privileged that Col has decided to share the remarkable stories of his life's adventures with us all.

This book will be launched at Col's ninetieth birthday party, to be held at the Marmong Marina on Lake Macquarie, NSW.

Jan Mitchell, 2011.

Glossary

Ambo	Australian slang for ambulance officer.
Anastomose	The act of re-joining blood vessels by stitching them together.
Armistice Day	Also known as Remembrance Day. The date World War 1 ended – 11.11.1918.
Bangalore Torpedo	An extendable pipe containing explosive near its far end, which can be pushed into obstructions like barbed wire entanglements and exploded to clear the way for an attack. First devised in 1912 in India, and used in World War 1 and subsequent wars.
Bobstay	Wire from the outer end of the bowsprit back to the bow near the waterline.
Calaboose	Native prisoner in New Guinea.
Camel	An air tank used to raise a sunken vessel.
Caulk	On a wooden vessel, you ram oakum into the seams between the planks, then coat the seams in tar.
Charabanc	An open air bus, usually constructed of timber.
Cong	Pidgin for a Chinaman.
Cop, Copper	Policeman.
Copra	The dried meat from a coconut.
Crackers	Crazy.
Dago	Australian slang for Italian migrant to Australia.
Degaussing	Reducing the magnetic field of a ship to avoid activating mines with magnetic triggers.
Demo	Australian slang for demonstration.
Dinkum	Genuine.
Doctor Boy	Native nursing assistant.
Go crook	Get angry about.

Great Depression	The world-wide economic depression of 1929-1932.
Gelly	Gelignite.
Gully Trap	The exterior drain, into which the interior building drainage flows. Can be either open or closed. In this case, wide open with a freshwater tap above.
Gunwale	Pronounced 'gunnel'; the edge around the outside of a boat's hull.
Haemolysis	Abnormal disintegration of red blood cells.
Hook	Punch.
JP	Justice of the Peace.
Kanaka	Native of New Guinea or other Micronesian islands in the South Pacific north-west.
Ketch	A two- masted vessel, where the aft mast is the shorter of the two and positioned forward of the rudder.
Knots	Nautical miles per hour. A nautical mile is 1852m. Therefore, 1kt =1.852 km/hr.
Krannie	The New Guinean word for a Malay.
Kunda	Cane for punishing natives.
Lap lap	A flap of fabric worn by men and hung over the genital region. The lap lap is secured around the waist with a cord.
Mary	Female New Guinean native.
NCO	Non Commissioned Officer (army).
Oakum	The roll of fibres obtained when worn hemp ropes are unpicked and re-worked for hammering between seams on wooden boats.
Pal, palled up, pally	A pal is a friend. To pal up with means become friendly with. Pally – friendly.
Perfusion	The pumping of drug-infused blood through an organ eg: liver.

Perky	Off colour, nauseous. 1930's slang.
Pinnace	A motor boat used as an auxiliary for a much larger vessel.
Port	The left hand side of a boat.
Pounds, pence	The currency before decimal currency took over in 1966. See shilling.
R & R	Rest and recreation leave for American servicemen.
Ropey	The man in charge of the ropes pulling the logs through the bush/forest.
Sat Nav	Satellite Navigation instrument, which preceded GPS.
Schooner	A sailing vessel with two or more masts of equal height, or with the foremast slightly shorter than the other(s.)Also New Guinean Pidgin for a ketch or other sailing vessel.
Shilling	Twenty shillings makes a pound. With the change to decimal currency, a pound became two dollars and each dollar was worth ten shillings or one hundred cents. Thus, a shilling [twelve pence] is worth ten cents.
Slipway	A sloping area with rails and a wire or chain winch. Boats are hauled out of the water on a cradle, which fits on the rails.
Smart Alec	A person who likes to show off.
Spinner	A fishing lure on a swivel.
Starboard	The right hand side of a boat.
Tambaran	A devil or evil spirit in New Britain.
The Prom	Wilson's Promontory on the SE corner of mainland Australia.
The Tivoli Theatre	The theatre was established in Melbourne in the 1800's. It featured vaudeville, variety shows and follies with a touch of nudism and 'spice'. Col mostly knew the theatre for its dancing girls dressed in glittering costumes. His

wife, Judy, was one of these dancers from 1950 to 1957. The shows were extremely popular before television and the cast toured all over Australia and New Zealand. In the early 1960's, the variety shows ceased and the theatre was used as a cinema for a short while, before it burned down in 1964.

Tickling the tills	Taking money from the till and not recording the income or spending.
Tidal rise and fall	In different places in the world, the tidal range is greater or lesser.
Trailing Log	An instrument which records speed through water. A trailing log dragged behind the boat.
Uni	Australian abbreviation for university.
Ute	Utility vehicle; small truck with a two seater cab and an open tray at the back; a pick-up.
Variac	A mechanism to control the speed of an electric pump.

Author Profile

Jan Mitchell was born in New Zealand in 1946, moving to live in Australia in 1970. She has retired with her Australian husband, Ian Mitchell, from Sydney to Rathmines, NSW, a semi-rural village in Lake Macquarie City, south of Newcastle. The couple has two sons and two grandsons.

Jan and Ian have sailed the world's oceans in their various yachts and it was during the six months they lived on their yacht in Marmong Marina, Lake Macquarie, that they met Col and Judy Kerby.

Jan has been an author for many years, mostly writing magazine articles about her family's yacht travels and experiences. She has been published in *Women's Day*, *Cruising World*, *Sea Spray* and *Cruising Helmsman* magazines. A secondary School teacher of English, during the 1980's, Jan re-trained as an alternative therapist, later teaching natural therapies at evening colleges.

Since moving to Rathmines beside Lake Macquarie, Jan has found friendship and inspiration with the members of the Lake Macquarie branch of the Fellowship of Australian Writers. She has another non-fiction book and some short stories planned for publication.

www.writingsfromjanmitchell.com

CPSIA information can be obtained at www.ICGtesting.com
Printed in the USA
LVOW012042090413

328375LV00032B/2518/P

9 781463 717216